Frank McGuin

'Another major playwright has full

Born in Buncrana, Co Donegal, Frank McGuin
Dublin and lectures in English at St Patrick's College,
Maynooth.

   *Observe the Sons of Ulster Marching Towards the
Somme* was first presented at the Abbey Theatre, Dublin,
in 1985; the first English production opened at Hampstead
Theatre in London in July 1986. The play has won many
awards including the London *Evening Standard* Most
Promising Playwright Award, the Rooney Prize for Irish
Literature, the 1985 Harvey's Best Play Award, the
Cheltenham Literary Prize, the Plays and Players Award
1986 (Most Promising Playwright), the Ewart-Biggs Peace
Prize 1982 and the London Fringe Award 1986.

   Other plays include *The Factory Girls* (Abbey Theatre,
1984); *Baglady* (Abbey, 1995); *Innocence* (Gate Theatre,
Dublin, 1986); Lorca's *Yerma* (Abbey, 1987); Ibsen's
Rosmersholm (National Theatre, 1987); *Carthaginians*
(Abbey, 1988, Hampstead Theatre, 1989); Ibsen's *Peer
Gynt* (Gate, 1988, RSC and international tour, 1994);
Mary and Lizzie (RSC, 1989); Chekhov's *Three Sisters*
(Gate and Royal Court, 1990); *The Bread Man* (Gate,
1991); Brecht's *The Threepenny Opera* (Gate, 1991);
Someone Who'll Watch Over Me (Hampstead, West End
and Broadway, 1992), won the New York Critics' Circle
Award and Writers Guild Award for Best Play; *The Bird
Sanctuary* (Abbey, 1994); Ibsen's *Hedda Gabler* (1994);
Chekhov's *Uncle Vanya* (a Field Day production in 1995).

FRANK MCGUINNESS

Plays One

The Factory Girls

*Observe the Sons of Ulster
Marching Towards the Somme*

Innocence

Carthaginians

Baglady

Introduced by
the Author

faber and faber
LONDON · BOSTON

First published in 1996 by
Faber and Faber Limited
3 Queen Square London WC1N 3AU

Photoset by Parker Typesetting Service, Leicester
Printed in England by Clays Ltd, St Ives plc

Observe the Sons of Ulster Marching Towards the Somme: The author
wishes to acknowledge the receipt of a bursary from the Irish Arts Council
towards the writing of this play.

For Celine and Packie McGuinness

Contents

Introduction

I started to write for the theatre in 1980 when I attended a
writers' workshop in Galway City, organized by the Irish
Arts Council and moderated by the director, Patrick
Mason. I'd seen Patrick's production of my favourite play,
The Winter's Tale, just before applying for the workshop.
Even if nothing were to come from the whole experience, I
was determined to meet the man who had transformed my
vision of Shakespeare as a playwright with his strange,
troubled, deep reading of a text I thought I knew, braving
the play's violence, hearing its plea for calm. That was the
beginning of a working friendship that continues today. I'd
like to acknowledge Patrick Mason's creative and
supportive advice in the writing and staging of many of the
plays in this book. He was the first to believe I could write
for the theatre, and you can never forget that recognition.

I hate writers rabbiting about their work. Just do it and
shut up. That is my motto, but believe me I don't live by it.
I have a few mates who, down the years, have endured
prolonged readings from work in progress. As they are
expected to nod appreciatively when eyed, murmur
benevolently at the jokes and generally behave with a
politeness that does not come naturally to them, there is a
strict rule that these readings do not last more than ten to
fifteen minutes. I would describe that time span as
prolonged when confronted with any work in progress, so
I'm grateful to them.

My first play was *The Factory Girls* (1982). I wanted to
write a play that celebrated the working class culture of
women in the part of Donegal I grew up in. My mother,
aunts and grandmother found employment in the local

shirt factories and I was brought up to appreciate a beautifully made shirt. A shirt is the most special gift I can give to anyone, woman or man. There is an erotic impulse behind all theatre. Actors put flesh on feeling and if you're lucky, you can find a special one who identifies with absolute precision the feeling, the flesh. I found Maurean Toal when she played Ellen in *The Factory Girls*.

Maurean is one of the great Irish actors. During *The Factory Girls* she was like a mother to me. In other words, she put serious manners on me, would listen to no bullshit, taught me that the rehearsal room was a place to work and work and work. She scared the living daylights out of me and I was, and am, cracked about her. I wrote *Baglady* (1985) for Maurean. I knew she would have the courage to tell the tale. She had. *Baglady* is a tough journey for any woman and was also a tough one for me. If I didn't have Maurean Toal's voice to accompany me, I doubt if I could have written it. One other person should be mentioned in the context of writing *Baglady*. Mairead Ni Domhnaill is the best Gaelic singer of her generation. She also works as a nurse. She told a company of friends at dinner one night a story that will always haunt me. Being the professional she is, Mairead totally respected the privacy of all concerned, but I know that the power of her compassion lies at the root of the play.

I wrote *Observe the Sons of Ulster Marching Towards the Somme* in Coleraine. The Irish Arts Council again helped me by giving me a grant to live there and research it. It was an eye-opener for a Catholic Republican, as I am, to have to examine the complexity, diversity, disturbance and integrity of the other side, the Protestant people. When the Abbey toured Patrick's first production of the play to Coleraine in 1985, I was there to hear Johnny Millen ask his fellow Coleraine man, Willie Moore, to take him home to the banks of the River Bann. I'll always remember that night.

All of these plays were performed by the Abbey. The next play, *Innocence* (1986), went on at Dublin's other leading theatre, the Gate. Michael Colgan wanted to do a new play, I wanted to work with him, and the subject matter was the life of Michelangelo Merisi, otherwise known as Caravaggio. It is fair to say that it took nerve for any theatre in Dublin in 1985 to stage *Innocence*, but no one could deny Michael Colgan's nerve. There was a fair degree of uproar, Patrick and I were branded as a disgrace to the nation and I got a number of anonymous warnings, but the play did reasonably well. I'd loved Caravaggio's paintings since I set eyes on them in Florence in 1977. I pieced together a fiction of his life based on a reading of clues I imagined he'd left in his paintings. As I was adamant the actor playing Caravaggio would not have to do a Rolf Harris impersonation, I tried to make him a poet and in his poetry would be his painting. I used the city of Derry as my model for the Rome of his day, which is near where I grew up and which is now about the same size as Rome was then.

Derry was also the centre for *Carthaginians* (1987). The events of Bloody Sunday ripped Ireland apart. In January, 1972, I was in my first year studying at University College Dublin. My adolescence ended that day. *Carthaginians* is my elegy to the dead and the living of Derry, the living who kept going, in Dido's words, 'Surviving. Carthage has not been destroyed.'

I don't want to say any more about the plays. They can talk for themselves. Many people were involved in their production. I owe them a lot. But, in the end, you stand on your own and do not look back. Of course, if you believe that, you'll believe anything. I like that in a person.

Frank McGuinness
August 1995

THE FACTORY GIRLS

For Celine, Cissy, Eileen, Roselean, Kathleen, Margaret
and Sadie
and Lizzie O'Donnell

Characters

Ellen, in her fifties
Rebecca, in her late twenties
Rosemary, sixteen
Una, in her sixties
Vera, in her early thirties
Bonner, in his forties
Rohan, in his late twenties

The Factory Girls was first performed at the Peacock Theatre, Dublin, on 11 March 1982 with the following cast:

Ellen Maurean Toal
Rebecca Nuala Hayes
Rosemary Martina Stanley
Una May Cluskey
Vera Kathleen Barrington
Bonner Peadar Lamb
Rohan Nicholas Grennell

Directed by Patrick Mason
Designed by Juliet Watkinson
Lighting by Tony Wakefield

SCENE ONE

Wednesday morning.
  Ellen, **Vera**, **Rebecca** *and* **Una** *are seated at their benches working.*

Ellen It's the second time in a fortnight.

Vera You're fairly counting.

Ellen It was me asked to get her in, Vera.

Rebecca Well it's not you has to watch her. Let her fight her own battles.

Ellen Don't worry, Rebecca. But I have to face her mother if anyone says anything to her.

Vera Tell her mother she should get her out in the morning.

Una If her mother had more to get out she would know what was sticking to her.

Ellen What are you talking about? Doesn't your big sister still get you out in the morning? I'm always expecting her to walk with us to the factory gate to make sure nobody runs away with you.

Una Susan's a born worrier. How do you manage to get your two out in the morning, Vera?

Ellen She manages, we all had to.

Vera I can answer for myself, you know. I'm not speechless.

Ellen Well she's always looking for news.

Una I was only asking.

  Pause.

7

Vera My bloody eyes. (*Pause.*) This new work is going to blind me.

Ellen You should have glasses.

Vera I know.

Ellen Why don't you?

Rebecca Because she's too bloody lazy.

Una Men never make passes at girls who wear glasses.

Ellen You would know all about that, wouldn't you?

Una Don't be so passremarkable.

Vera I'm sorry I opened my mouth. But do the rest of you not find this rate sore on your eyes? This is rotten work.

Rebecca It's work, isn't it? Before this order weren't we three days in, three days out? This is a week's work at a time.

Ellen No. Vera's right. This is the worst work. Not one of us can keep up this rate. Rohan's a right pup.

Una If this factory is in such a bad state why was a young fella put in to do a man's job?

Ellen Because he's cheap.

Vera Just like the material he buys.

Rebecca And we're as cheap in his eyes. Put a plaque with a B.Comm. on their door and they think they're God Almighty.

Una This place has never recovered since the Buchanans left. You know what they say, new bosses, new rules, and, stupid or not, Rohan's the new boss.

Ellen The Buchanans were as bad as any.

Una They were not. They never had us doing a dozen shirts in sixteen minutes, did they? And there was never this muck of material. Once the Protestants hotfoot it out of a factory, you can forget it. Since they went, not one of the regular orders have reappeared. That's Freemasons for you. They stick together.

Ellen Are you saying that if Rohan was a Protestant we'd have better work?

Una No, I'm not saying that. Sweetieball Rohan doesn't own this factory, whoever might. He may be the first Catholic we've had over us but he's worse than all the Buchanans rolled into one. I'd rather work for a Protestant than not know who exactly you're working for, no matter who they put over you.

> **Rosemary** enters, wearing a red duffle coat.

Vera Christ, look who it is. Santa Claus. You're a bit late this year, Santa.

Rebecca Where did you get the red duffle coat, Rosemary?

Ellen Never mind the red duffle. You're late again, woman. The second time in less than a fortnight. You're very lucky nobody came checking to see if your orange skull was bobbing about. Get me some more work or my complaint goes to Rohan.

Rosemary Run on and tell, big mouth. I don't give a tinker's curse.

Ellen You'll know that when you're out on your ear.

Rosemary Go and shite.

Una Charming. Lovely-spoken girl.

Rebecca Where did you get the red duffle?

Vera In the jumble sale for the blind.

Rosemary Anything you say to me is in one ear and out the other. But then you'd know who bought what at jumble sales. You're always first in the queue. Jesus, I dread to think how long since your weans had a clean stitch on their backs.

Rebecca Rosemary, start working.

Vera And watch it, small fry, or you get my fist in that beck of yours.

Rebecca Leave her alone. She's only in the door and everybody's at her.

Vera Poor wee Rosemary. Poor wee soul. Leave her alone.

Rosemary Leave me alone, that's right. The whole lot of you can go to hell.

Una Temper, temper. It must have been a late night last night.

Ellen All she ever thinks about is gallivanting.

Vera That's all they ever think about, gallivanting.

Ellen Her poor mother's heart's broken.

Vera If I was her mother, I'd tie her up.

Rosemary If you were my mother, I'd tie myself up.

Ellen You see, no respect even for her mother.

Vera A girl with no respect for her mother never has luck.

Una I always say that too, and so does Susan.

Rosemary You always say that too, and so does Susan. You and Susan aren't right in the head. Just lay off me, and for everybody's information I wasn't out last night, gallivanting or anything else. Now get your own work. I don't give a damn. Tell that to Rohan too, big faced Ellen.

I'm going out for a smoke, yous do it often enough.

Vera Cheeky wee bitch.

Rosemary exits: short pause.

Ellen That one will have to learn something soon. She'll have to learn she can't come saddling in here half an hour late and then storm out to the toilets after five minutes, no matter what kind of temper she's in. The way this factory's in at the minute, she's going to be flung to the streets if she's found out. There's a big enough queue waiting to take her place. By Christ she's changed her soft tune since she came in here first. She's getting a tongue that could tar roads.

Rebecca I wonder where she learned it from.

Ellen You can be right cheeky as well, Rebecca.

Rebecca I wonder where I learned it from too, Ellen.

Ellen Listen you, you're doing her no favours by sticking up for her. If she thinks she has one silly enough to take her part, she'll walk on you.

Una Young people today would eat you alive if you let them.

Vera Jesus, she's not joking. Did any of yous read in the paper two Sundays ago about a gang fight, one fella bit the ear off another and ate it?

Ellen Sweet mother of Jesus, what kind of cannibals are they?

Vera He ate the ear.

Pause.

Una I saw in a picture once where a man cut his ear off. He wasn't right. He was a painter.

Ellen A lot of them go that way. It's the lead fumes from the paint. A man that lived down beside us towards the end of his life could only do whitewashing.

Una He wasn't that kind of painter, he painted pictures.

Ellen I suppose he did Christmas cards. You sometimes get them from the handicapped.

Una No, he just did paintings. Kirk Douglas was acting the man who cut off his ear. I love Kirk Douglas.

Vera I never knew Kirk Douglas had one ear.

Una Jesus Christ, Vera, Kirk Douglas was only acting –

Vera Who would cut off his ear just for a picture? Kirk Douglas must have only one ear.

Una I've seen him in other pictures where he had two.

Vera That must be a dummy one he uses to let on he has two.

Una Holy God, I always thought Kirk Douglas was lovely and now you say he has only one ear.

Rebecca Una, you are an innocent eejit of a woman. Vera's mocking you. Kirk Douglas has two ears.

Una Vera, you bad bitch. Taking a hand at an oul woman.

Ellen An oul woman's right. A woman oul enough to be Kirk Douglas's granny. You think he's lovely. You're getting worse as you're starting to dote. You should be at home saying your prayers, you stupid bitch.

Una I beg your pardon, nobody has to tell me to say my prayers. Me and Susan are at first Mass every Sunday.

Ellen Taking in anything and everything that moves. The two of yous see enough there to keep yous in gossip for a week.

Una My sister has always minded her own business.

Ellen And everybody else's if she had the chance.

Una Susan's in her late seventies, she notices very little of what goes on about her.

Ellen Not when she's sober.

Una God forgive you.

Vera This is some morning. Not ten o'clock yet and two fights.

Rebecca I mean it, we're going to have to start bringing in a bell and ring it to start and end the boxing matches.

Vera Jesus, can you just see it? The two old dolls in the wee white vests and silk shorts. Falling on top of each other like two pigs in a parachute.

Ellen You can be very fucking funny, can't you? If Una and me are to take up boxing, maybe you and your fighting man might teach us all we need to know. If the noise that's supposed to come out of your house is anything to go by, you're well able to talk about boxing and insult other people.

Vera Thanks, Ellen, you could always laugh at yourself. They say it's a great gift.

Ellen You weren't given much of it yourself.

> *Pause.*
> *Rosemary enters: sees the glum faces, pauses, works.*

Rosemary What's the big joke?

Una They're taking a hand at innocent people as usual.

Rosemary You don't need to tell me. I know them too well. You can say nothing in this place but they're at you.

Vera Look, if you've cooled down a bit, could you do your job for a minute and give us our work? I'm nearly finished with this lot.

Ellen I asked you for work before you went out, so move it.

Rosemary Are you OK for work, Una and Rebecca?

Una I could do with some, pet.

Ellen What do you mean, you could do with some, pet? You're not halfway through that batch yet. There's not much point you starting to hoard work. There's none of us reaching our quota as it stands. And for that matter, since when has pigeontoes been your wee pet?

Una Rosemary, give the work first to Godzilla.

Rosemary All right, Una dear.

Una Thank you, pet.

Rosemary starts to pile shirts on Ellen's bench.

Ellen Thanks, wee pet. You're too good, wee pet. You're a living saint, wee pet. Vera, what would we do without our wee pet?

Vera I don't know. Just don't know. Maybe we should take up a collection for her. She might think it was a going away present.

Una Don't listen to them, Rosemary.

Rosemary Don't worry, Una. I hear nothing that passes between the two magpies. They're farting with their big mouths into the wind.

Long pause. The women continue working. Rosemary goes around collecting and delivering work.

Vera Jesus, I cannot understand how the rest of yous

haven't the eyes burned out of you with this work.

Una You have bad eyes because you didn't eat enough carrots when you were a wean.

Vera And you did?

Una I certainly did. That's why I have eyes like Grace Kelly.

Vera Well, if Grace Kelly will excuse me, I'm going to the toilets for a smoke. Becky, are you coming now or are you waiting?

Rebecca I'll come with you.

Ellen What if they see the two of yous are out?

Una We'll tell them one can't pee without the other. Run on.

Rebecca Thanks, Una, we'll bring you back something nice.

Una If you see any sailors, I have first pick.

Ellen Get out to hell and don't be long. We'll want to go soon.

Rebecca and Vera exit. Rosemary follows. Short pause.

Una Do you think Vera might be looking for another man, God forgive me for saying it.

Ellen What do you mean?

Una Well, you said yourself she and him were always fighting, you know.

Ellen Don't drag me into your dirty stories.

Una She won't get glasses and I always heard it said that men never make passes at girls who wear glasses.

Ellen Woman, will you shut your big mouth?

Una I was just asking.

Ellen You were just hoping.

Una I wouldn't wish it for a minute, a woman with two weans.

Ellen And a big man that would knife her.

Una Oh no, don't forget him.

Ellen You better not. If he heard you, he might do the same for you.

Una He'd only hear me if somebody repeated it.

Ellen You should watch your tongue.

Una Look who's talking.

Ellen They're well matched. One's as bad as the other, as quick-tempered.

Una Just like you and your man.

Ellen We won't speak of the dead.

Una What stopped you before?

Ellen He was as rotten an oul shite as Vera's.

Una And you were as mild a woman.

Ellen Since when did you start to stick up for him? At least I never haired one to the ground over a man like Vera did. Do you remember in the toilets before she was married? I suppose you would have been the same, given the chance.

Rosemary enters.

Una Thank Jesus, no fear. Me and Rebecca has the right idea.

Rosemary Do you think Rebecca's never going to get married?

Una Well, she's no spring chicken.

Ellen I don't think Rebecca's the marrying kind.

Rosemary Rebecca's a lovely name, isn't it? I'm going to call my first baby Rebecca if it's a girl.

Ellen You're a bit young to be chatting about babies, aren't you?

Una You had one when you were eighteen.

Ellen And the third before I was twenty-two. I might not have had them long but I know too well what they bring. Stay away from babies, woman. There's plenty of time. Rebecca does right to wait. The same one has no shortage of men who want her.

Rosemary She says no man is good enough for her.

Una She's right. Do you remember that time and study fella, Nigel, the Englishman? He was mad about Rebecca, asked her out, but she wouldn't go. Who would blame her? He was a right plaster of Paris.

Ellen You didn't think so at the beginning. Who used to run every morning to him with a packet of peanuts?

Una I soon stopped after our rate went haywire. Nigel was working our fingers to the bone. Something had to be done, Rosemary.

Rosemary So what happened?

Una Well you know we all down tools at twelve o'clock and say the Angelus when it's on the wireless? This day Ellen decided that when we downed tools, they'd stay down.

Ellen When Nigel saw no movement for ten minutes, he came over to Rebecca.

Una And he still thought he had a soft mark in our quiet Rebecca.

Ellen Right. So he whispered to her, 'Are you still praying, dear?'

Una Rebecca looked at him and said, 'Go away and shite.'

Ellen He nearly did. I think Nigel was never the same in here afterwards.

Rosemary Rebecca wouldn't let you away with anything. She's great. I'm wild about her, everybody is.

Ellen Well, if you're that wild about her, get out to the toilets after her and Vera. We're not covering up for them if they're out much longer.

Rosemary Hold your horses. I'm not here just to answer your beck and call. What'll you give me if I go?

Ellen These clippers up the nose if you don't. Hop it.

Rosemary All right, Godzilla.

Ellen Cheeky fucker.

Rosemary exits.

You started that Godzilla name. I hope you know that.

Una You started plenty of names as well. There never was much to stop your big mouth.

Ellen Just leave my mouth out of it. You should put a zip on yours. That Rosemary has been as bold as brass since you had your wee talk with her.

Una What wee talk?

Ellen The wee talk in the toilets a wheen of months after she started, when you told her she would either have to face up to me or leave the factory. Don't deny it. My ears were burning when yous were out and I could tell by your sleekit face what yous were up to.

Una Well, Jesus Christ, when she came in here first she could do nothing right by your. Everybody has to learn, you know.

Ellen I was doing it for her own good.

Una You were doing it because you're a bad tempered bitch. It did you good too. When she faced up to you, I thought the shock was going to kill you. You're getting worse with age.

Ellen It's better than getting senile. Jesus, where are those two? I'm gasping for a smoke.

Una I think I'll give up smoking. It ruins the skin.

Ellen Your skin can take it, dear. It's hard to ruin a Brillo pad.

Una It's better than being shaped like a Dettol bottle.

Ellen What's that supposed to mean?

Una I don't know, but I'm glad it annoyed you.

Darkness.

SCENE TWO

Wednesday lunchtime.
   Rosemary sits on Ellen's stool, affectedly combing her hair. Ellen enters.

Ellen Off my stool, crab.

Rosemary Sorry, big arse.

Ellen You could trim a fair few slices off your own. What's this?

She picks up a few of Rosemary's combed out hairs.

Are you going bald?

Rosemary What do you mean?

Ellen It's very bad for a girl your age to be shedding hair.

Rosemary I am not losing hair.

Ellen You're casting, woman. Look at that. There's only one cure.

Rosemary What?

Ellen Old maid's piss.

Rosemary What?

Ellen You heard me. You have to wash your hair in it. Ask Una to bring you in her sample.

Rosemary I will not.

Ellen starts to laugh.

That's you all over, isn't it? Mocking people. Nobody should speak to you.

Ellen Wouldn't that save me a lot of bother? The only time you speak civil is when you come girning you want something done that only the old horse can do for you. Where's the rest of them?

Rosemary Rebecca's doing Una's hair and Vera went home.

Ellen Vera always goes to the canteen on Wednesdays and her mother gets her weans their dinner.

Rosemary Her mother's at a wedding.

Ellen Who's getting married?

Rosemary Don't know.

Ellen Is it a relative?

Rosemary Don't know.

Ellen Where's the reception?

Rosemary I don't know.

Ellen Thank you and that is the end of the news.

Pause.

Rosemary Ellen?

Ellen What?

Rosemary Do you think there'll be redundancies?

Ellen *You* needn't worry about redundancies.

Rosemary Why not?

Ellen Because you're going to be sacked for timekeeping. Every time you're late, young lady, it's down on your sheet.

Rosemary It's not you know. I get someone to stamp my sheet when they see it's not.

Ellen So you're out to lose two jobs instead of one? And who's stupid enough to do it?

Rosemary Wouldn't you like to know?

Ellen Keep it all to yourself. Just don't send your ma crying to me when you're out on your ear.

Rosemary Why should anybody come crying to you?

Ellen That's very true. Why should they?

Rosemary Will the union do anything?

Ellen About what?

Rosemary Redundancies.

Ellen Why all this chat about redundancies?

Rosemary Well, Mr Rohan was down –

Ellen Has Mr Universe been flexing his muscles again?

Rosemary It's no joke. Rohan was down with the collars section and the banders yesterday. He told them they'd either take the new rate or there'd be no work for them. They said they never saw him as angry.

Ellen His shiny smile must have stopped blinding them then.

Rosemary He said times had changed in this factory. The way of working had changed and it should have done years ago. If we can't modernize, we don't survive. So we'll go under and take all with us. He said there was no orders on the books and the only way he could get them was to offer firms cheaper work.

Ellen He should try dazzling them with his B.Comm.

Rosemary He said too he couldn't afford opposition and that there were ways and means of getting rid of it. Everybody thinks there's definitely going to be redundancies and pay-offs.

Ellen Well, if that's what everybody thinks there must be some truth in it.

Rosemary Do you think there must be truth in it?

Ellen I don't know.

Rosemary You do so.

Ellen Well, I just know that I've heard the same rumour every year for the past thirty. Sometimes it's true, sometimes it's not. I wouldn't worry too much.

Rosemary He can't get rid of us all. The union would do something. What do we pay them for?

Ellen Listen, Rosemary, unions work like big business, they have to if they're going to tackle big business, and in every big business there are priorities. We're not at the top of anybody's priorities and to get there we have to fight our own way up every time. If not you learn the hard way how things will turn out.

Rosemary What do you mean?

Ellen Something happens in this factory. We ring Andy Bonner at the Union. He thanks us for ringing and he rings Dublin. Dublin says, 'Where? Donegal? Donegal?' Dublin gets a map of Ireland, looks for Donegal, Jesus that's it, the jiggeldy-piggeldy bit at the top of the country. They think we dropped off years ago, Donegal's been that quiet. Dublin ringadings Andy Bonner, says, 'we'll support them but you do the talking, Andy.' Andy Pandy ringadings us, says, 'shut your mouths, I'll do the talking.' And we've learned to shut our mouths. Like good weans, be seen but not heard. It would be bad manners to interrupt. Fortunately I've never prided myself on my manners. But remember one thing, if the worst comes to the worst, it's always the way with redundancies and pay offs that last in is first out. So all you can do is pray there'll be none.

Rosemary There will be, I just know it.

Ellen Oh for Christ's sake, woman, if it's any consolation to you, I've heard bigger threats than any Rohan could come up with. Look, there's no point in worrying about what hasn't happened yet.

Rosemary OK.

Rebecca and Una enter. Rebecca carries a box full of hair curlers. Una's hair is still very slightly damp. She carries a towel. She sits on her bench and Rebecca starts to curl her hair.

Ellen Animal crackers in my soup, monkeys and tigers loop the loop –

Una Have you finished?

Ellen Would you do mine on Friday, Rebecca?

Rosemary I was going to ask her to do mine today. This place is like a hairdressers on Friday.

Ellen I asked her first. It's not often I ask.

Rosemary What does an old woman need her hair done for?

Ellen Less of the old woman.

Rebecca One moment, please. Vidal Sassoon hasn't checked the appointment book yet. I think I can fit both ladies in on Friday. Ellen, you at the dinner-break, Rosemary, you in the evening.

Ellen If it's too much bother, then don't.

Rebecca Shut your mouth. If I didn't do it, I wouldn't have the living of a dog.

Una You're far too goodnatured, Rebecca. You should refuse once in awhile. That would – aah! Did you jag me with that steel comb?

Rebecca I did. That's for you to shut your mouth too.

Rosemary Rebecca's better than any hairdresser. She should do it full-time. That's why her hair is so lovely.

Una Ellen, do you remember when your hair was as nice as Becky's?

Ellen No. It was as long as Rebecca's, but it never had her colouring or strength. Mine was too straight. Good hair's a Godsend. Do you remember Veronica Lake?

Rosemary Who?

Ellen Veronica Lake. She was a film star. A perfect face. I saw her a few years ago on TV and God help her, she was that drunk she couldn't stand. She was a dead old woman. They shouldn't have let her on. I think she died just after that.

Una Do you remember the one worked in here thought she looked like the image of Veronica Lake? She had long stringy hair and she used to keep it all over one eye until one day it caught in her sewing machine.

Ellen Jesus, who could forget it? The squeals of her.

Rosemary The poor woman. What did yous do?

Ellen What could we do? We cut her hair. Looked like Veronica Lake. She looked more like my arse.

Vera enters.

Vera Your best feature, Ellen.

Ellen Between you and Rosemary, my arse is having some day of it.

Vera What?

Ellen Forget it.

Vera Anyway you better move it. I met Rohan on the way in. He wants to see you in his office.

Ellen What does he want to see me for?

Vera In an effort to improve management-workers co-operation, he's organizing a quiz. He wants to test your general knowledge.

Ellen What does he want to see me for?

Vera I didn't ask him. Pleasant as he is, we're not on familiar terms. My husband would not approve.

Ellen He can wait until we start work. I'm not giving up my dinner-break for him. I'm worked hard enough.

Vera You better go up. He said it was urgent. You know when he asks to see you, something's on the cards.

Una Oh God, do you think something desperate has happened?

Vera Shut your mouth, alarmous Kate. We'll only know when Ellen goes up to see him.

Ellen Rosemary, I'm nearly finished with this work. Get me a fresh batch. I don't suppose I'll be long.

Ellen exits. A short, tense pause, then the sound of the factory horn. Una and Rebecca clean up quickly. The women go back to work. The pause continues briefly.

Rosemary Why do you think he wants to see her?

Rebecca When Rohan sends for her, it's not good.

Pause.

Vera I think one of mine might have the measles.

Una Poor wean.

Vera He was scratching the whole time. I didn't know what he might have picked up, you know weans at school. So I looked through his clothes. There was nothing there. I saw the beginnings of a red rash. I don't think it's hives. Measles is all I need.

Rebecca Did you keep him at home?

Vera I wasn't going to but I thought it better. My mother's at the wedding, so there's nobody to look after him. I couldn't stay at home with the way the work is here, so I had to keep the other one home too.

Una She's very long out of the room, isn't she?

Vera She's hardly out of the room for two minutes.

Una I just hope it's not bad news about somebody belonging to us and they're asking Ellen to break it to us. That's all I hope.

Rebecca Una, will you go and put a plastic bag over your head?

Una The laugh will be on the other side of your face if anything has happened.

Vera Nobody's laughing, Una.

Pause.

Rosemary She is there a long time.

Una That's what I said.

Rebecca I think we heard you. Look, she hasn't had time to walk to the office and back. Do yous think she's flying there by helicopter?

Una I wonder what he's saying to her.

Vera He's lost without his mother. He wants her to adopt him.

Una I just wonder what they're doing.

Vera Playing marbles.

Una I'll know it's bad news if she walks in with red eyes.

Vera Give my head peace, Una. You'd sicken a dog girning.

Una I'm just worried.

Vera You're just whining.

Rosemary When was the last time he sent for her?

Rebecca When they threatened to get rid of me for giving backchat to Nigel, the Englishman.

Rosemary What happened?

Rebecca I had to make an apology, a formal apology.

Rosemary What did you do?

Vera She went up to Nigel, and she said, 'Did I tell you to go and shite? Well then don't bother now'. He didn't ask for another apology.

Rosemary You're a bad bitch at times, Rebecca.

Rebecca I know.

Una Poor Nigel.

Vera Fuck poor Nigel. It was that bollox started this whole caper with his bloody stopwatch. I think he imagined he was working with a pack of greyhounds. I ripped more shirts trying to keep up with his time and motion and he was supposed to be increasing production.

Ellen enters and immediately starts to work.

Well?

Ellen Well what?

Rebecca Tell us, Ellen.

Ellen Yous will have to miss your teabreak tomorrow morning. But just for tomorrow.

Una That's why he sent out for you?

Ellen We're having a meeting with him and Bonner from the union tomorrow at eleven. I know no more, so ask no more.

Pause.

Una Is it bad news, Ellen?

Ellen What do you think, Una?

Pause.

Remember what I was saying to you, Rosemary? Well you better start saying your prayers.

Darkness.

SCENE THREE

Thursday morning.
  The women, with the exception of the absent Una, are all working.

Ellen I hope she doesn't think she's going to sit this out in the toilet.

Rosemary She'll be back in time.

Ellen It's nearly eleven.

Rebecca Will they be here on the dot?

Vera Likely.

Ellen Did yous notice Bonner's car outside the factory this morning?

Vera He must have been here before nine.

Ellen Something's cooking and we're going to get the

smell. Rosemary, will you do me a message?

Rosemary What?

Ellen Go up to the manager's office, knock on the door, tell Rohan and Bonner that Ellen sent you and she said that if they want to talk to her they'll have to come down and see her, not her up to see them. All right?

Rebecca You said they were coming to see all of us down here.

Ellen A little white lie. Rohan tried to palm me off yesterday with just me meeting Bonner. I agreed because I was saving my ammunition for this morning. I am not moving to that office. The fight is on home ground. Tactics, Rebecca dear, you have to have tactics. Move, Rosemary.

Rosemary Will they not be wild angry?

Ellen Not as much as I will be if you don't hop it. Go.

Rosemary exits as Una enters.

Una My chest is still going. (*She starts to work.*)

Ellen Well, if it finally goes, that'll stop you chatting about it.

Una Does anyone think we should say a decade of the rosary for luck?

Ellen The joyful mystery strikes again. Maybe you'd be better off thinking of ways to save your job. Just shut your mouth, do you hear?

Una I won't open my mouth.

Vera I wonder what Rohan's up to.

Ellen I wonder more about Bonner. Since the Buchanans sold out he's changed his ways. I would just like to know why him and Rohan are in such cahoots. Bonner knows a damn sight more about this place and the running of it than he'll tell us.

Vera You definitely don't think Rohan part owns it?

Ellen You can forget that rumour. That edgy little bastard couldn't buy a kennel when he came here, let alone a factory.

Rosemary enters.

Rosemary It's them.

Ellen Are yous ready?

Rebecca Yes.

Vera I'll start off.

Ellen Good. Come in then when yous are needed.

Rohan *and* **Bonner** *enter, at the dialogue's beginning the women keep working.*

Rohan Good morning, ladies, hard at it? (*pause*) I see you've taken us for a short stroll, Ellen.

Vera Exercise is great for the figure, Mr Rohan.

Rohan We could all benefit from it, couldn't we?

Vera Thanks.

Rohan You all know Mr Bonner.

Vera and all (*sing*) Hello, Andy, well hello, Andy, it's so nice to see you back where you belong.

Ellen Are you looking for a job, son, or is this a social visit?

Bonner Just a visit, Ellen.

Ellen You're looking well, your shirt's lovely. Very well made.

Bonner You've always noticed a good shirt, Ellen.

Ellen The shirt never made the man though, did it, Andy?

Bonner I see.

Vera You better.

Rohan We did want to talk to you on your own. You know that, Ellen. I think we might get on with this better if we didn't have to compete with your choir of factory women.

Vera Excuse me, Mr Rohan, not factory women, factory girls. Everyone here is a factory girl. Factory girls never grow old and they don't fade away.

Rohan Are you coming to the office, Ellen?

Ellen No, I'm not going to the office.

Rebecca Anything either of you have to say to her you have to say to everyone here.

Una You will not use Ellen as your message girl.

Vera Speak to all of us or to none of us.

Rosemary We're all ears.

The women stop working.

Rohan I thought there might be a fairer chance of a hearing if I could speak with you first and explain this in detail.

Vera Well, now you're going to speak and explain it to everybody.

Rebecca That's what we call fair.

Rohan Right, well, I don't need to tell you we've been living from order to order. You know too well how things have been going in this factory.

Ellen We've noticed.

Rohan What work's coming in has to be shared. The three-day week and all.

Ellen Have you noticed you're trying to get twice the work out of us in half the time?

Rebecca You have some of us nearly blinded at the rates you expect us to keep up.

Vera It's hardly work anymore. It's slave labour.

Rohan Can I continue without these interruptions?

Ellen Well, as you're hardly going to answer them, you better.

Rohan Ellen, I didn't particularly enjoy putting anyone on a three-day week. I have to take orders too and get a certain amount of work out in the time I'm given. Would you prefer I rejected contracts?

Ellen I would prefer you got better contracts. That's what you're paid to do, isn't it?

Rohan Where do I find these better contracts?

Ellen You look for them. Look for regular orders. They were always there before. Let us do good work for people who will come back wanting us to do more work for them. Don't deal with fly-by-nights whose shirts for all their big labels fall apart with one pull. Learn your market, man. Learn something about the work you're doing. Is it not about time?

Rohan I'm sorry, it's not as simple as that, Ellen. This factory is no different from any other in the textile industry, the textile industry is the whole cloth –

Vera We know what textiles means.

Rohan Then do you know what a flooded market means? Shirts selling for half nothing from Korea, Taiwan –

Bonner And that factory in Bundoran is managing to get its feet on the ground.

Una Korea and Taiwan?

Rohan Yes.

Una And Bundoran?

Bonner Yes.

Una Jesus, if it wasn't for Bundoran, you'd swear you were watching Miss World.

Rohan We can continue?

Una Please do.

Rohan We are no different from any other business. We have quite simply been hit, badly hit by the recession.

Ellen We seem quite simply to be permanently hit by recession. And since you arrived, wonder boy, we seem quite simply to have been really hit. The only ones not really hit are yourself and Mr B. I'm sure your hearts went out to us when we were on the three-day week, so I'm just dying to know what changes you've come up with to see us through.

Rohan Clever Ellen, yes, there will have to be changes, I've explained as much as he'll listen to to Mr Bonner. He knows too well there is nothing left to do but what I'm about to propose.

Bonner I know nothing too well. I know what's acceptable if this factory is to survive.

Rohan I'm not getting into another slagging match. This time it's too serious. The factory is on its uppers. What's to

34

be done? Back to three-day weeks? Nobody could be satisfied with that. The whole factory needs a clean sweep.

Vera Here it comes.

Bonner Girls, I want to save jobs, jobs that are worth saving.

Rohan Sometimes to save jobs you have to lose them. And some jobs here will have to be lost.

Bonner I know too well how you're going to react to the word redundancy. It's the way I react. That's why I know how you're going to think I'm a liar when I say I'd advise you to face up to the fact there will be, there must be, redundancies. The Buchanans might have been the best in the world, but in the long run they couldn't run their factory. The books in this place have to be seen to be believed. They are in such a state I don't know why anybody took it over. I can assure you I'll fight to the last breath in my body that it'll be voluntary redundancy, with everybody getting as much money as can be squeezed out of the firm.

Ellen And that's blood from a stone if it's correct that this factory is on its uppers.

Rohan I will do my best to see that anybody accepting voluntary redundancy does not go short.

Ellen And if nobody does?

Rohan They'd be very foolish.

Una Who exactly might you be asking to accept it?

Rohan Older workers would obviously be asked to volunteer.

Una Would they indeed? I'm not going, put that in your pipe and smoke it.

Rohan Una, this will all have to be discussed privately and quietly.

Una I'm telling you loudly and publicly. No. N-O spells no.

Ellen I think you might find Una is not an exception, Mr Rohan, B.Comm.

Rohan Whether she is or not the exception that's not my concern, but even with redundancies, there will have to be a new rate.

Slight mayhem.

Bonner There's a lot of talk to be made before this is settled.

Rohan It better be made clear here and now that for the sake of new orders –

Vera I do not believe this.

Bonner There's no point in panicking. I've said a lot of talk –

Vera I just do not believe this. Did you not hear what Rebecca's told you? We can't work faster, we can't reach our percentage as it stands.

Rebecca What do you want now?

Rohan A dozen in thirteen minutes.

All What?

Ellen Andy, he's bluffing. A dozen in thirteen minutes.

Una What did he say?

Ellen A dozen in thirteen minutes. Listen, Rohan, show me a shirt. Here, take a look at this. (*She throws a shirt.*) What do you see when you look at that, what do you see?

Rohan A simple piece of coloured cloth, stitched together.

A unit of production that I need to see go out this factory quicker and in greater numbers if against all the odds I'm to make this hole of a place survive.

Ellen Let me tell you what I see. I see a collar. Two cuffs. Eight buttons. Eight buttonholes. Bands. A back. Two sides. A lower line. When I look closer, do you know what else I see? A couple of thousand stitches. Why do I see it? I've been trained to see it. I've trained other people to see it. That's my job, Rohan, and I know my job cannot be done in the way and the time you want it done, and I won't do it that way.

Bonner Christ Almighty, this is not agreed on. This eejit of a man thinks he'll get away with pushing his luck, but he'll have to learn. He won't learn if all he has to fight against is a pack of hyenas squealing about what they learned thirty years ago. So cool it, will you? Nobody could be happy about this rate –

Vera Oh Andy, nobody could be happy? A higher quota and less money. I am only delighted. I am over the moon, just at the very thought of it.

Bonner Come back down to earth then. Nothing whatsoever has been settled.

Ellen Look, the factory's going down, it's on its uppers. Who put it there, Andy? Who? A simple piece of cloth stuck together, heh? This man knows nothing about a shirt. What in hell's name is he doing running a shirt factory? Rohan, the only way you'll let us reject a shirt is if there's a hole as big as your fist in it. You are pulling this place down about your ears and about our ears because you know fuck all about what you're working with, let alone who you're working with. You can talk big talk about production, about quotas, about contracts, but what do you care about our work or about us? What do you care about this factory? Damn all. That's why it's on its uppers.

Rohan It would of course be all different if the Buchanans were still here.

Ellen The Buchanans could always be seen through. They feathered the nest and flew. They were no different from the rest, but Jesus when they were here at least you were fighting against ones that knew what they were talking about. Do you?

Rohan That is not the issue.

Ellen I think it is.

Rohan I say it is not. Oh, forget it, there's no reasoning with you.

Rebecca With your kind of reasoning it's a bloody good job there's not.

Bonner Women, let me ask you straight, are you willing to destroy this factory?

Rebecca We're not willing to destroy ourselves.

Rohan Then what the hell are you doing? Will you not listen to facts and figures?

Vera The one fact we grasp well is that we have a job. The one figure we're most interested in is our week's wages; interfere with that fact and figure anymore and see what happens. Because I for one have had enough.

Rosemary Hear, hear.

Rebecca It was about time you said something.

Rosemary You weren't that talkative yourself.

Rohan Your own union knows the state of this factory.

Ellen I ask again, did any woman here put the factory into that state?

Rohan Each and everyone has to share responsibility.

Ellen Right so. Who'll be the first to apply for redundancy? Will we all trot in sympathy to the dole? No. I don't think so. Gentlemen, yous have your work cut out. Andy, we've lost our teabreak over this and you know we're entitled to it. I'm sure you'll ask Mr Rohan to give us our due.

Rohan You know what you're entitled to, take it.

Ellen Andy, isn't it great to have an understanding boss? You must be doing a great job with him for us. Take your break. You too, Rosemary. Vera, I want to talk to you.

Each of the women exit, except Ellen.

Rohan No matter what happens, you're finished here.

Ellen (*sings*) I hear music and there's no one there. (*She exits.*)

Rohan You might hear a lot more soon.

Ellen (*off*) So might you.

Long pause. Bonner lights a cigarette.

Bonner Can I give you some advice?

Rohan Surprise, surprise, that's all you seem to give.

Bonner You might very shortly be glad of it.

Rohan If I want to deal with you, deal straight. Is that it?

Bonner That's it. Don't ever forget it.

Rohan The new rate?

Bonner What else?

Rohan I lost my head.

Bonner A bad habit to develop.

Pause. Rohan sits on workbench.

Rohan For Christ's sake, you know these women. I never know what they'll come out with next. You know all about them. Where they're from – What they are – You can use that to give as good as you get. But with me, it's – Andy, since I arrived in this factory nobody listened to me. I tried being reasonable. I tried to cushion them. I've tried everything. You know what I mean. You've heard what they say about you.

Bonner Water off a duck's back to me. Let them rabbit on. But you, you'll have to face a lot more than wagging tongues if you try to pull a fast one on me. That's all I warn you and your pals across the water.

Rohan The same pals are no pals of mine. They'll chuck this place over if they don't get what they want. One bad mistake and we're fucked.

Bonner Correction. You're fucked.

Rohan This place might bring me down with it, but watch out the ones in it don't see to it that you go with me.

Bonner Oh no, son, that's not the way it works. You might have learned plenty from your copy books, but you still have to learn how to work with me. And I can tell you it won't be by backslapping. No more than it was with the crowd of charmers that have just left. You might go, and they might go, but will I?

Rohan Do you want to see this factory survive in any shape or form? If you do, you better keep your wildcats controlled.

Bonner The same wildcats might have torn their bit of

flesh. Leave them to run around in circles. When they're exhausted, they'll lie down.

Rohan I hope they weren't just sharpening their claws.

Bonner Live and learn, tomorrow's Friday. A lot can happen over a weekend. It's been a hard morning's work, but I've a harder day ahead of me. I'll leave you to your factory. I won't wish you good luck. It's a bit early for that yet.

Bonner exits. Rohan remains.
Darkness.

SCENE FOUR

Thursday lunchtime.
Rosemary sits on a stool reading Bunty, not noticing Rebecca's entrance. Rebecca sneaks up behind her and speaks in a deep voice.

Rebecca Not working, young lady.

Rosemary Oh God!

Rebecca Yes.

Rosemary jumps from the chair, sees Rebecca, starts to roll up comic. Rebecca races to her own stool, followed by Rosemary who gives her three blows on the head with the comic.

Rosemary That'll teach you not to put the life and soul out of innocent people. I swore you were Rohan. I've been expecting the brute in here since the showdown. There's not been a stitch of a shirt looked at.

Rebecca I think Mr Rohan might have seen enough of us for one day.

Rosemary Did you see the look of him at times? His eyes go like a cat's in a dark house.

Rebecca Are you scared of him?

Rosemary Yea, I think he must scare Andy Bonner a bit too.

Rebecca It might be the other way about.

Rosemary How do you mean?

Rebecca Just a feeling. (*She goes back to her work.*)

Rosemary It's round the factory you know. All hands are talking about redundancies and bigger work rates.

Rebecca I wonder who told them.

Rosemary I've just been sitting here reading the Bunty.

Rebecca Is that what you're reading? Give us a quick look. I haven't seen it in ages.

Rosemary A woman your age shouldn't be reading the Bunty.

Rebecca Look who's talking. Give us a look.

Rosemary No. Go away.

Rebecca Rosemary, you know I can't stick someone defying me. I see I'm going to have to come and get it.

Rosemary Just try.

Rebecca Right you are.

> *Rebecca chases Rosemary, stops. Pretends to see Rohan. Startles Rosemary. Rebecca snatches the comic from Rosemary.*

Rosemary You bitch.

Rebecca Now all I wanted to know is if the Four Marys are still in it.

Rosemary I could have told you they weren't. Give it back.

She tries to snatch the comic back. Rebecca evades her.

Rebecca Wait a minute until I see if I know any of the others. Oh Christ, look, the dancing life of Moira Kent. Moira Kent must be as old as Una by now. Oh, I remember that one too, Sonja and her pony, Magpie. (*pause*) Rosemary?

Rosemary Shut up.

Rebecca Why have you scored out the name Sonja and wrote in Rosemary?

Rosemary Shut up.

Rebecca Go on, tell us.

Rosemary You'll tell everybody.

Rebecca I won't.

Rosemary I love horse stories.

Rebecca What's this one about?

Rosemary Sonja's a gypsy and she has a pony, Magpie, but this rich girl who's spoilt buys Magpie and Sonja has to get a job in her stables to be with him. This week (*she takes comic*) she won a rosette in a show-jumping competition and the rich girl takes away the rosette but Sonja doesn't care. At the end there, you see her kissing Magpie and Magpie is smiling. It will all end happily. It always does in Bunty.

Rebecca I never knew you liked horses.

Rosemary I've never been on one and likely if one came near me I'd die but I think horses are beautiful. Over jumps must be like flying. I'd rather have a horse than get married.

Rebecca It might be easier.

Rosemary Why the hell does anybody get married?

Rebecca Not everybody wants a horse.

Pause. Rosemary sits.

Rosemary What do you want, Rebecca?

Rebecca Neigh.

Rosemary That's not an answer.

Rebecca That's my answer, so take it or leave it. (*She goes back to her work.*)

Rosemary I don't want to get married. I mean listening to Vera talking about her man, or Ellen giving off about her's that's dead, you'd swear they couldn't stand the sight of each other. Knowing the gulpin Vera's saddled with, I wouldn't blame her for giving him the worst word in her stomach.

Rebecca You don't know what way people get on together when they're on their own. So mind your own business.

Rosemary I'll be like you, Rebecca. Just work and support myself. Look at the way you keep working even when there's nobody else there.

Rebecca Take the money when they're still offering it.

Rosemary No. I think you enjoy it.

Rebecca Sitting here going demented looking at what some get's going to wear? Thanks. Every day a holiday.

Rosemary Still, you are definitely a career girl, you know.

Rebecca Just like Una.

Rosemary I wouldn't put it like that.

Rebecca I would.

Rosemary Oh well, I suppose we'll all need a man to support us soon.

Rebecca Where will they get the work to support us?

Pause.

Rosemary Isn't it funny the way these things go round in circles?

Rebecca When do you get your pension, granny?

Rosemary Listen to me. When my mother worked in the factory there were big pay-offs too. Most of the girls, even ones my age, had to take the boat or get married. Can you imagine it?

Rebecca I can imagine it only too well.

Rosemary I just know one thing. I am not going into another factory as a message girl. A year of that is enough for any woman. Whatever I do, it's not that. Ah to hell with it, I'll run away and join the circus.

Rebecca Steal a horse and release the gypsy in your soul, Sonja?

Rosemary Watch it you.

Rebecca Would I do that to you?

Rosemary You better not.

Una enters.

Una Are they not back yet?

Rosemary Ellen and Vera?

Una Who else, stupid?

Rebecca I thought you were with them.

Una No, I wasn't asked. I took a run up home and saw no sign of them. Whatever the secret confab is I'm not let in on it.

Rebecca Ellen was in tough form today.

Una The same one might not have started yet.

Rosemary You mean she could get worse?

Una Or better, depending how you look at it.

Pause. Una goes back to work.

Yous never knew her man. When they were younger they used to batter the lining out of each other, but Ellen was smarter. She never fought with him unless he was drunk and she could flatten him from behind. After all the weans died, the life went out of him too. He talked about nothing else. They had no more fights. She had to carry him home and put him to his bed most nights.

Rebecca How did she ever get over that?

Una Who knows? She cried at the graves but not a murmur out of her apart from that. She nursed them all. It was the only time she missed her work in this factory since coming into it.

Rosemary What was it?

Una TB. There was no cure for it then. I don't know how Ellen and the man missed it. But she got over it.

Rebecca That woman will never crack.

Una She's getting on. We all crack.

Rebecca You're getting very serious –

Una In my old age? That bastard Rohan.

Rebecca He can't force nobody to do anything.

Una Can he not? Him and his type? For all we argue and

46

fight we've always been walked on. Does it make any difference what we do? You know that, Rebecca, as well as I do. They give with one hand and take with another. (*pause*) Ah well, I'll think about it tomorrow.

Rosemary It's funny though, when you think it's all about to go, you know how much you'll miss it, bad and all as it is.

Pause. Una stops working.

Una What time is it?

Rosemary It's near dinner time.

Una I don't want to do any more till after dinner.

Rebecca I couldn't face that canteen today with questions firing from all sides.

Una Do yous all want to come up to our house for tea? Susan'll kill me, but sure what odds.

Rosemary All right.

Rebecca I wanted to see Vera first.

Una Leave a note telling where we are in case they come back looking for us.

Rebecca starts to write a note on a discarded shirt sleeve. Una and Rosemary look on solemnly. Vera enters, sees the general gloom. Silence, then shouts.

Vera Hello angels. (*She giggles.*)

Una I'm glad somebody's got something to laugh about.

Vera Life's a laugh, Una dear.

Rebecca Where were yous?

Vera Obtaining some small refreshment.

Una What if Rohan came in here looking for yous?

Vera You could have told him where we were and he might have come up and stood us one.

Una At this hour of a working morning in a pub.

Vera You're just raging because you weren't in it.

Una Why all this secrecy?

Vera Ellen needed a small brandy to revive her nerves. We also had something to discuss initially in private.

Rosemary What?

Una If it's that private, you needn't bother to tell us.

Vera I won't. It was all Ellen's idea. She did all the talking and if I was consulted first, then you'll have to have it out with Ellen, won't you?

Rosemary Where is she?

Vera Aaah! That would be telling.

Una Just how many small brandies did she need to revive her nerves?

Vera Not that many. Have patience.

Una The two of them are drunk.

Vera I never felt as sober.

Ellen enters singing 'Somewhere over the Rainbow'.

Ellen Have you said anything?

Vera Not a dickiebird.

Ellen Vera, I'd trust you with my life.

Una Come on, tell us.

Ellen Well, I've decided I'm very tired. I need a good rest. I don't know for how long, but of course I couldn't go on my own. So if yous want to come, I'll take you. I'm not saying where, but you can say we'll all be moving up in the world.

Una Jesus, what happened today deranged her.

Ellen Oh no. If you want to hear more, all hands back to my house. There's work to be done outside here this afternoon. That goes for you too, Rosemary.

Rosemary Are we not coming back here after dinner?

Ellen We are not, lambchop. But believe me you might see enough of this place soon to last your life. Get your coats. Move. Action.

All exit dancing, Ellen and Vera singing 'We're off to see the wizard, the wonderful Wizard of Oz' making the others join in.
Darkness.

SCENE FIVE

Friday afternoon.
The office. Two doors. One leads to a toilet. Another leads to the factory floor. Two desks. On each a telephone. Behind each a swivel chair. Near to the door leading to the factory floor a large filing cabinet. On the smaller desk a call system apparatus. On the wall, framed, Mr Rohan's B.Comm. Ellen enters, surveys office, exits, then leads in all the women, except Una. Throughout this scene, there is a constant flurry of activity as they unpack and move between office and toilet.

Una (*thud. Off*) Oh sweet Jesus (*thud*). Sweet Jesus.

Ellen Vera, you're the one best to give her a hand to cart in that menagerie she's brought. Go out and haul her in.

Vera exits.

Rosemary I wonder did anybody see us.

Ellen Who cares if the whole factory saw us. They'll soon hear about it. Right. Get behind this cabinet, Rebecca. The minute those two are in we'll get the room blocked. We'll move that big desk over beside the door in case Rohan gets a crowd of men to ram it.

Vera and Una enter, dragging the coffin-like case.

Una Sweet Jesus. I thought I was going to breathe my last dragging this up all them stairs. Thanks very much, Vera, you were the only one to give me a hand.

Ellen That's big enough to bury yourself in. Could you not have got something wee-er?

Una It's mostly things for other people that were left to the responsibility of the packhorse to carry.

Ellen Well, who was that big mouthed to offer to carry so much?

Rebecca Look, shift this cabinet quick.

Una You can count me out of shifting that. I've done my bit of weight lifting. I haven't a spunk left.

Ellen At my age it's kinda dangerous to risk straining yourself.

Vera You'll risk straining my fist if one of yous doesn't get behind this cabinet. Jesus, what has he in it or what is it made from? It's the weight of a steam roller.

Ellen, Vera and Rebecca try to move the cabinet.

Ellen Vera, it's no good, I'm useless. I'm panting like a stuck pig.

Vera Becky, this is not going to beat me. Roll your sleeves up.

Vera and Rebecca manage to shift the cabinet with one prolonged heave.

Are you putting your bastarding elbow in it?

Rebecca I'm putting my bastarding elbow into it. Save your breath for pushing.

The cabinet is finally behind the door.

Rosemary What about the desk?

Vera What about the desk?

Rosemary We were going to put that in front too.

Vera Forget about the desk. If he gets past that cabinet he's bloody superman.

Ellen Right. Stage one completed. Now Major Tom to ground control.

Rosemary There are two phones, do you notice?

Ellen I don't mean the phones, you stupid bitch. I meant the call system. (*She goes to the desk and switches on the system. She reads prepared statement.*) Good afternoon, ladies. This is the representative of the action committee, consisting of the examiners and their message girl. We have decided to take action over proposed unfair working conditions. Our first step is the takeover of the office until such times as better conditions are offered. This is our last communication with the outside world until then. Good afternoon and good luck. (*She switches off the system.*) Well, with luck, one or two people will have shit themselves in the rush to get to Rohan.

Rebecca How long will it take?

Ellen Not long I imagine. Come on. All hands start getting the stuff out.

*The women begin to unpack making improvised
conversation. Food, clothes, cigarettes, crockery,
cutlery, pots, a kettle, two small gas canisters and a
stove. Rosemary has brought an inordinate amount of
clothes, some of which she holds up against herself,
admiring them in an imaginary mirror. Out of Una's
case may appear any variety of objects, the only specifics
being those mentioned.*

Rebecca Why did you bring an electric fire, Una?

Una It still gets very cold at nights, Rebecca.

Ellen Woman, did you ever realise why you don't bring a
fire to work with you? This place is heated by oil, central
heating. Have you heard of it?

Una I've heard of it well enough to know central heating
can go wrong. I'm glad I brought my fire.

Rosemary Two hot water bottles?

Una Quite sensible as well. One's for my bad stomach and
nobody's borrowing it.

Vera Oh sweet Jesus, she's brought a chip-pan.

Una You'll thank me when you're dying for a chip.

Rebecca We are not frying chips in this place and that is that.

Ellen Rosemary, what exactly or where exactly do you
think you are? Standing there admiring yourself, do you
think this is a bloody fashion show?

Rosemary I'm just looking at this skirt. I don't suit blue as
a rule but I think this is very nice. My mother bought it for
me this morning when she heard I was definitely going
with yous. Isn't she not right in the head? I said to her who
would see me locked in Rohan's office, but she said you
could always have an accident.

Rosemary and Vera talk, Una has started to remove at least two bottles of Bushmills interspersed with large packs of toilet rolls.

Rebecca The bare necessities of life I see.

Una Mock on. I'll have the best laugh. I know yous are all hiding the drink you brought. I didn't expect to see that. But if this is a long stay, I notice there's a dire shortage of the other lady (*pointing to toilet rolls*). Don't come crying to me when yous are skiptipalooring from the shithouse.

A loud rattle is heard. Rohan's voice is heard off.

Rohan Ellen?

Ellen Hold it.

Rohan Ellen, are you in there?

Ellen Yes, Mr Rohan, I've come up as you asked me.

Rohan What in Christ's name are you about?

Pause.

Ellen, what are you doing?

Pause.

What in hell's name are you up to?

Ellen Our purpose has already been made clear.

Rohan Our? How many of you are in there?

Ellen One.

Vera Two.

Una Three.

Rebecca Four.

Rosemary Five.

Pause.

Rohan Now ladies, be sensible, open the door.

Pause.

Open the door.

Pause.

I warn you to leave this office.

Ellen You leave.

Rohan Right, you're out of a job, each and every one of you.

Ellen OK. We'll take yours.

Rohan You're out of your minds, do you hear me, you're mad.

Ellen Aah, is your head beginning to go?

Rohan Jesus Christ, what are you trying to do?

Pause.

Now look, I'll ring Mr Bonner, we'll reason this out around a table. Open the door.

Vera Go to hell.

Rohan I ask you calmly once more, get out of my office.

Ellen That's right, calm down. Even men your age can get heart attacks. Don't die on us, that would be too easy. We're not leaving until you improve your offer.

Rohan You stupid bitches.

Una Good evening, Mr Rohan, and good night.

Rohan You leave me with no alternative.

Ellen You left us with no alternative.

Rohan Oh no. You're going to find out who gives orders here. Christ damn you, I tried to be fair all along, but now the kid gloves are off. You're going to learn the hard way who you're up against.

Ellen I'm trembling with fear.

Rohan Every worker in this factory is being sent home now. If I can't get into work there, nobody else will.

Vera That doesn't make much of a difference, does it? When you could work here there still wasn't many working.

Rohan Laugh on, we'll see who has the last laugh.

Ellen I'm bursting my sides. Go home and get your nappies changed.

Pause.

Una Poor Mr Rohan. I thought he was going to cry.

Vera Do you think he'll do it?

Ellen Naa.

Rebecca He might. When the bully doesn't get all his own way, he'll stop other people doing anything.

Ellen We'll wait and see.

The siren goes.

Jesus, I think we might be in for a long session.

Vera All hands are being sent home. He's definitely done it.

Rosemary They'll be delighted. Friday evening off and they were paid yesterday.

Rebecca They might stop being delighted if we keep on in here. There'll be no more money coming in.

Vera Isn't that exactly what Rohan's working on? He gets them to do his dirty work. Well, he's far mistaken if he thinks that'll shift us. Whatever about the rest of you, I meant what we all said yesterday.

Una You can only be walked on so much.

Ellen Aye. It's about time we did the walking. See if they like a feel of their own medicine.

Rohan Ellen.

Ellen Jesus, he's back.

Rohan Ellen.

Ellen What?

Rohan You have until four o'clock.

Ellen We have all the time in the world.

Rohan All right, enjoy your little escapade for a few hours more. Even if you last out a day, I can freeze the arses off you. Every heater in this place will be switched off.

Una holds up fire.

Ellen We've brought electric fires. A very enlightened gesture on the management's part to pay its workers' bills.

Rohan Very well. I'll turn off the electricity.

Ellen What about your alarm system? You're scraping the barrel a bit.

Rohan I warn you straight. This is the last time any of you will see the inside of this factory. Four o'clock and then the guards are called in. I mean that.

Ellen Rohan, wise up. Guards never get involved in local fights, not until they have to, and it will take you longer than you might think to force them into doing that. Push off.

Pause.

Una Do you think he'll get the guards?

Ellen Not yet. He knows them as well as anybody. It's too early for them. They need time for the blood to boil.

Pause.

Rosemary Will I make tea?

Ellen What?

Rosemary Tea?

Ellen I'll make it. Vera, give me a hand to stack the rest of this stuff in the toilet. The rest of yous start getting the beds down.

Ellen and Vera exit. The others start to spread sheets, blankets, and pillows. Ellen enters. Ellen picks up the sheet Una has brought.

Ellen Is that the sheet you packed for us two? How are the two of us going to share this? It's fit for a wean's cot.

Una Oh God, I never thought. It is very small. I just pulled it off my bed.

Rosemary Me and Una would fit it. You take my sleeping bag, Ellen.

Ellen Thanks, I suppose I have to. (*She exits.*) Stupid bitch, Una, you can be trusted with nothing.

Vera enters.

Una I could be trusted long enough with you.

Ellen (*off*) The bloody kettle's leaking. I think there must be a hole in it. Who brought it?

Vera I think it was you.

Ellen enters.

Ellen There is no hole in my kettle.

Rebecca Ellen, it was you said you'd bring a kettle.

Ellen There is no hole in my kettle. I should know.

Vera Ellen, I've just brought it in.

Una Just one moment please, ladies.

Una lifts out another kettle. She places it on the floor near Ellen, and smiles at her.

Fetch it, Fido.

Ellen Thank you, head the ball.

Darkness.

SCENE SIX

Saturday morning.

Vera I slept like a log.

Rebecca You were out the minute your head hit the pillow.

Ellen It was all the excitement.

Rebecca How did you fare in the sleeping bag, Ellen?

Ellen I didn't know you were supposed to get into them until it hit me in the middle of the night what the zip was for. I was foundered until four o'clock and I never warmed. I'm stealing another blanket off Rosemary and Una. Jesus, you'd think they were heading for the North Pole the way they're wrapped up. What are they doing in that toilet? Are yous not nearly finished in there? What are you doing in there, Rosemary?

Rosemary (*off*) I'm cleaning my teeth.

Ellen I'd let them fall out, if I was you, Bugs Bunny.

Rosemary enters.

Rosemary I do not have buck teeth and even if I did, they'd be my own, toothless Meg. I don't go around at night scaring the life out of people with my gummy face. (*She exits.*)

Ellen Watch out or I'll knock the same teeth down your throat.

Una (*off*) Leave her alone.

Ellen I'm glad to hear your voice. You're in there that long I was beginning to think you'd flushed yourself away.

Una No fear of you flushing yourself away.

Ellen No. No fear. Come on the two of yous. I'm starving and gasping for tea.

Una There's tea made.

Ellen Vera the vulture's drunk it.

Una enters.

Well, no harm to swanky Rohan, but that toilet I think is like a byre. Ellen, it can't be hygienic cooking in a lavatory.

Ellen Since when were you hygienic? We're cooking in there.

Una Why?

Ellen Because I can't stand anybody looking at me cook. (*She exits.*)

Una Who says you've to do all the cooking. Do you think we're going to poison you?

Vera You can hardly make a cup of tea.

Una So I'm supposed to be useless about a house?

Vera Your big sister has the baby spoilt.

Rebecca You and Rosemary can do all the dishes.

Una Thanks.

Rebecca I wish to God he had a shower installed. We'll all be stinking by the end of this.

Una What do you want a shower for? Isn't there a wash handbasin and you can boil the kettle for water.

Rebecca You need to take a bath once in a while.

Una I do. Every Good Friday.

Vera Why do you take it just on Good Friday?

Una It's very unlucky to break a habit like that.

Rebecca When I get you out, I'm dumping you into the nearest tub.

Ellen enters.

Ellen I'm telling you, yous don't know how to rough it. Me and Una will last this better than any of yous.

Rebecca Yous probably will.

The phone rings.

Ellen You answer it, Rebecca.

Rebecca Why me? Nobody's going to phone me.

Ellen You never know. It might be the TV. You're the best spoken.

Rebecca answers phone.

Rebecca Hello, yes, yes . . . This is me . . . She's here if you want to speak to her . . . She's a grown woman, I put her up to nothing, she makes up her own mind . . . Now look, I don't have to put up with your abuse. You want to speak to your wife, I'll put her on now . . . Vera, guess who?

Vera Who?

Rebecca Who else?

Vera What does he want?

Rebecca It's not to wish you support.

Ellen I'll face up to him.

Vera Thanks, I can handle it myself. (*She goes to the phone.*) Yeah? . . . Lower your voice, all I can make out is bitch . . . What? Christ Almighty. Is my mother not down with them? What do you mean, they want their mother, have they not got their father? They're yours too . . . Then do whatever she tells you . . . No, I'm not coming up . . . You'll have to learn. I had to . . . I was not swearing like a trooper yesterday. Who give you this inside information? The man with you, was it indeed? . . . Do you believe all Andy Bonner tells you? Well, I'll tell you what. You get your pal Bonner to get the best doctors for your weans if you're worried about them . . . What do you mean you haven't got a clean shirt for Sunday? Bonner knows a man with a whole factory full of shirts. Get him to give you a clean one . . . Fuck off yourself.(*She slams down the phone and walks to her seat. Pause*) Jesus. (*pause*) The two of them now have measles. Jesus, you'd think they were going to die with measles. My mother must be run off her feet. I shouldn't have kept the eldest home from school.

Ellen You never think of these things till afterwards.

Vera No. He's a right to be angry. It's my fault in the long run. He is worried, but what the hell was he doing with Bonner? That made me see total red. My mother will know everything. They'll be OK. It never rains but it pours.

Pause.

Una Ellen, did you say you were making tea?

Ellen I'll put it on.

Una Wouldn't it be desperate if they cut off the water? Can you imagine what it would be like without tea?

Ellen We'd have to open your stock of Bushmills.

Una You're not that badly supplied yourself. No. I mean it. I couldn't live without tea.

Rebecca This is from the one who's used to roughing it.

Una Well, you wouldn't have water in your handbasin, let alone your fancy shower, would you?

Ellen Girls, no fights now.

Una You're that peaceful, right enough.

Una lights a cigarette and glares at Ellen as she takes a mug. The phone rings.

Ellen Jesus, this is getting like an emergency ward.

Vera I'm not talking to him, Rebecca. Will you get it?

Rebecca No.

Pause. Ellen goes to the phone.

Ellen She is indeed. Una, it's your sister, Susan.

Una Oh my God. (*She quickly extinguishes the cigarette.*)

Ellen Susan doesn't know she smokes.

Una She'll hear you, she misses nothing.

Ellen I know she misses nothing, but not even she can poke her eyes down a phone.

Una goes to the phone.

Una Hello . . . hello, Susan, It's me, Una.

Ellen She hardly thought it was a grizzly bear.

Una What, Susan, it's a very bad line . . . I'm not to worry about missing Mass tomorrow, you're going to two . . . God love you, I'll tell them. She's having a Mass said for our intentions by a priest home from the foreign missions . . . What do you mean he's stood you a drink? Are you in a pub? How long have you been there? . . . How many have you had? . . . As many as are stood to you? You know you're never supposed to have more than two . . . Listen you to me. Get down that street quick. I warn you there's people posted to make sure you don't make an eejit out of yourself. Susan, I know you're drunk when I hear you laughing like that. Susan . . . She's put down the phone. What am I going to do with her? A woman over seventy with a man in a pub on a Saturday morning.

Ellen It'll be the life of her.

Una It's all right for you. She can't be trusted at her age.

Ellen Well, there's not much to be trusted with her, is there? You're hardly going to be left with a baby niece.

Una Don't be disgusting about my sister.

Rosemary Ellen?

Ellen What?

Rosemary What are we going to do about Mass? My mother would kill me if she thought I missed it. She must have forgot about Sunday.

Vera I forgot about it too.

Una Did we all forget?

Pause.

Ellen We've got a radio. We could hear it on that.

Una That's only for the sick and incapacitated.

Ellen That's us, incapacitated.

Una We are not. You need to be in something like a Communist jail to be incapacitated.

Ellen What kind of jail are we in?

Una We are not in jail. We can walk out of here.

Ellen And be put in jail for being in here? Look, we can't go to Mass, should they bring Mass to us?

Una Who?

Ellen The clergy.

Una Are you off your head?

Ellen But they must know we can't go, so will they come to us?

Una For God's sake they won't come to us.

Ellen Why?

Una You don't expect a priest to come running to a crowd of women who've locked themselves in a shirt factory.

Ellen Oh, but I do expect that.

Una Ellen, we'll be the talk of the town if we asked that.

Ellen We're already the talk of the town. Where's that directory? (*She finds directory.*) There's only one way to settle this.

Vera You wouldn't ring them.

Ellen walks to phone.

Ellen I would. Which one will I ring?

Vera The youngest.

Ellen Mitchell?

Una *Father* Mitchell.

Ellen finds number and dials.

Ellen Hello, hello, could I speak to Fr. Mitchell, please . . .
No it's not a sick call, more an incapacitated call . . .
Listen, dear, could I speak to the priest himself, not his
henwife, so would you have the manners to bring him to
the phone . . . Thanks . . . Father Mitchell, Hello, father.
I'm ringing from the shirt factory . . . I am . . . Oh you
heard . . . the whole town's talking about it . . . Well,
father, you know what this town is like . . . you didn't
know how bad until this . . . Father, I may as well ask
straight out, would you come and say Mass for us? None
of the five of us want to miss – (*As she receives his answer
her face registers little. Midway through the long pause she
says*) There's two sides to everything.

*The pause resumes until she speaks, immediately before
placing the receiver down slowly.*

I don't think I'll be on my knees this week anyway. (*She
watches the phone, saying nothing.*)

Una He's not coming.

Ellen No, he's not coming.

Vera What did he say?

Ellen He just thinks we should go home where we belong
and be down on our knees thanking God we have a job,

seeing the times we're in. He also thinks we might do something to help the factory, something constructive, now that for the first time we have a Catholic manager.

Vera What does he think the rest of us are?

Pause. Una walks to phone.

Una Do you remember that number?

Ellen 2367.

Una dials.

Una Father Mitchell, please . . . You heard me, bring him . . . this is another of the factory women. I know you've just heard from us. I've just heard your answer. I'd just like you to know, father, I think you are very, very cruel. (*She calmly replaces the receiver.*)

Darkness.

SCENE SEVEN

Saturday night.
   The women are getting ready for bed. Already in her slip, Vera sits on one of the makeshift beds, smoking. Rebecca is combing Ellen's hair, Ellen is sitting on one of the swivel chairs. Una, with a mug of tea, sits on the other. Rosemary is in the toilet. As the lights come up there is a short pause, then Una coughs.

Una You'd wonder at them still, cutting the phone.

Pause.

I mean if anyone took sick and needed a doctor quick.

Vera Don't talk about sickness. Have I not got enough to worry about.

Ellen They better not be looking for a priest, phone or no phone.

Vera I wish my mother had rung before it happened.

Pause.

Una Will he cut off the heat?

Rebecca Give him time, he will.

Una One electric fire won't be much good, will it?

Ellen Summer's coming.

Pause.

Una I wish I hadn't eaten that blackcurrant jam.

Pause.

I should never eat blackcurrant jam. It affects my stomach.

Ellen Well, at least it doesn't affect your feet.

Una I never mentioned my feet since coming in here.

Ellen If you have, nobody's listened to you.

Pause.

Una We never have blackcurrant jam at home.

Vera Why the hell did you eat it on the bread then? Your eyes are bigger than your belly, that's all that's wrong with you.

Una I was just trying to save butter, that's all I was doing. If you're anyway trying to do something here, all you get is abuse.

Vera Are you two soon going to be finished so we can put the light off and get to our bed?

Ellen Can you not sleep with the light on?

Vera I can't sleep with the light on.

Rebecca We'll be finished in a couple of minutes.

Vera Speed it up then.

Una Rosemary's still doing herself up in the bathroom.

Vera She can find her way in the dark.

Una I never knew anyone that had to make themselves up to go to bed.

Pause.

Una Did you think they'd be down with us today, Ellen?

Ellen I thought Bonner would have made some appearance by now.

Rebecca Will there be somebody from Dublin with him?

Ellen Likely.

Una The Dublin union man will have no truck with Rohan.

Ellen He'll have truck with us, so he'll have truck with Rohan. Salvation falls from the skies of Dublin. Mr Rohan might even get him to lead a procession of prayers around the factory.

Pause.

Vera I wonder did my mother try to get through here and couldn't.

Rebecca Vera, if anything had been badly wrong, you would have heard. Hearing nothing is a good sign.

Vera How would you know what kind of a sign it was? Since when did you become the expert? Have you a wean tucked away somewhere we know nothing about?

Una Jesus Christ, Vera.

Vera I wish people would keep their noses out of other people's business.

Rebecca I was only wondering –

Vera Don't bother your arse wondering.

Rebecca All right, I won't, you crabbit old bitch.

Ellen Look, Vera, you've been like a bag of cats since dinnertime. We can hardly speak to you without getting the face torn off us. If you want to go up and see them, slip out well on in the night and come down early in the morning. It'll put your mind at rest. I know how you can worry about them. Didn't I have to go through it too?

Rosemary enters.

Vera Are you implying mine might get what yours had?

Pause. Vera rises.

Are you saying to my face that mine have what yours had?

Ellen No. I'm not saying that.

Vera You better never think it even, do you hear? You're a big woman, Ellen. You can face up to anyone and anything. You say whatever you like. You got us in here, no matter what hardship it took or it will take. Not only for us, but for everybody else that you locked out of this factory. But remember one other thing. You're tough, but that does not give you licence to say what you like to me, because I know, tough as you are, you are not fair. You can batter down any body you want to because you're only a bully. But you won't bully me. I can face up to you. I can – FUCK IT.

Rebecca goes to Vera.

69

Vera My head, Rebecca. My head. I'm sorry. I don't know.

Ellen All right.

Una Ellen.

Ellen I don't want to talk about it.

Una goes and opens a bottle of Bushmills.

Una Cracked open Fort Knox.

Una pours Ellen some whiskey.

For you, Ellen.

Ellen Thanks.

Una Rosemary, get some cups. Get that into you, Vera.

Rosemary enters with three cups, Una fills two.

For you, Rebecca.

Rosemary What about me?

Una There's a big tap out there and plenty of cold water. Good luck folks.

Una and Rebecca drink. Vera and Ellen remain silent, then Ellen lights a cigarette.

Vera I'm the biggest bully, not you. I'm worse than a bully. That's why I said what I did.

Ellen What did you say? What did you say but what you thought? Weans, weans. Fuck them. They're not worth it. Three buried in a year. What loss. Believe me, behind all the handshaking and tears, people were saying a lot worse than you could, Vera. When I went near a woman that had a wean with her, you could see her panicking in case I touched it. The very look of me might affect them. I began to think I was a walking carrier. If it hadn't been for Una,

I'd have been in a mental home. I spent the day cleaning everything. Going off my head cleaning. If I cleaned everything, I thought nobody else would have to go through it. Can you believe how knocked stupid I was?

Una That's enough, Ellen. Vera said she was sorry.

Ellen Do you remember, Una, tearing in one morning and nearly dragging me by the hair of the head down the street?

Una I would have done it too, you stupid bitch.

Ellen She battered me down the street. We were like two drunk woman.

Una Who said we weren't?

Ellen There's just one thing, Vera. I don't think I forced anyone into coming in here.

Vera I know you didn't. It's just my big mouth.

Ellen Let me finish. We all know why we're locked in here. For once they can't put us out. We put them out. I think this is going to be our last chance to get them on their knees. I want to see them crawl, and that's the only way they'll get us out of here. Jesus, I'd work for nothing if I could see that.

Una Well, I wouldn't. I'd rather go off my head sitting in the house than sit here for nothing.

Rebecca That's right. We're not in here for nothing. We're in here to get the best for ourselves. And nobody can get that for us but ourselves. That's why we're in here. Isn't it?

Pause.

Una Well, God's good.

Ellen Unfortunately, he doesn't pay our wages.

Una If we're going to start on either religion or politics, I'm leaving this night. There's been enough fights for one evening. What difference does it make to people like us what happens?

Ellen It's people like you have the country the way it is.

Una It's people like me the country has the way I am. I've as much interest in it as it has in me. Would anybody like another?

Ellen You're going strong. I haven't touched this.

Vera I've only started this. It's OK.

Rebecca I wouldn't mind a drop more, Una.

Una Good girl, give us your mug.

Rosemary What about me?

Una I told you about the tap.

Ellen Give her some, Una. Shut her mouth. Go and get plenty of water. I'll pour her a taste that'll do her no harm.

  Rosemary exits.

Una Right then, you tell her mother who started her off when she comes in staggering after a dance.

Ellen I will.

Vera Una, you have this. I'm not keen on whiskey. Rosemary?

Rosemary (*off*) What?

Vera Look in my case out there. There should be some gin and some tonic. Bring in some.

Rosemary OK.

Ellen What kind of night is this turning into? I'm glad

Rohan is not here to see it. He'd think we came here on some kind of picnic.

Rebecca He went for enough picnics on our time.

Rosemary enters with gin, tonic and mug.

Rosemary I think I'd rather have gin.

Ellen You'll take what you're given and shut up.

Rosemary Well, if I taste the whiskey first, then can I taste the gin?

Ellen NO.

Rosemary I'm not asking you. I'm asking Vera.

Vera We'll see.

Ellen Could I have another drop?

Una Do you ever think of opening your own?

Ellen Don't worry. I've already counted what I owe you. You're a great big-hearted Arthur. Everybody else gets it with a smile, but I know rightly I'll have to pay.

Una takes Ellen's mug and pours her a drink.

Una I'm far too soft.

Ellen Just like a big iced caramel. You could swallow you, you're that sweet. I hate a big night without a song. Who's going to start? Rosemary?

Rosemary I can't sing.

Ellen Anything?

Rosemary Nothing. Ask Rebecca.

Rebecca This forcing is going to go on all night. I hate it. We better get it over with. Vera, come on.

Vera You mean the only song I know is the one you're going to sing? You're a smart bitch at times, Rebecca. All right, wait one minute. (*She finishes her drink.*)

Vera and Rebecca (*sing*)
Do you love a soldier, do you love a Tan,
Do you love a strong and a big Englishman?
But still I love him, can't deny him,
I'll go with him wherever he goes.

Una Good man Nigel.

Vera and Rebecca (*sing*)
He bought me a handkerchief, red, white and blue.
I caught it and ripped it, I tore it in two.
But still I love him, can't deny him,
I'll go with him wherever he goes.

Una and Ellen Nigel strikes again.

Vera and Rebecca (*sing*)
He stood at the corner, shirt tail hanging out.
He lifted his hand and he hit me a clout.
But still I love him, can't deny him,
I'll go with him wherever he goes.

Ellen You can handle him, Vera.

Vera and Rebecca (*sing*)
Before I was married, I was bright and gay,
But now that I'm married the cot's in the way,
But still I love him, can't deny him,
I'll go with him wherever he goes.

Ellen For Jesus sake, why are yous singing about Black and Tans?

Rebecca A private joke.

Ellen You should be ashamed of yourselves.

Una Oh, for Christ's sake, one soldier's no different from another. Irishmen kicked the shite out of plenty as well. If the English hadn't been doing it for them, they would have made a good job of doing it themselves.

Ellen A blow from your own's different.

Una Aye, because they're the ones you don't heal from.

Ellen She wasn't always that hard on soldiers. What about that Yank in the naval base in Derry during the war? She had the road wore out travelling to dances.

Vera Una, tell us.

Una Mind your own business.

Ellen She wouldn't leave her own native land.

Una It never went as far as that and you know it, you bad bitch. He wrote, but it just petered out. The way things go. Listen, talking of dances, there's always a good jazz programme on at this time. Where's your wireless, Rebecca?

Rebecca What do you know about jazz?

Una Haven't you just heard that Marlene Dietrich here was nearly a G.I. bride? I didn't come down the Mississippi in a bottle bath.

Rebecca fiddles with the radio switch and finds the station. The introduction of 'So Do I' is heard.

That's Kenny Ball. Leave it on, he's all right. Who's for a dance, anybody?

Ellen Sit down, you eejit.

Una Come on, is anybody dancing?

Una dances alone, the others watching.

Oh God, there's nothing like a good jazz band. It was once all jazz. Ellen, pour us another one, go on.

Ellen What do you think I am? Some kind of bunny girl running to serve you?

Una Go on. I poured yours twice.

Ellen Where's your mug?

Una I don't know.

Rebecca Here it is. I'll get it for you, Una.

Una You're a living saint, Rebecca.

Rebecca Go away and shite.

Ellen Now, now. I'll complain to head office. I don't have far to go.

Rebecca Sorry, I didn't know he was back. Could we stop talking about Nigel? I was beginning to enjoy myself.

Vera You were stupid not to take him for every penny he had.

Una Cheers to Rebecca. The only one to land one from management.

Rebecca Just cut it. I had enough stick when he was here.

Ellen Cut it's right, folks. It's been a long day. We'll call it a halt. I'm done.

Una Come on. One more.

Ellen Listen to her, go away and sober up.

Una We haven't to get up in the morning.

Vera No. I'm going to hit the sack.

Una Yous are no crack.

Rosemary, who has been helping herself to drink since the music, starts to laugh suddenly, increasing in volume.

Vera What's wrong with you?

Rosemary It's the thought of seeing Ellen in a bunny suit. The wee tail.

Ellen starts to laugh and the others follow. Rosemary stands quickly.

Ellen Remove her immediately.

Ellen and Una escort Rosemary off. Vera and Rebecca sit on, saying nothing.

Vera Are you tired?

Rebecca A bit, are you?

Vera Yes. You're being very quiet.

Rebecca No, I'm not. You haven't been listening.

Vera Are you still angry?

Rebecca No. I'm not still angry.

Vera I've a big mouth, haven't I?

Rebecca The biggest, woman, the biggest.

Vera You're still not angry?

Rebecca Vera, I'm not angry.

Sounds of Rosemary being violently ill.

Vera Will they want a hand?

Rebecca They can handle it.

They laugh lowly.

Vera We'll go to our bed. Leave on the light till they come in.

Rebecca OK.

Ellen (*off*) Vera, I cannot face this. Will you come in and help Una?

Vera No rest for the wicked.

Rebecca I'll warm the bed for you.

Vera Big-hearted, aren't you?

Rebecca Maybe.

Ellen enters as Vera exits.

Ellen Rather you than me, dear. Her whole life's coming up.

Vera Thanks.

Pause. Ellen notices Rebecca's stare at her. She smiles.

Ellen Why are you devouring me with them big eyes?

Rebecca Una's drink and a song and a dance won't always save us.

Ellen You're no crack. There's fights in the best of houses.

Rebecca We're not in a house now, Ellen. We're in here.

Ellen Are you going to turn against me next? (*pause*) Are you?

Darkness.

SCENE EIGHT

Ellen is sitting alone in the dawn light. Una turns around in the makeshift bed.

Una Can you not sleep, Ellen?

Ellen I'm not tired.

Una What's wrong with you?

Silence.

I think I'm beginning to wander.

Ellen You'll be all right.

Una Do you think so?

Silence.

Will you go to your bed?

Ellen Stop worrying about me.

Una Are you hungry?

Ellen No.

Una You've barely put a mouthful into you this two days.

Ellen I'm grand.

Una Why are you not eating?

Ellen I'm grand, Una. Go to sleep. Is Rosemary all right?

Una Not a stir. Vera was good to her.

Ellen Aye.

Una She's not a bad wee girl, Rosemary.

Ellen You're definitely wandering.

Una I had a very funny dream, Ellen. You were in it. I don't know if you were laughing or crying. You were wearing that cream blouse. Do you remember it?

Ellen How would I remember it?

Una You were married in it.

Silence.

79

What happened to it?

Ellen I burned it. I burned every stitch. After the burials. Am I cursed, Una?

Una No. Go to sleep, Ellen. It's the middle of the night.

Ellen It's nearly daybreak.

The phone rings. Ellen stands up.

Sweet Jesus, say the word is good.

Vera rapidly gets to her feet.

Vera Rebecca.

Ellen answers it. Silence.

Ellen It's gone dead.

Vera What?

Ellen There's nobody there.

Vera Give it to me. Hello, who is it? Hello. Who's there?

Silence.

It rung. It did ring, didn't it?

Ellen There was nobody there.

Vera Somebody must have been there if the phone rang.

Ellen They put it down again.

Vera Why?

Ellen I don't know.

Vera Why would they put the phone down?

Silence.

Who was it, Rebecca?

Rebecca Someone trying to contact us, I suppose.

Vera Who?

Rebecca They'll ring back. Put down the phone.

Vera replaces the receiver. Silence.

Vera Something's wrong.

Rebecca What makes you so sure?

Vera Definitely wrong.

Rebecca Go up and see. I'll come with you.

Ellen She can't. Nobody can leave until the morning.

Rebecca What?

Ellen Nobody moves –

Vera Get that cabinet out of my road.

Ellen I mean it, Vera.

Vera Mean what?

Ellen Until Bonner –

Vera Fuck Bonner. My weans –

Ellen Will live, Vera. Nobody's leaving.

The phone rings. Vera grabs the phone.

Vera If there's anything wrong, tell us.

Silence.

Hello, it's me, Vera, who's there?

Rebecca I think I know who's there.

Una Why is the phone reconnected?

Rebecca It's him. It's Rohan.

Vera He wouldn't do that to us. He couldn't do this to me.

Rebecca He could. How dirty can you fight?

Vera replaces the receiver.

Vera If anything happens –

Rebecca Nothing's going to happen, Vera.

Vera How do you know?

Rebecca You're panicking over nothing.

Ellen Leave her alone.

Rebecca I just know –

Ellen I told you, leave her alone. We're all tired. If the phone rings again, leave it. Or I'll answer it –

Rebecca And say what, Ellen?

Ellen Would you like to tell me?

Rebecca I might tell you to shut your mouth and let him stew –

Ellen Don't talk to me like that, Rebecca.

Rebecca If Vera wants to go –

Ellen Let her go, let her go.

Silence.

We can all go. Nothing to stop us. Go out that door –

The phone rings. Ellen goes to answer it. Rebecca stops her.

Rebecca Leave it. Let him ring. Let him waste his time.

Vera Are you sure it's him?

Ellen grabs the phone.

Ellen For Christ's sake, who is it? What do you want? It's the middle of the night. We can't sleep. Will you let us sleep?

Ellen throws down the receiver. Silence.

Vera I better go.

Rebecca Why?

Vera You never know –

Rebecca You do.

Vera Rebecca, I've two weans –

Rebecca And a man.

Vera What about him.

Silence.

What about him?

Rebecca It's for him you're going.

Vera What do you mean?

Rebecca Go back to your big man, Vera. He's your biggest wean. It's him you want to look after. Run on home to him.

Vera Do you ever listen to yourself?

Rebecca Do you?

Vera What's happening to us? Am I going off my head? We have to leave. We have to leave.

Rebecca No.

Ellen Rebecca, Vera has two sick weans –

Rebecca Do not use Vera as an excuse.

Ellen I'm not looking for excuses.

Rebecca One minute nobody's leaving, Ellen, the next we're all going. Well, I'm not going, Ellen. I'm not leaving.

Ellen You're keeping this on single handed?

Rebecca Not single handed. They're all staying.

Ellen If they're staying –

Rebecca It will be without you, right? Maybe we're already without you.

Ellen I know where I'm needed.

Rebecca I don't need you anymore, Ellen.

Ellen Whose side do you think I'm on?

Rebecca I don't care. I don't know what the sides are anymore.

Ellen Then you don't know much.

Rebecca I know you. Why do you want to leave?

Ellen All right, I'll tell nobody to stay or leave. If they want to stay, I'll stay. Do you all want to stay?

Rosemary Do you think we're beaten, Ellen?

Una I don't know what it's like not to be beaten. What it's like to win. I don't know what it's like to even fight to win. And I want to know what it's like to stand your own ground to the bitter end. I'm staying.

Silence.

Rebecca Vera?

Vera Ask Ellen.

Rebecca I'm asking you, Vera.

Silence.

Vera Stay. I'm tired. I'm very tired, Rebecca.

Ellen Listen, big woman, do you know what you are going to do next?

Rebecca I don't know.

Vera Jesus, Becky, you must have some idea.

Rebecca I told you, I don't know. All I can tell you is I'm sticking it out.

Rosemary But what exactly are you going to do?

Rebecca I've already said I don't know.

Ellen Just a minute you. Don't bloody think you're going to crawl back into your shell again. You were full of the sound of your own voice five minutes ago, you're not going to lose it now.

Una She's right, Rebecca. You owe it to us to tell us what you see us doing.

Rebecca I owe you nothing.

Ellen You owe us a reason –

Rebecca Why do we always think that we owe each other something? Why do we have to think we owe each other something? Is it because we're too scared to stand on our own two feet? You want us scared, Ellen. You think and we think that if you take away your hand, we'll fall on our faces. That's why you flatten us, so you can lift us up when you feel like it and we'll be thankful. Why do you want our thanks?

Ellen I've never asked for thanks.

Rebecca Then what are you asking for?

Ellen I'm asking that you use whatever brains you have and walk out that door –

Rebecca Where? Into Bonner's arms, so you and him can keep up your private fight. Do you realise it's different this time, Ellen?

Ellen We have to stand together –

Rebecca We are, damn you Ellen, we are.

Ellen How long do you think we're going to last in here?

Rebecca We'll last.

Ellen Let me finish.

Rebecca I've let you finish too long. Why don't you leave, Ellen? Why don't you just go? Walk out that door. What's stopping you? That's what you want. You're scared, Ellen. You want us scared. Why? I've been watching you. I've watched you since coming in here. You've wanted to leave since that siren went. You want to leave now. Do you know why? If this factory is closed on your account what happens, Ellen? The whole town blames you and you never want to face blame again. I did today what you couldn't do. If I owe you anything, it's to defy you, because you owe us nothing and Ellen, you owe the dead nothing

Una It's time to climb down, Ellen. You've met your match. You were a long time looking but you've found her at long last. I mind when the first one was buried. You opened your mouth. Whatever sound came out of it, I heard you cursing your own life. The curse has been lifted. Fight on. We all need you to, but you'll have to stop fighting yourself. That had to be said, Ellen. And I'm not going to be sorry for saying it.

Ellen Don't any of yous waste your time being sorry, I

threw sorry out the window years ago. I suppose you live and learn. Well fuck yous, I'm still capable of living, whatever about learning. Maybe I'm not that interested. Maybe it's not worth knowing. Is that why I wanted to leave here? To get out into fresh air. Rid myself of the smell of this place. But how could I get rid of the smell of myself? A nobody that has nothing, beaten the day she walked into this godforsaken factory. Would I have been somebody if I never set foot in it? It would have taken luck, and I never chanced my own. A wasted life. Heartbreaking isn't it? Another martyr for old fucking Ireland. Well here's one martyr that's going to be carried to her grave squealing. And it'll take a damn sight more than you, big lady, to dig that grave. I started this, you're right. So I'm damned sure I'll finish it. But just one thing. You better think fast what we're going to do next, because if you don't come up with something you'll answer to me, and you should know me by now, daughter, I'm a tougher nut to crack than the other boyos.

Ellen exits, closing toilet door. Short pause. Una looks at Vera, glances at Rebecca, then back to Vera, and exits to Ellen.

Rebecca Go and lie down a while, Vera.

Pause.

I won't blame you if you go.

Vera Go? I wonder where. I'm a foolish woman. I'll do the foolish thing now. I won't leave, Becky. (*pause*) Not today anyway.

Rebecca Sleep.

Vera Rebecca, what about Bonner?

Rebecca Vera, I've just tackled Ellen. Let me get my breath back.

Vera He's a bastard.

Rebecca Are you worried about him?

Vera No.

Rebecca Why not?

Vera So are you.

They laugh.

Rebecca Sleep.

Vera I'm sleeping. I'm sleeping.

Rosemary Do you have any idea, Rebecca, what's going to happen?

Rebecca They'll try first to starve us out, but they won't.

Rosemary How?

Rebecca We could eat you.

Rosemary What are we going to do, Rebecca?

Rebecca What are you going to do, Rosemary?

Rosemary What everybody else does.

Rebecca Rubbish, you don't need anybody to tell you what to do. Steal a horse and get out. Get away as far as you can.

Rosemary Why don't you?

Rebecca Tell me why didn't I?

Rosemary I don't know why. Nobody can read anybody else's mind.

Silence.

Rebecca I read something once. I didn't know what it meant, but I learned it off by heart. It's stayed in my mind.

'I saw a woman sleeping. In her sleep she dreamt Life stood before her and held in each hand a gift – in the one Love, in the other Freedom. And she said to the woman, Choose. And the woman waited long and she said, Freedom. I heard the woman laugh in her sleep.' Yes, I heard the woman laugh in her sleep. (*She closes her eyes.*)

Rosemary Come on, Rebecca, waken.

Rebecca opens her eyes.

Rebecca I have, woman, I've wakened.

Darkness.

OBSERVE THE SONS OF ULSTER
MARCHING TOWARDS THE SOMME

In memory of Michael Hayes

Characters

Kenneth Pyper, as an old man
Kenneth Pyper, in his thirties
David Craig, in his late twenties
John Millen, in his thirties
William Moore, in his thirties
Christopher Roulston, in his thirties
Martin Crawford, in his early twenties
George Anderson, in his thirties
Nat McIlwaine, in his thirties

Observe the Sons of Ulster Marching Towards the Somme
was first performed at the Peacock Theatre, Dublin, in
February 1985. The cast was as follows:

Kenneth Pyper (*as an old man*) Geoff Golden
Kenneth Pyper (*as a young man*) Bosco Hogan
David Craig Lorcan Cranitch
George Anderson Oliver Maguire
Mat McIlwaine Ian McElhinney
Christopher Roulston Tom Hickey
Martin Crawford Michael Ford
William Moore Mark Lambert
John Millen Niall O'Brien

Directed by Patrick Mason
Designed by Frank Hallinan Flood
Lighting by Tony Wakefield

The play subsequently opened in London at the
Hampstead Theatre in July 1986, directed by Michael
Attenborough.

Part One: Remembrance

Low drumbeat. The **Elder Pyper** *wakes.*

Pyper Again. As always, again. Why does this persist? What more have we to tell each other? I remember nothing today. Absolutely nothing.

Silence.

I do not understand your insistence on my remembrance. I'm being too mild. I am angry at your demand that I continue to probe. Were you not there in all your dark glory? Have you no conception of the horror? Did it not touch you at all? A passion for horror disgusts me. I have seen horror. There is nothing to tell you. Those willing to talk to you of that day, to remember for your sake, to forgive you, they invent as freely as they wish. I am not one of them. I will not talk, I will not listen to you. Invention gives that slaughter shape. That scale of horror has no shape, as you in your darkness have no shape. Your actions that day were not, they are not acceptable. You have no right to excuse that suffering, parading it for the benefit of others.

Silence.

I will not apologize for that outburst before you. You know I am given to sudden fits like that. The shock you gave never left my system entirely. I still see your ghosts. Very infrequently. During daylight now. Dear Lord, you are kind in your smaller mercies. Did you intend that we should keep seeing ghosts? It was the first sign that your horrors had shaken us into madness. Some were lucky enough to suffer your visions immediately. Those I belonged to, those I have not forgotten, the irreplaceable ones, they kept their nerve, and they died. I survived. No, survival was not my lot. Darkness, for eternity, is not survival.

Silence.

There is a type of man who invites death upon himself. I thought once this is the stuff heroes are made from. I enlisted in the hope of death. I would be such a man. But mine was not the stuff of heroes. Those with me were heroes because they died without complaint for what they believed in. They taught me, by the very depth of their belief, to believe. To believe in you. What sense could you make of their sacrifice? I at least continued their work in this province. The freedom of faith they fought and died for would be maintained. There would be, and there will be no surrender. The sons of Ulster will rise and lay their enemy low, as they did at the Boyne, as they did at the Somme, against any invader who will trespass on to their homeland. Fenians claim a Cuchullian as their ancestor, but he is ours, for they lay down for centuries and wept in their sorrow, but we took up arms and fought against an ocean. An ocean of blood. His blood is our inheritance. Not theirs. Sinn Fein? Ourselves alone. It is we, the Protestant people, who have always stood alone. We have stood alone and triumphed, for we are God's chosen.

Silence.

Leave me. Do not possess me. I do not wish to be your chosen.

Silence.

Leave me. Must I remember? Yes, I remember. I remember details. I remember the sky was pink, extraordinarily pink. There were men from Coleraine, talking about salmon fishing. A good man who wanted to enter the Church gave me an orange sash. We sang hymns and played football. That is true, football. Someone said the sky is red today. David said it's pink. And I looked and I could see again. I saw the sky in him. I knew he would die, for he was turning from earth into air.

Silence. As the light increases, Pyper sees the ghosts appear, **Craig**, **Roulston** *and* **Crawford**.

You have bestowed your parting gift. Welcome. You look angry, David. Have I hurt you by speaking? I can't understand your silence. Can you, Roulston, you, Crawford? I envy your happiness together. But you must call as and when you wish. This place is yours when you wish it to be. I want you here. I want you to stay with me. Where are the others? Is Moore still searching for John Millen? Will he never believe Millen cannot be found? If he were found, would he not return here? Moore must stop searching. It is time to rest. I would rest, but when he frees you from his darkness, he asks questions, as if he wishes to remember. Where is Anderson? Still attending McIlwaine? I saw that, you know. Cut in two. Anderson falling on him as if his body could hold McIlwaine's body together. I looked and saw his blood was the same colour as my blood. When I saw that colour, I felt my blood on fire and no water would ever quench it again. You were right, David. The last battle. I died that day with you.

Silence.

The house has grown cold. Ulster has grown lonely. We discourage visitors. Security. Men my age have been burned in their beds. Fenian cowards. They won't burn me out with their fire. I have defeated fire before. And you will always defend me. You will always guard Ulster. I miss you. Each day that increases. Is that because I'm coming closer to you? Am I at last leaving earth for air? Tell me. Give me a sign. Touch me. Why are you silent with me? Have I said too much? Have I said enough? Tell me.

Silence.

I want to ask you something. I need your answer before I turn into air. Answer me why we did it. Why we let ourselves be led to extermination? In the end, we were not led, we led ourselves. We claimed we would die for each other in battle. To fulfil that claim we marched into the battle that killed us all. That is not loyalty. That is not love. That is hate. Deepest hate. Hate for one's self. We wished ourselves to die and in doing so we let others die to satisfy our blood lust. That lust we inherited. The true curse of Adam. I was born knowing there was something rotting in humanity. I tried to preserve that knowledge, David. To die willingly, to die clutching it, but you defied my death. I need defiance now, David. Ulster lies in rubble at our feet. Save it. Save me. Take me out of this war alive. Evil is come upon us. The temple of the Lord is darkness. He has ransacked his dwelling. The Protestant gods die (*sings*) 'Fare thee well, Enniskillen, fare thee well for a while, and when the war is over –'

Pyper sees more ghosts rise, **Moore, Millen, McIlwaine, Anderson.**

You are here at last. Your rest begins. Moore, Millen, Anderson, McIlwaine. I have remarkably fine skin, Anderson. Remarkably fine for a man. Look, David, I've cut myself peeling an apple. Kiss it better.

Pyper holds his arms to the ghosts.

Dance in the deserted temple of the Lord. Dance unto death before the Lord.

Pyper sees the ghost of the **Younger Pyper.** *As if introducing that younger self to the other ghosts, he beckons it towards them, invitingly.*

Myself. My soul.
Dance. Dance.

Part Two: Initiation

*A makeshift barracks, bedclothes in heaps along the floor.
Already in uniform, apart from his jacket, the Younger
Pyper has already sorted out some bedclothes. He sits, his
army kit beside him, peeling an apple. He cuts himself.*

Pyper Damnation. Blood.

Pyper sucks his thumb. David Craig enters.

Hate the sight of it.

Craig Sorry?

Pyper What for?

Craig I thought you said something.

Pyper I did.

Craig To me?

Pyper No, so don't apologize.

Craig Ah, right.

Pyper I was talking to my blood.

Pyper shows Craig his bleeding thumb.

I was telling it I hate the sight of it.

Craig Never pleasant to see from man or beast. Lord, this
place hasn't much order about it. Do we have to sleep on
the ground?

Pyper It's the amount of volunteers from our beloved
province. They can't keep up with us.

Craig How will they train us all?

Pyper They won't.

Craig We can take any of these bedclothes?

Pyper I did.

Craig Right.

Craig sorts out some bedclothes, starts to make up some sort of sleeping space.

Pyper It won't stop for hours now.

Craig It's only a cut, man. You're not in your grave.

Pyper You're making yours.

Craig What?

Pyper I could have taken the finger off myself.

Craig But you didn't.

Pyper That's not the point. I could have. And why? For the sake of peeling an apple. I was hungry. I had an apple. I wanted to eat it. I had to peel it. And I almost cut my thumb off. You have to take risks in this life.

Craig You find peeling an apple's a risk?

Pyper I cut my finger, didn't I?

Craig Thumb.

Pyper Thumb, finger, it's all the same. Kiss it better, will you?

Craig Get away home out of that.

Pyper I can't go home. I've signed up. The army has me. Once you're in, there's no getting out.

Craig Well, you'll see a lot more than a bleeding thumb before you're out.

Pyper screams.

Pyper Now look what you've done. You've really scared me.

Craig Who the hell are you?

Pyper Pyper, sir, Kenneth Pyper.

Craig Are you sure, Pyper –

Pyper Call me Kenneth.

Craig Kenneth, are you a fit man for this life?

Pyper Yes, sir, I wish to serve, sir.

Craig I'm not sir. I'm the same rank as you. I'm Craig. David Craig.

Pyper David –

Craig Call me Craig.

Pyper I prefer sir.

Craig You're a bit of a mocker, aren't you, Pyper?

Pyper Me, sir?

Craig They'll soon knock that out of you.

Pyper I sincerely hope so.

Craig So do I.

Pyper Like a piece of apple?

Craig I've work to do.

Pyper I can't tempt you?

Craig Get on with your business and stop this foolishness.

Pyper Have you ever looked at an apple?

Craig Yes.

Pyper What did you see?

Craig An apple.

Pyper I don't. I see through it.

Craig The skin, you mean?

Pyper The flesh. The flesh. The flesh.

Craig What about it?

Pyper Beautiful. Hard. White.

Craig Not if it's rotten.

Pyper What?

Craig The apple. You know the saying. One bad apple spoils the barrel.

Pyper You forgot your shirt, son.

Pyper leaps off his bed, races to Craig carrying a shirt.

Craig I did not forget my shirt.

Pyper Yes, you did. Here.

Craig My shirt is here.

Pyper Then whose is this?

Craig It must be your own.

Pyper No not mine. I'm wearing mine.

Craig Take your shirt, take yourself and get out of my sight.

Pyper You don't want your shirt?

Craig I don't want your shirt.

Pyper Please yourself.

Craig begins to undress, Pyper watching him intently.

Craig glares at Pyper. Pyper shrugs, turns his back. When Craig is undressed, Pyper turns rapidly. Craig starts.

Craig Will you for God's sake –

Pyper You're as scared of me as I am of blood.

Craig I am not scared of you.

Pyper Then what are you doing here?

Craig My country's at war. I –

Pyper Did you not join up to die for me?

Craig For you?

Pyper It'll be good sport.

Craig You're a madman, Pyper.

Pyper Am I, David?

Craig Well, you're a rare buckcat anyroad.

Pyper Funny word that.

Craig Buckcat? It's a –

Pyper No. Rare. Are you rare, David?

Craig When I want to be. Army's no place for rareness though.

Pyper Why not? It takes all sorts to make an army.

Craig True enough. You never know. We could end up dying for each other.

Pyper No, we couldn't. I won't anyway.

Pyper throws Craig the shirt.

A little gift, don't argue. There's plenty more where they come from. Get into uniform, David. You'll catch your death. Then I'll have to follow suit.

Craig gets into uniform. William Moore and John Millen enter, Moore punching Millen forward playfully.

Millen You never laid a hand on her.

Moore Think what you like.

Millen You wouldn't know where to put it if I wasn't there to tell you.

Moore Would I not?

Millen goes to attack Moore. Moore dodges by greeting Pyper and Craig.

Good morning, chaps. My name is Moore, Willy Moore. This specimen is Millen, John Millen.

Craig Hello.

Craig goes to shake hands, Pyper abruptly intervenes.

Pyper Mr Moore? Mr Millen?

Millen Yes?

Pyper You know where you are, I take it?

Millen Supposed to be an army barracks.

Pyper It is such. And why are you here?

Millen Who are you?

Pyper I asked you why you were here, Mr John Millen. I see I had better tell you. You are here as a volunteer in the army of your king and empire. You are here to train to meet that empire's foe. You are here as a loyal son of Ulster, for the empire's foe is Ulster's foe. You are here to learn, Mr Millen. Learn to defend yourself and your comrades, and while you are here, you will learn to conduct yourself with respect, respect for this army, respect for your position in this army, and respect for all other positions above you. Since there are no ranks beneath you, you will never be at ease again until you leave this army. Do you understand that clearly?

Millen Yes.

Pyper At ease, man.

Pyper salutes and leaves them. Moore and Millen stare at him. Pyper sits cross-legged on the bedclothes, motionless, ignoring their stare. Millen and Moore take bedclothes, start to unpack kit. Millen goes to Craig, mouths the question, Who is he?, nodding at Pyper. Craig shrugs innocence.

Moore You boys just volunteered?

Craig Aye, I have anyway.

Moore Where are you from?

Craig Enniskillen, Fermanagh.

Millen Know a family Rushton there?

Craig Can't say I do. Where do they live?

Millen A bit outside your own town. Tempo.

Craig Should know them.

Moore We're Coleraine men.

Craig None better. I'm Craig. David Craig.

Moore and Craig shake hands. Millen goes towards Pyper.

Pyper David's the name, David Craig.

Moore That's a funny thing. Two boys with the same name.

Craig His name's Pyper.

Moore Then why does he call himself –

Pyper I have remarkably fine skin, don't I? For a man, remarkably fine.

Craig and Moore rapidly start getting their beds together.

Millen Have you indeed? (*He notices the others at work. He does so also.*)

Pyper Quite remarkably fine. Soft. I've never done a day's work in my life.

Moore Lucky man. This is a desperate kip to house us in. Will we have to make these up every morning?

Millen Where do you think you are? Home? Have you never made up a makeshift bed in your life?

Moore Woman's work. You don't join the army to do woman's work.

Pyper No, not a single day. I once nearly starved rather than do a day's work. In fact I did starve. You wouldn't think that to look at me, would you?

Millen Indeed you wouldn't. Willy, do you sleep on your left side or right?

Moore Why?

Millen Your ma warned me you snored. I'm wondering if I should change places.

Moore I don't snore.

Millen How do you know?

Moore I know.

Millen How could anyone know if they snored?

Moore My Ma never told me I snored. How come she tells you?

Pyper I remember that time in France.

Craig What?

Pyper In France. I nearly starved there.

Craig You've been there?

Moore When were you there?

Millen What's it like?

Pyper That time I thought my end had come. Well-deserved bad end. Absolutely friendless. It was a Friday. I hadn't eaten for two weeks or so. I kept seeing things. Maybe they were there. I felt miles away from everybody. I thought I was dying. Not just in the way we're all dying, but suddenly and unprepared. I thought I was growing wings. But I made a vow I wouldn't die. I vowed that if I survived, I would never go back to France. If I did go back, I asked that I be struck blind. I made a covenant, and I survived.

Moore You had no money at all or people to pull you through?

Pyper None.

Millen How did you make it home from France without money?

Pyper Remember I thought I was growing wings? Well, I flew.

Moore Can I ask you something?

Pyper Anything.

Moore What's a rare boyo like you doing in an army?

Pyper What's a rare boyo like you doing in an army?

Moore If I'm rare, what does that make you?

Pyper Cigarette?

Moore If you have one to spare.

Pyper I don't smoke.

Millen Is this a barracks or an asylum?

Pyper begins to whoop.

Pyper Sorry. Don't worry, I'm certified as fit and sane for work as any of you in this army.

Millen and Moore start to change into uniform. Craig goes to Pyper.

Craig Why did you enlist, Pyper?

Pyper The name is Kenneth, David.

Craig If you don't want to answer –

Pyper I enlisted, before I was conscripted, because I'd nothing better to do. No, that's wrong. I'd nothing else to do. I enlisted because I'm dying anyway. I want it over quickly.

Craig I thought you said you were certified fit.

Pyper Fit for dying. Fit for the grave. Fit for pushing up the daisies. Point proved.

Millen Look, we're going to have to share this place for the training time, Pyper. I've only met you. And I don't like you already. Now I don't care what you're going on about, but no more chat about dying. It'll be looking at us straight in the face soon enough.

Pyper I'm looking at you straight in the face.

Millen And I don't care much for what I see.

Moore We won't argue for the first day, Millen.

Millen That silly chat has no place here. Get enough of it at home. It's more fit coming from crying women. You should have heard them on the stairs this morning. All the superstitions of the day. A red sky in the morning. A warning. We should wait.

Moore Where did that saying come from about red skies?

Craig Shepherds.

Pyper Lambs to the slaughter. Baaaa. OK, Millen. That's French for sky.

Craig It's not.

Silence.

Ciel. Le ciel. Right?

Pyper Right. Le ciel rose.

Craig Rose? Pink! Are the skies in France pink?

Moore How do you get a pink sky?

Millen Shut your mouth. I often saw a pink sky in Coleraine. So must you.

Moore Red maybe, but not pink.

Millen He's blind as a bat anyroad.

Moore What's wrong with my eyes?

Millen You've eyes like your granny.

Moore That woman could see as well at eighty as she could at twenty.

Millen Did you see the old witch at twenty?

Moore Respect that woman's memory.

Millen What have I said against her exactly?

Moore You said plenty.

Millen I just said you've eyes like your granny. It's only a saying. Eyes like your granny. Feet like your granny, brains like your granny.

Moore That woman could buy and sell you up to her dying day. She had brains in her boots. You've some neck –

Millen Will somebody take that thick horse outside and –

Moore I don't need to be taken outside. You might want to be taken outside and taught manners. Have I ever upcasted your family at you?

Millen You have nothing to upcast.

Moore I might have plenty, but that's not the point. Have I ever done it?

Millen No.

Moore Exactly.

Silence.

Pyper To answer your interesting question, David, yes, you get pink skies in France. Not as pink as Coleraine, but still pink.

Millen Give it a rest. I've lived there all my life and I doubt if I've seen one pink sky in the hole.

Moore Then why say you did and start this bother?

Millen I was only sticking up for my place.

Moore I was only sticking up for my family.

Millen I know. Your granny was a decent old woman.

Moore A stupid old bitch and an old rip. Well rid of her. Do you want a cigarette?

Millen Have you enough?

Moore Aye.

Millen Right.

Moore What about yous boys?

Craig Yes.

Millen Pyper, you'll recall, doesn't smoke.

Pyper Why not? In celebration?

Moore Celebrate what?

Pyper Peace. Perfect peace.

Moore Pay no heed to fights like that.

Millen We have them all the time.

Moore Over in a minute.

Millen All forgotten then.

Craig Best way to have fights.

Moore Far the best. No grudges.

Pyper What way do you fight, Craig?

Craig Fight?

Pyper Fight. Flare up, get it all out, then forget about it. Or are you a grudger?

Craig What makes you ask?

Millen I'd say he's a grudger, that boy.

Craig Why?

Moore Quiet boy. Still waters run deep, right?

Millen Worst men in a fight.

Moore Depends on the fight.

Craig I don't have many fights.

Pyper You should be at home here.

Craig Give me time.

Pyper Why spend your time here?

Craig It goes without saying.

Pyper Say it.

Craig I'm in this for Ulster.

Moore Like ourselves.

Millen For the glory of his majesty the king and all his people.

Moore Exactly.

Pyper For your religion?

Craig Yes.

Pyper My religion too.

Pyper offers Craig his hand. They shake.

Millen You haven't told us yet, Craig, what you're like in a fight.

Craig Good.

Millen Say so. Strong-looking boy. What are you working at?

Craig The father works a forge. I've been working with him since I was a child. He's getting no younger. I've taken a fair share of the heavier work.

Moore Sore work that.

Millen When you're used to it, no.

Craig It's a dying skill. I've been at him to get into the motor business. This pal of mine, he's been learning about engines and the rest of it outside Belfast. That's where the future lies. If I'd the money, I'd start up with him. But you know what it's like working for your own people. Once they get to a certain age it's all clinging to whatever's there in their time. Nothing else. Father lives for the place as it is. That and his greyhounds.

Pyper Greyhounds?

Craig You know about dogs?

Pyper We bred, the family bred greyhounds.

Moore You wouldn't have struck me as a greyhound man.

Pyper Beautiful animals. Precise. Lethal.

Craig You should meet the father.

Millen And you think the blacksmiths have had their day?

Craig Not yet. But soon.

Moore How soon?

Craig Twenty years at most.

Pyper Will there be twenty more years?

Moore My heart goes out to the horses.

Millen What?

Moore What's going to happen to all the horses?

Millen They'll line them up and run motors over them.

Moore Could never kill a horse.

Craig You might soon kill a man.

Moore I'll face that as soon as I have to.

Craig Sooner than you think maybe.

Silence.

Moore I saw a horse being killed once.

Pyper Why?

Moore It was blind.

Millen Who did it?

Moore Who else? Brewster, the boss of the factory I worked in. Decent enough if you keep to the right side of him and give him his money's worth, but one sign of slackening and bang, that's you out.

Craig What did you work at?

Moore Weaving. Well, I'm a dyer.

Millen For a man half-blind he's a great eye for colour.

Moore Funny that, isn't it?

Pyper No.

Moore I always thought it was.

Pyper And you, Millen?

Millen I'm in the flour mills.

Moore He's a baker.

Millen I'm a miller.

Moore He bakes cakes. Wee buns. He's a pastry chef. That's what his wife calls him when she's getting swanky.

Millen Give it a rest.

Moore Give him a skirt and he'll run you up a four-course dinner.

Millen Enough of that.

Moore laughs.

Craig And you breed the greyhounds, Kenneth?

Pyper My family did. Like yours, for pastime.

Craig They don't any more?

Pyper I don't know.

Millen What do you turn your hand at?

Pyper I work with stone.

Millen Were you some kind of labourer?

Pyper You could say that.

Millen Casual work.

Pyper Yes, a sculptor.

Moore nods.

Craig I'd say you're a dangerous man in a fight, Kenneth.

Pyper Would you, David?

Craig I'd say so.

Moore How do you fight, Pyper?

Pyper Dirty.

Millen I think I hear someone coming.

Moore Top brass maybe. Move.

They stand to attention by their sleeping spaces with the exception of Pyper, who reclines on his.

Millen Get yourself up, Pyper. You'll land yourself in it on your first day.

Pyper remains motionless.

Moore On his own head be it.

Christopher Roulston enters. They relax. He ignores them, gathers bedclothes, starts to unpack kit.

You give us all a shock there, boy.

Roulston Shock?

Moore We thought you might be top brass.

Roulston I'm not in the habit of lying about my rank.

Moore Who accused you of lying?

Pyper Aren't you speaking to the poor, Christopher? You don't remember me, Roulston? Look hard.

Roulston Pyper?

Pyper I hoped you'd never forget my face.

Craig Yous two know each other?

Moore Must often happen with the amount volunteering.

Roulston We schooled together.

Pyper But we never shared together. Roulston's best friends were always much younger.

Roulston You've kept your tongue.

Pyper Are you asking to see it?

Roulston I've heard little of you.

Pyper Impossible. You've heard everything.

Roulston I try to avoid scandal.

Pyper Then what do you preach against?

Roulston I no longer preach.

Pyper That's why you're here?

Roulston Pyper.

Craig I've met you too, Mr Roulston. Well, I've seen you before.

Roulston Where?

Craig Our meeting house. I heard you preach in the kirk.

Moore Funny the way paths cross?

Millen I'm Millen, Roulston. John –

Roulston Where did you hear my sermon?

Craig Enniskillen.

Roulston Yes. I remember my few occasions there, Mr –

Craig Craig, David Craig. You certainly shocked us into changing our ways.

Roulston I thought I had tempered that sermon well.

Craig Yes, indeed. You've left off the collar, I take it.

Roulston Yes, I – You thought me too impulsive that day?

Craig Not that, I didn't mean that.

Pyper What was the subject? Pride?

Roulston A vice you are sick with.

Craig No. Sin.

Moore Just sin?

Craig Yes.

Moore Sorry I missed it.

Roulston Enniskillen is a beautiful town.

Craig It is. Did you manage to get on any of the islands in Lough Erne?

Roulston Unfortunately no, but I have happy memories of your homeplace.

Craig So have I.

Roulston To be expected. To be expected.

Pyper Well done, Christopher. You're developing a good line in polite clerical nonsense.

Roulston returns to his unpacking. He takes out a Bible.

Sorry, Roulston. Didn't mean it. Don't cry. We have to be big boys here. Tough men on the training ground.

Moore Can't wait to get at it.

Millen I'm sure they'll start us with the guns.

Craig Doubt it.

Moore Why?

Craig We've just arrived and all that. Might not trust –

Moore We're no strangers to guns.

Millen Your mouth is going to get you into trouble.

Moore Why? We're all the same here. Even Pyper has admitted he's one of our own kind.

Craig You boys are Carson's men?

Moore Too true we are.

Craig The North County Derry Battalion?

Millen That's the one.

Craig Who were yous under?

Millen You're looking at one of them.

Moore Best soldier for fifty mile.

Millen Good support in Fermanagh anyway.

Craig Plenty. But it was needed. Every man had his job to do, even if it was only to keep his eyes opened. We have our fair share of Fenian rats. I did a few runs to collect and deliver the wares. We've a couple of vehicles. Was near enough to your part. I could have supplied yous with stuff.

Moore The same stuff was badly needed.

Craig Compared to ours, your part is safe enough.

Moore No part's safe this weather.

Roulston has gone to Pyper.

Roulston (*sotto*) Are you going to keep up this attack?

Pyper Do you want me to?

Roulston leaves.

Moore Getting a bit too big for their boots everywhere. Tell him about the pup we had to deal with.

Millen We went out one morning, himself and myself, one Saturday, not that long ago, early-morning training session, near Bushmills.

Moore The smoke from a Papist chimney will never darken the skies of Bushmills.

Millen Am I telling the story or you? Gathering near the lodge, first thing we saw, painted on the left wall, would you credit this, a tricolour.

Moore A tricolour. Painted on an orange lodge.

Millen Green, white and gold.

Moore Green, shite and gold. It wasn't there for long.

Pyper Go on.

Millen You listening?

Pyper Every word.

Millen We tracked down the artist. Sixteen years old. Wanted to die for Ireland.

Moore The mother a widow woman, decent enough creature for a Papist.

Millen We rounded him out. Her crying not to shoot him, he was only a wain.

Moore Did better than shoot him.

Pyper What?

Millen Battered him down the streets of Coleraine.

Moore Shaved every hair off his head.

Millen Cut the backside out of his trousers.

Moore Painted his arse green, white and gold.

Millen That cured him of tricolours.

Pyper roars with laughter. Martin Crawford enters. He stops at the pile of bedclothes.

Crawford Is this where we're supposed to be?

Craig What?

Crawford This is where we sleep?

Millen Looks like it, doesn't it?

Moore Better grab what's going.

Crawford Thanks.

Millen Who are you, son?

Crawford I'm Crawford. Martin Crawford from Derry Town, sir.

Millen Whereabouts?

Crawford Foyle Street.

Millen What number?

Crawford Number 27, sir.

Millen Do you sleep on your right side or your left?

Crawford Sorry?

Moore Nothing.

Craig has gone to Pyper. Crawford gets bedclothes, tries to unpack kit and make up a bed at the same time. Moore and Millen watch his efforts.

Craig So you didn't enjoy France?

Pyper Didn't I?

Craig You said you nearly starved there.

Pyper Yes, I'd forgotten that.

Craig What part were you in?

Pyper Paris, I think.

Craig You don't know?

Pyper Let me think about it.

Millen You're not making much of a fist with that bed.

Crawford I'm not.

Millen Might be handier if you tried one thing at a time.

Crawford Yes.

Millen takes the bedclothes.

Millen Show us them. Watch me.

Crawford Yes, sir.

Craig What were the women like?

Pyper French women?

Craig Aye.

Pyper Whores. Everyone of them. Whores. Wonderful whores.

Moore Go on, Pyper.

Pyper I married one.

Moore A French woman?

Pyper Yes, a whore. A Papist whore. I married her out of curiosity.

Roulston Do we need details of your foul life here?

Moore Don't listen if you don't want to.

Roulston There's a fellow here no more than a lad.

Moore Crawford?

Pyper He means himself.

Roulston I mean –

Moore Shut your mouth. What were you curious about, Pyper?

Pyper What they're like when they're naked. Papists.

Roulston Turn your mind away from this evil, young man.

Crawford I've enough to do without listening to that.

Moore If she was a whore, you could have seen her naked without marrying her.

Pyper What do you take me for? Do you think I have no respect? I married her to make an honest Protestant out of her.

Moore Of course, of course. Go on what was she like?

Pyper Unusual.

Moore How?

Pyper You've heard the rumours?

Moore Every one. Wait, are you listening to this, Millen?

Millen I'm coming over. Now Crawford, have you got the hang of it?

Crawford I think so.

Millen thoroughly unmakes the bed.

Millen Then make it yourself now, right? (*He goes towards the others.*) Go on. I've been listening.

Moore Right, Pyper.

Pyper She started to take off her clothes very slowly, but very shyly. Well, I imagined it was very shy for a woman of her experience. When she was down to her petticoat, she stopped.

Moore Why?

Pyper She asked me if I'd ever been alone with a woman like this before. A standard question for one of her profession, so I lied and said, yes, but never a Papist. When she heard this she told me I had a surprise coming. She took off her petticoat and there they were.

Moore What?

Pyper Three legs.

Moore What?

Pyper She had three legs. The middle one shorter than the normal two.

Craig starts to laugh.

Moore Don't laugh. That's the truth.

Millen You believe that?

Moore I've heard that three-legged rumour before, but only in relation to nuns. There's this big convent in Portstewart –

Pyper She could have started out as a nun. I don't know. I never got a chance to find out about her. She died on our wedding night.

Moore What happened?

Pyper She bled to death.

Moore How?

Pyper I sawed her middle leg off.

Moore Why?

Pyper My duty as a Protestant.

Moore Where did you get a saw on your wedding night?

Pyper I've heard the same rumour as you, Moore. In France I always carried a saw with me. It's overridden by nuns.

Moore Did you bury her after you murdered her?

Pyper No. I ate her. Do you not remember I was starving in France?

Moore Pyper?

Pyper What?

Moore I'm staying well clear of you.

Millen That makes two of us. Come on, Willy.

Moore and Millen go off. Craig remains.

Craig You're some boy, Kenneth.

Pyper Am I, David?

Craig I've never met anybody like –

Pyper Neither have I.

Craig There'll be sport with you about.

Pyper Will there be?

Craig Go easy on Roulston a bit.

Pyper Why?

Craig He's nervous.

Pyper David.

Craig What?

Pyper So am I. Have you a cigarette?

Craig I thought you didn't smoke?

Pyper I didn't. I do.

They smoke in silence. Millen has been examining Crawford's bed. Moore flicks through Roulston's Bible. Roulston watches him.

Millen Do you call that making a bed?

Crawford I did my best.

Millen Make it again.

Crawford Look, it's my bed. I've made it. I'll lie in it. Now

I've got my kit to get sorted out. Let me get on with it.

Millen Then do it and make it snappy.

Crawford I'll do it in my own sweet time. You're not over me.

Millen Fighting back, Crawford?

Crawford I'm standing up for myself.

Millen You're fighting back, man. You won't be much good against the Kaiser if you've no gumption, will you? Get on with it.

Craig You didn't marry a French whore, did you?

Pyper What makes you doubt it?

Craig You don't strike me as a married man.

Pyper Nor you me. Women in France are very beautiful. Like women everywhere, as I'm sure a man of your experience has found out.

Craig I don't have much experience. Well, not that much.

Pyper No, not that much. Like men everywhere. Beautiful.

Craig Men or women?

Pyper What's the difference?

Craig Why ask me? Do you expect me to know?

Pyper I think you are a rare boy, David. When you want to be, as you say. (*Pyper begins to put on his jacket.*)

Craig Feeling a draught?

Pyper I felt it a long time ago. I'm growing warmer.

Craig What were you doing before enlisting?

Pyper Whoring.

Craig With three-legged French nuns?

Pyper No. I was the whore.

Roulston Do you often read the good book?

Moore This is yours, Roulston?

Roulston Yes.

Moore Well thumbmarked.

Roulston It should be. This Bible has been in my father's family for four generations.

Moore Four? Good work.

Roulston Is there a particular book which interests you?

Moore No.

Roulston I could recommend some of the psalms.

Moore Don't bother. I wasn't reading it. I was only looking for the dirty pictures.

Roulston snatches the Bible violently. He roars.

Roulston Do you dare defile the word of God? Do you dare blaspheme against my Father?

After Roulston's outburst there is a sharp silence. Roulston sits on his bed, buries his head in his hands. The Bible falls to the floor.

Millen You're going to burst your skull, son, before you give the Huns a chance to do it.

Crawford goes and picks up Roulston's Bible.

Crawford Your Bible, Mr Roulston.

Roulston Thank you.

Crawford It's all right.

Roulston I don't know your name. I'm sorry.

Crawford Crawford, Martin Crawford, from Derry Town. And you?

Roulston Roulston. Christopher Roulston.

Crawford No, I meant where are you from?

Roulston Tyrone. Sion Mills. I was born there. Then the family moved.

Crawford I know it, Sion Mills. Good cricket club there.

Roulston I never played, I'm afraid.

Crawford I haven't played much cricket. But I'm interested in games, all games. Boxing and football especially.

Roulston Yes. Thank you.

Crawford I play for the town team every Saturday. Well, I played every Saturday. I don't know whether the army will let us play.

Craig We'll get a game up here soon.

Crawford You play? What position?

Craig Goals.

Millen You've stolen my position, Craig.

Moore You're a rotten goalie.

Millen I'm not that bad.

Moore You're pathetic. Anyway, Craig's the goalie.

Crawford Will we get permission to play a match?

Millen If today's anything to go by.

Moore They must be easing us in.

Craig We'll get a game.

A loud roar. George Anderson and Nat McIlwaine enter, tossing their kit bags to each other.

Anderson We're here, we're here. No cause for panic, ladies. The men are here.

Moore Belfast.

Millen You'd never think it they're that quiet.

McIlwaine Line them up, line them up. We're ready for them.

Anderson I spy a Taig. I spy a Taig.

McIlwaine Where? Tell me where?

Anderson Use your nose, lad, use your nose. Have I not trained you to smell a Catholic within a mile of you? Get him.

McIlwaine flings back his head, howls, rushes for Crawford.

Tear his throat out.

McIlwaine hurls Crawford on to the bed, snarling and snapping. Anderson throws McIlwaine off Crawford.

Mad dog, mad dog, mad dog.

Anderson hurls McIlwaine off the bed.

Millen What the hell do yous two think you're doing?

Anderson Defending this part of the realm –

Millen Keep your defending for where it's needed across the water. Let that young lad go.

McIlwaine He's a Catholic bastard, he has no place in this regiment.

Millen He's no Catholic. He's one of ours.

Anderson Look at his eyes.

Moore Are you a Catholic, son?

Crawford No.

Millen Let him go. Do you hear?

Craig He said, do you hear?

Anderson I hear. I hear clearly.

Anderson lets Crawford off the bed. Crawford stands, then sits, turning his back on them all. He rises suddenly and exits. Soon afterwards Roulston follows him.

McIlwaine He might deny he's a Catholic, but he wouldn't walk in our part of the shipyard.

Moore We might have known.

McIlwaine Known what?

Moore Shut up, you Belfast mouth.

McIlwaine Friendly company, eh Anderson?

Anderson Warm as your mother's fireside, McIlwaine.

Pyper Boys?

McIlwaine Look at this buckcat.

Anderson I know they're taking on all types, but are things that desperate?

Pyper I'd like to show you something.

Anderson I'd say you would if you'd one to show.

Craig Leave it alone, Pyper.

Pyper I want to be friendly. Watch this. Let me entertain you, boys. (*He rolls up his sleeve.*) I observed to the company earlier how remarkably fine my skin is. They agreed. Do you?

Anderson What kind of milksop –

Pyper Now, I want to show you how someone with my remarkably fair skin can perform magic. A trick. A wee trick. Do you want to see it? Never mind. I'll show you. Here, look at my hands. Empty. Aren't they? Right. And nothing up my sleeve. Right. Feel my arms if you like. Feel them. Go on.

> *Anderson briefly feels Pyper's arms. McIlwaine tries to squeeze them into submission. Pyper hurls his effort aside.*

Now that's cheating. None of that. Two bare arms. I clench each fist like this. Inside one of my hands something has appeared. I'll give it to whichever one of you guesses the correct hand. Come on, guess.

> *Silence.*

Come on, guess. Guess, guess.

> *Anderson touches Pyper's right hand. Pyper punches him in the groin. Anderson screams.*

McIlwaine You dirty bastard,

Pyper That makes three of us. Warm as your mother's fireside, right, McIlwaine?

> *McIlwaine helps Anderson on to a bed.*

McIlwaine All right, Anderson, old boy? All right?

Anderson Where is he?

McIlwaine Get your breath back. There'll be time to give him the hiding he's looking for. More than enough time. Get you breath back.

Pyper Moore?

Moore What?

Pyper Still going to stay clear of me?

Moore Clearer.

Pyper What are you like in a fight, Moore?

Moore Clean. I fight clean. I fight straight.

Pyper You're not going to survive.

Millen We'll all survive. This is the best army on God's good earth.

Pyper But we're the scum of it. We go first.

Craig Not if we fight together.

Pyper We will go first, David.

Craig Pyper.

Pyper We will go first, David.

Roulston and Crawford enter.

Millen Is that what you want, Pyper? Death? I've heard about maniacs like you. The ones who sign up not to come back. If that's what you've done, I'm warning you –

Pyper I need some sense kicked into me, right?

Moore Right. More than right.

Pyper Very much more than right. And I might get that kick right here. I might survive from what I learn here. Right? And who'll teach me? Other sons of Ulster, marching off to war. A good war. A just war. Our war. The war of the elect upon the damned, right? God's chosen will rise up and fight. Will you rise up with me? The elect shall bond in God's brotherhood. Right? Right. More than right. It's good to be right. I'm sorry. I get carried away when I'm right. I'm especially sorry for my violence against you, Anderson. Will you accept my sorrow?

Anderson McIlwaine, don't let that mad bastard anywhere near me.

Pyper I've studied anatomy. Perhaps I can ease your pain. (*He opens his penknife.*)

Anderson Keep your hands away from me. I hate all doctors.

Pyper Why are you afraid?

Anderson I said keep away from me.

Craig Kenneth, for God's sake.

Pyper This is not the stuff we fashion heroes from.

Roulston Pyper.

Pyper stands to attention and salutes. Crawford enters.

If you are responsible for one more disturbance of the peace in this barracks, I will be left with no option but to report you.

Pyper What, Roulston? What will you report? What have you been doing, Christopher?

Roulston Get out of the army now. Go to a doctor. You're mad. He'll sign you out. Don't stay in this company. Get out. Go.

Pyper I will get out, Roulston, and do you know how? I'll die willingly. Will you? Yes. (*He raises his knife to Roulston's throat.*) You can feel that. Death. You fear that. Death. And I know death. I'll let you know it. I'll take away your peace and that's the only disturbance I'm responsible for in this company. Right? Right. More than right. (*He pretends to slash Roulston's throat.*)

  Silence.

Millen I've no time for superstition.

Moore He'll learn the hard way. Are you all right, son?

Crawford As I'll ever be.

Millen Good man.

> *Millen lies on his makeshift bed, as does Moore.*
> *Roulston goes to his bed and begins to read the Bible.*
> *Crawford goes over to read it with him. McIlwaine*
> *looks after Anderson. Ignored by all except Craig,*
> *Pyper raises his left hand and with his penknife slits the*
> *front of it. Craig takes the shirt Pyper had given him.*
> *About to toss it at him, Craig hesitates, tears a sleeve*
> *from the shirt and attracts the others' attention by so*
> *doing. They watch as Craig bandages Pyper's bleeding*
> *hand.*

Craig Red hand.

Pyper Red sky.

Craig Ulster.

Pyper Ulster.

Part Three: Pairing

Ulster: Boa Island, Lough Erne, carvings [Craig and Pyper]; a Protestant church [Roulston and Crawford]; a suspended ropebridge [Millen and Moore]; the Field, a lambeg drum [McIlwaine and Anderson].

The sound of water. Light up on Boa Island. Craig rests, smoking. Pyper enters.

Craig Well?

Pyper Good. Good place.

Craig I hoped you'd like it.

Pyper You rowed out here every day?

Craig When I had the chance and I wanted to be on my island.

Pyper Your island?

Craig Sorry. Boa Island. I stand corrected. I meant when I wanted to be on my own.

Pyper Nobody ever comes here?

Craig Very few.

Pyper Strange.

Craig This place? Yes.

Pyper The place is definitely strange, but strange too, people shouldn't come.

Craig Why should they come here?

Pyper The carvings.

Craig What are they?

Pyper Signs.

Craig Signs? Could you sculpt here again?

Pyper What makes you ask that?

Craig Just wondered.

Pyper That's why you brought me here?

Craig I just wanted to show it to you. That's all. I'm not puting any pressure on you.

Pyper laughs.

Why the laugh?

Pyper Because I'm happy.

Craig Good.

Pyper Thanks.

Craig What for?

Silence.

What for?

Pyper You know.

Craig No.

Silence.

Pyper Saving my life. I want –

Craig Kenneth, I don't want that brought up ever. Hear me? I only did what you would have done if it had been me. Not just me. Any of us. We need to forget.

Pyper Do we?

Craig Listen. I want to get away from the war. We're on leave. That long five months is behind us for a while. Leave passes quicker. I'm home now. I've brought you home. Home with me. I might never be able to do that again. When I walked into the Erne this morning, I just wanted to wash the muck of the world off myself. I thought it was on every part of me for life. But it's not. I'm clean again. I'm back. All right?

Pyper You're going to shut me up?

Craig Calm you down?

Pyper Same difference.

Craig I won't succeed.

Pyper You might.

Craig Tell me about the carvings. You're the smart boy. I always wanted to know about them.

Pyper What?

Craig I don't know. Tell me.

Lights fade on Boa Island.

Lights up on the church. Roulston kneels.

Crawford I think we should leave this church.

Roulston I can't leave this church.

Crawford It's not helping you in here.

Roulston I'm not asking for help. I'm asking for strength.

Crawford You proved your strength beside me.

Roulston No.

Crawford Why ask for more?

Roulston No, no. I have to.

Crawford Are you afraid to go back?

Roulston Have I left the front?

Crawford You're strong already, man. Now prove it. Leave this church with me.

Roulston I can't

Crawford Why not?

Roulston Because – because I have to give thanks. That we're alive. All of us. Does that not strike you as God's will?

Crawford Why God's will?

Roulston The day we joined up, all eight of us, still living. How many other days were as blessed? How many other days were as lucky?

Crawford So you admit there was luck in it?

Roulston There's more to it than that.

Crawford Such as what? Such as?

Roulston Why do you always question?

Crawford Because you never do.

Roulston That's not true. I never stop asking myself questions. Why do you think I'm not still a clergyman?

Crawford Because you don't believe.

Roulston What?

Crawford You don't believe.

Roulston I believe too much.

Crawford You don't believe in Christ. You don't believe in

God. You don't believe in yourself. If you do, prove it.

Silence.

Roulston How?

Crawford Leave.

Roulston I can't.

Crawford You see, you don't believe.

Lights fade on the church.

Lights up on the bridge. Millen and Moore stand on one end.

Moore I can't cross it, Johnny, I can't. I want to but I'm not able.

Millen You have to try.

Moore Tomorrow.

Millen No, you have to do it now.

Moore I'll fall.

Millen You won't.

Moore Why have we been spared?

Millen Spared what?

Moore Johnny, I can't go back.

Millen You've told me that already.

Moore I wouldn't tell anyone else.

Millen Get to your feet and start walking to the bloody rock and back.

Moore I'm getting sick just looking down.

Millen Don't look anywhere but straight in front of you.

Moore You do it first.

Millen It'll make no difference. Walk.

Moore No.

Millen We're not leaving till you cross it.

Moore I'm tired. I'm frightened. I don't want to go on. I can't.

Millen Come on.

Moore All the dead.

Millen You've said we've been spared. You won't fall.

Moore I'll die first.

Millen No.

Moore Why did you bring me here?

Millen Walk.

Moore I can't.

Millen Then stay where you are.

Moore I keep hearing the dead.

Millen It's only the water beneath you. You've heard it before.

Moore It's guns.

Millen The guns are over there. You're home.

Moore The guns are home.

Millen Stand up, come on, stand up.

Moore I've lost my nerve, you bastard. Do you not see I've lost my nerve? I can't move. Leave me alone. I want to fall here. I want to die.

Millen shakes Moore.

Millen You've lost your nerve, have you? Get over there and get it back. Get over there and come back in one piece.

Moore is now standing on the bridge.

Moore I won't make it.

Millen You will. I'm with you.

Moore Where's the rest of them?

Millen They're with you. They want you to cross.

Moore Pyper, Roulston, Craig.

Millen I said they're with you.

Moore Anderson, Crawford.

Millen They're all here.

Moore McIlwaine.

Millen Every one of them.

Moore Millen.

Millen I'm behind you. I'm here.

Moore Johnny.

Millen I'm here. I'm listening. You've missed one out.

Moore Who?

Millen Think.

Moore Who?

Millen He's a weaver. A Coleraine man. Half-blind. So he won't see much if he looks up or down. Do you remember him? He saw a horse being shot. His heart went out to the horse. Now he's seen men being shot. He came back. His heart hasn't come back. It was cut out of him. His heart's over there. Do you know who he is?

Moore Yes.

Millen Walk over to him.

Moore Are you with me still?

Millen No. You're by yourself.

Moore takes another step on to the bridge. Lights fade on the bridge.

Lights up on the Field. McIlwaine and Anderson sprawl on the ground. Beside them a lambeg drum.

McIlwaine Good day.

Anderson Beautiful.

McIlwaine How was she sounding?

Anderson Perfect.

McIlwaine Great drum.

Anderson The best.

McIlwaine See this, this is holy ground.

Anderson The Field?

McIlwaine The Field. Holiest spot in Ulster. I'm glad we come here, laughed at or not.

Anderson Who was laughing at us?

McIlwaine They all were.

Anderson I didn't hear them laughing. If I had, I'd have knocked their teeth in. When did you see them laughing?

McIlwaine Everyone. Every single one.

Anderson Who?

McIlwaine Willy Moore for one. And his pal, Millen. I asked them to march with us. And they refused. And why? Because it wasn't the Twelfth of July. Look, said I. We weren't here on the Twelfth of July. We were over across. We couldn't march. Now we're back. We can march in battalion. I'll carry the drum. Yous carry the banner. Romp up a bit of support. We'll make a fair show of Orangemen. We'll march to the Field. The bastard laughed at me.

Anderson Moore?

McIlwaine When was the last time you heard Moore laugh?

Anderson How should I know? Anyway, I didn't hear them laughing.

McIlwaine Then why would they not join us?

Anderson They'd marched on the Twelfth.

McIlwaine Why shouldn't they march again? Why shouldn't they march with us? We're the returning heroes. We should be marched with. We are the boys. We should be celebrated. Shouldn't we? I'm asking shouldn't we? Are you going to answer me?

Anderson Hold your tongue. You've had enough I see.

McIlwaine I haven't started. And don't preach to me.

Anderson You want more?

McIlwaine If I can find it.

Anderson Look beside you. It's there.

McIlwaine finds the bottle of Bushmills, opens it, is about to take a slug from it, roars with laughter, leaves down the bottle, cups his hands into fists.

McIlwaine Georgie?

Anderson What do you want? I know you're up to some badness when you use my Christian name. I'm warning you.

McIlwaine No badness. Just a trick. Remember this?

Anderson Remember this? Remember what?

McIlwaine I have remarkably fine skin for a man. The others agree. Do you?

Anderson What's got into you?

McIlwaine I'll close my empty hands. If you guess which one there's something –

Anderson Cut that out.

McIlwaine You'll get it –

Anderson I said cut it out.

McIlwaine You walked into that one, boy.

Anderson You mightn't walk out of it.

McIlwaine He's some fighter though. Pyper. Who would have thought it?

Anderson Who indeed?

McIlwaine You said he was a milksop.

Anderson There's still something rotten there. That time Craig threw himself on him to save him.

McIlwaine What about them?

Anderson The look on their faces. Something rotten.

McIlwaine What?

Anderson Who gives a Fenian's curse? Show us that bottle.

McIlwaine Hold your horses. Here. Pour us a drop in here.

Anderson pours whiskey into McIlwaine's cupped hands. He opens his hands and whiskey pours to the ground.

Something rotten.

Anderson What the hell are you doing? Waste of good whiskey.

McIlwaine It's no good. It's no good.

Anderson The whiskey?

McIlwaine Everything. It's no good here on your own. No good without the speakers. No good without the bands, no good without the banners. Without the chaps. No good on your own. Why did we come here to be jeered at? Why did we come here, Anderson?

Anderson To beat a drum.

Lights fade on the Field.

Lights up on Boa. Pyper studies the stone carving. Lights up on the church. Roulston stands.

Craig Well, what are they?

Pyper Don't rush me.

Craig You've had enough time.

Pyper I don't think these have anything to do with time.

Roulston When I came through this battle, do you know what I felt?

Crawford Blessed?

148

Roulston More than that.

Crawford What?

Roulston Chosen.

Craig They don't look like men or women.

Pyper Depends on the man or woman.

Craig They could be either.

Pyper They could be both.

Roulston Saved.

Crawford To survive?

Roulston Something else.

Crawford What?

Craig What do you think they are?

Pyper Men and women? Men and women are gods.

Craig Gods?

Crawford I asked what.

Roulston I realized for the first time what it means to be of the elect.

Crawford What does it mean, being of the elect?

Roulston That you're the Son of God. Son of God, Son of Man, I can't preach any more.

Crawford I don't want your preaching.

Craig I want to understand this place. To understand you. Explain yourself to me here.

Pyper I could only explain myself when I could see, not just with my eyes, but with my hands. They've stopped.

Craig See. See now. See what's in front of you.

Pyper How?

Craig Start again. With your eyes. Carve. Carve me.

Crawford Why did you bring me here?

Roulston I grew up in this church.

Crawford You grew stunted in it. Didn't you? Well, didn't you?

Pyper You're on this island.

Craig Who's with me?

Pyper I am. Flesh. Stone. David. Goliath. Why did David save Goliath's life? For Goliath diminished into nothing through David's faith and sacrifice. Was David cruel to save Goliath from death? Because Goliath in his brutality, in his ugliness, wanted death. David would not let him die. He wanted to rescue Goliath from becoming a god. A dead god. A stone god. And this stone destroys whoever touches him.

Roulston In the beginning is the word.

Pyper I turn people into stone.

Roulston And the word is within me.

Pyper Women and men into gods.

Roulston And the word is without me.

Pyper I turned my ancestors into Protestant gods.

Roulston For I am the Word and the Word is mine.

> *Throughout Pyper's next speech Roulston lowly whispers, 'For I am the Word and the Word is mine'.*

Pyper So I could rebel against them. I would not serve. I

150

turned my face from their thick darkness. But the same gods have brought me back. Alive through you. They wanted their outcast. My life has been saved for their lives, their deaths. I thought I'd left the gods behind. But maybe they sent me away, knowing what would happen. I went to Paris. I carved. I carved out something rotten, something evil.

Craig What evil, Kenneth? Tell me.

Light fades on Boa Island.

Roulston There was once a boy. This boy spent so long in church they said he was born there. The boy only wanted to please his fathers, earthly and heavenly. But neither father believed, by word nor passion, in him, the boy. The father's lack of belief stunted the boy. He could not grow in his faith. Without faith how could the boy grow into a man? For the only men he knew were men of firm faith. Faith in themselves. In their world. In their own heavenly father. The boy tried to assert his faith in their world by serving the church of his heavenly father. He failed. He turned instead to serve the army of the king, his God's anointed. He served. He lived. He lives. Now he realizes – he recognizes – . Yes. Yes. Do you not see who I am? I am Christ. Son of Man. Son of God. (*He continues softly and simultaneously with Pyper's speech.*) In the beginning is the Word. And the Word is within me. And the Word is without me. For I am the Word and the Word is mine.

Crawford Who cares?

Silence.

Who cares what you think you are? I don't give a damn. What kind of boy do you think I am? You seem to think I'm soft in the head. Just like Anderson and McIlwaine did on the first day to me, you're doing now. Trying to knock the living daylights out of my mind and senses – through ganging up. They ganged up with each other. You gang up with Christ. Well, listen, keep him to yourself. I'm not interested in either of you. Christ never did much for me, and I don't think he's done much for you. What did he give me? Look at it. What am I? I'll tell you. I'm a soldier that risks his neck for no cause other than the men he's fighting with. I've seen enough to see through empires and kings and countries. I know the only side worth supporting is your own sweet self. I'll support you because if it comes to the crunch I hope you'll support me. That's all I know. That's all I feel. I don't believe in Christ. I believe in myself. I believe in you only in so far as you're a soldier like myself. No more, no less. That's what I have to say about your outburst. It was a disgrace. Do you have anything to say to defend yourself?

Lights fade on the church.

Lights up on the bridge. Moore has commenced his crossing. Lights up on the Field.

Moore No more.

Millen You have to move one way or the other.

Moore I can't see where I'm going.

Millen Keep going. Don't look down. Don't listen. Just get to where you're heading.

McIlwaine beats the lambeg drum with his fist.

Moore I'm back there again.

Millen You're here with me now.

Moore You were there, I didn't want to leave it alive.

Millen I said don't think of anything. Just move.

Moore No.

Millen Move.

Moore I'm going to die. They're coming at me from all sides.

McIlwaine beats louder on the lambeg.

Anderson Are you going to play it?

McIlwaine What for?

Moore Keep them away from me.

Anderson Celebrate.

McIlwaine What?

Millen Keep them away from yourself.

Anderson Us.

Moore I can't keep on much longer.

McIlwaine kicks the lambeg.

Anderson Why did you do that?

McIlwaine Get it out of my sight.

Anderson It's only a drum.

Millen Close your eyes.

McIlwaine Know what I'm thinking about?

Millen Keep taking your breath.

McIlwaine The boat.

Moore I see nothing before me.

Anderson The *Titanic*?

Millen The end's in sight.

Anderson What brings the *Titanic* into your mind?

McIlwaine The drum. The noise of it. It's like the sound she made hitting the Lagan.

Anderson We weren't to blame. No matter what they say.

McIlwaine Papists? (*He spits.*)

Moore I'm drenched.

Millen That's with sweat.

Moore Not with muck? Not with flesh? Not with blood?

Millen Just with sweat.

Moore I think it's blood. But it's not my own. I never saw that much blood, Johnny.

Millen It's not ours.

Moore The whole world is bleeding. Nobody can stop it. (*He slowly continues his crossing.*)

Anderson Every nail they hammered into the *Titanic*, they cursed the Pope. That's what they say.

McIlwaine There was a lot of nails in the *Titanic*.

Anderson And he still wasn't cursed enough.

McIlwaine Every nail we hammered into the *Titanic*, we'll die in the same amount in this cursed war. That's what I say.

Anderson What are you talking about?

McIlwaine The war's cursed. It's good for nothing. A waste of time. We won't survive. We're all going to die for nothing. Pyper was right. I know now. We're on the *Titanic*. We're all going down. Women and children first. Women and children. Damn the Pope. Let me die damning him.

Anderson Catch yourself on. You're not dying. None of us are dying. Here.

McIlwaine grabs the whiskey bottle, slumps back.

Moore Are you a soldier, Millen? Are you a good soldier? Am I? I think there's no such thing any more. There are only cowards, and the worst learn to hide it best. I can't hide it any more. I won't be back. Let me go. Let me fall.

Millen Here, take my hand. Take my hand.

Millen holds out his hand. Beyond its reach, Moore raises his hand. They do not meet.

Have you got hold of it?

Moore I don't know.

Millen Just feel it. Feel around it.

Moore's hand feels the air.

Can you touch the fingers? Can you get the feel of the palm? Do you find its strength? Come on, Willy, can you find it?

Moore Yes.

Millen Right, that hand's holding you up. You won't fall if you move. Do you believe that?

Moore Yes.

Millen Walk to the other side. There's people waiting for you over there. Who are they?

Moore All the dead people.

Millen No. All the living. Do you see them? Who are they?

Moore I don't recognize them.

Millen You do. Name them. One by one. Who are they?

Lights fade on the bridge.

Anderson Are you all right now? I said it before, and I mean it this time, you've had enough, boy. I want to hear no more chat like this.

McIlwaine Give my head peace.

Anderson You're raving drunk.

McIlwaine Just raving.

Anderson We should be getting back soon.

McIlwaine I can't leave here. Not yet anyway.

Anderson Do you want to pitch camp here for the night? If you do, you're on your own.

McIlwaine I'm always on my own. Always have been.

Anderson Because you're a hateful git.

McIlwaine It was a sign of what we're in for. What we've let ourselves in for.

Anderson The bloody *Titanic* went down because it hit an iceberg.

McIlwaine The pride of Belfast went with it.

Anderson You're not going to meet many icebergs on the front, are you? So what are you talking about?

McIlwaine The war is our punishment.

Anderson There's more than Belfast in this war.

McIlwaine But Belfast will be lost in this war. The whole of Ulster will be lost. We're not making a sacrifice. Jesus, you've seen this war. We are the sacrifice. What's keeping us over there? We're all going mad. Some of us, like Pyper, were mad before going. Others are getting that way, look at Moore. He won't be back. He'll be in a home for the rest of his life. Where I'll be too. Crawford's turning into a machine and I'm going lunatic –

Anderson I'm listening to no more of this drunken rambling.

McIlwaine It is not drunken rambling. You're listening to no more of what I have to say because you've already said it yourself. You already know what's happened to yourself, but you won't admit it, will you? You can't admit it, and I can. *I can*. Oh, for Christ's sake, Georgie, stop me talking like this. Drown me out, will you? Stop me. Give me noise. Give me the docks. Give me the yard. Steel banging against steel. Hammer in my hands. Fill me with noise, man. Stop me hearing myself. Stop me.

Anderson grabs McIlwaine's fists, brings them down heavily and repeatedly on the lambeg, until McIlwaine shakes him off and falls heavily against the drum.

Lights up on all areas. There is stillness. McIlwaine rises from the drum.

Anderson All right?

McIlwaine (*looks at his hands*) They're not bleeding. To play this brute of a drum your flesh must bleed. Mine isn't. I'm doing it wrong and I'm going to do it right this year above all others. Help me into this. (*He grabs the lambeg by its straps.*)

Anderson For God's sake, man, it's late.

McIlwaine Help me into this, I'm telling you.

Anderson helps McIlwaine into the drum.

Anderson Will you go after this?

McIlwaine We'll see.

Anderson Will you at least sleep it off?

McIlwaine When was the last time I slept?

Anderson How do I know?

McIlwaine When was the last time you slept?

Anderson I sleep sound.

McIlwaine I think I've been asleep for years. I want the sound of this boy to rouse me. If it doesn't, I can't go back there.

Anderson You'll go back to the front, if I've to carry you. You won't disgrace yourself or your breed or where you work. Now get it over with, will you?

McIlwaine You've to do your bit as well.

Anderson How?

McIlwaine Speak. Speak loud and clear. Let them hear you in Belfast. Let the Fenians hear it everywhere. Let the Hun hear the sons of Ulster preaching war.

Anderson You are off your head.

McIlwaine Speak, do you hear me? Roar it out, Anderson.

McIlwaine hammers on the drum. Light fades on the Field.

Roulston I'm cold. We'll leave.

Crawford We'll stay.

Roulston Why?

Crawford Do you not want me to say my prayers? Wait there. Wait until I'm ready.

Crawford kneels. Light fades on the church.

Craig Why have you told me about her? Why have you told me about her?

Pyper To let you know what you saved.

Craig rises.

Perhaps I misjudged.

Light fades on the island.

Moore Craig?

Millen Craig's there, yes. Do you know him?

Moore Courage of a lion. Blacksmith. Risked his life for Pyper's. Together for eternity now. Good man, Craig. Two of them. Good men. Did Pyper come back from the dead that time he fell? I saw it. I saw Craig, what he did. He blew his own breath into Pyper's mouth. It was a kiss.

Millen Who else is there? Is Roulston there?

Moore I think he is, but I can't fathom him. I don't think he's a holy man, but he tries to be. Crawford keeps his feet on the ground. They make a funny pair. Not like you and me. Not like Anderson and McIlwaine. Anderson is turning his back on me. McIlwaine is still looking.

McIlwaine Walk to them.

Moore continues his crossing.

Moore I've seen you all my life, Millen. You could always lead me where you wanted. I was afraid of not doing as you bid. Who leads you?

Millen Top brass. I do as I'm told. I make no complaints. If they order me to put my hand in the fire, for the sake of what I believe in, what they believe in, I'd do it willingly. You have to do that as well, Moore. That's the only way you'll come back alive. Keep crossing. Keep working at it.

Moore This bridge is a piece of cloth. It needs colouring, I'm a dyer. When I step across it, my two feet are my eyes. They put a shape on it. They give it a colour. And the colour is my life and all I've done with it. Not much, but it's mine. So I'll keep going to its end.

Millen Once you've done that, nothing can stop you coming back.

Moore Except top brass.

Millen How?

Moore If they order me to fall?

Millen You fall.

Moore has arrived at the bridge's end.

Moore Millen? When I touched your hand, I smelt bread off it. I smelt life.

Millen Mine or yours?

Moore The two. Two lives. We're going to lose them. We're going to die.

Silence.

Millen No.

Moore Die together as we lived together. I can see death as sure as I can touch your hand. Your hand's cold, but death will warm it. It's like an oven. It's roasting. It's waiting for all of us. You're turning white. You're like ice. But you'll melt in the oven. You'll bake there. You'll lose your smell of bread, and you'll find the smell of death. You'll burn.

Millen Stop this. Come back here, Moore, to me. Do you hear me? Come back over to me. Come back from the dead.

Lights fade on the bridge. Light on the church.

Crawford Christopher?

Roulston Yes.

Crawford Do you hear confession?

Roulston Confession?

Crawford A Papist sacrament. You tell your sins and secrets. To a priest. I want you to hear mine. Remember when Anderson smelt a Catholic? He half did. My mother's Fenian. She never converted. I'm sure I was baptized one sometime. No one else knows that. Can you keep a secret?

Roulston I don't believe your secret.

Crawford I'll break your mouth if you tell it.

Roulston This is not funny, Martin.

Crawford I challenge you to keep your mouth shut.

Roulston Challenge?

Crawford Come on, I'll fight you for it.

Roulston Where do you think you're standing? A public house? This is a church.

Crawford Who gives a damn? It's not my church.

Roulston It's mine.

Crawford Come on then, Proddy. I'll fight you for it. Come on, planter. Winner takes all.

> *Roulston turns to leave. Crawford grabs him in a stranglehold.*

Do you submit? Or do you resist?

> *Roulston hurls Crawford aside.*

Roulston I'm warning you.

Crawford I'll do the warning.

Crawford trips Roulston, rapidly breaking his fall, spreadeagling him.

Fight back, Can you?

Roulston Please stop.

Crawford No, fight. Fight me.

Roulston lashes out at Crawford. It is no use.

Roulston Let me up. If anyone enters this church –

Crawford Tell them I'm a Fenian. They'll join in.

Crawford slaps Roulston violently about the face.

Come on, Christ, turn the other cheek.

Roulston spits into Crawford's face.

As good a beginning as any.

Crawford releases Roulston. Roulston rises slowly. Suddenly he attacks Crawford, who makes a feeble attempt at defence.

Roulston Don't ever attempt to humiliate me again. Do you hear? I said, do you hear?

Crawford Yes, Pyper. Yes, Anderson. Yes McIlwaine. Yes, lout. They're all one, aren't they? And now you're one with them. You're one with us. Blasphemer, brawling in the church. No better, no worse. Sorry about that. You had it coming. One or the other would have given you the same lesson someday. Weren't you lucky it was me? Weren't you lucky it was here? Now you can march out of it with me, a soldier, a man, a brute beast. You're not Christ. You're a man . One man among many. (*pause*) Want to join me someday in a game of football? I've got you boxing.

Lights fade on church. Light rises on the island.

Craig Why did you kill her?

Pyper I had to. And she killed herself.

Craig You drove her there. You drove her to do it, if all you say is true. Is this another test? Another riddle? See if I can answer a shocking one? Well, I can't. You've got me. So tell me straight why you killed her.

Pyper She killed herself. She killed herself. She killed herself. Because she was stupid enough to believe that I was all she had to live for. Me. What would I have brought her? The same end, but a lot later, and not with the dignity of doing it with her own hand. I'm one of the gods, I bring destruction. Remember?

Craig Don't try that smart talk to get yourself out of this.

Pyper What more's to be said? She took her life. She did something with it, finally and forever. I thought I was doing the same when I cleared out of this country and went to do something with my heart and my eyes and my hands and my brains. Something I could not do here as the eldest son of a respectable family whose greatest boast is that in their house Sir Edward Carson, saviour of their tribe, danced in the finest gathering Armagh had ever seen. I escaped Carson's dance. While you were running with your precious motors to bring in his guns, I escaped Carson's dance, David. I got out to create, not destroy. But the gods wouldn't allow that. I could not create. That's the real horror of what I found in Paris, not the corpse of a dead whore. I couldn't look at my life's work, for when I saw my hands working they were not mine but the hands of my ancestors, interfering, and I could not be rid of that interference. I could not create. I could only preserve. Preserve my flesh and blood, what I'd seen, what I'd learned. It wasn't enough. I was contaminated. I smashed my sculpture and I rejected any woman who would

163

continue my breed. I destroyed one to make that certain. And I would destroy my own life. I would take up arms at the call of my Protestant fathers. I would kill in their name and I would die in their name. To win their respect would be my sole act of revenge, revenge for the bad joke they had played on me in making me sufficiently different to believe I was unique, when my true uniqueness lay only in how alike them I really was. And then the unseen obstacle in my fate. I met you.

Craig What do you want from me?

Pyper What you want.

Silence.

Craig You said you wanted to die. I know what you mean. I didn't want to die, but I know what you mean. I wanted war. I wanted a fight. I felt I was born for it, and it alone. I felt that because I wanted to save somebody else in war, but that somebody else was myself. I wanted to change what I am. Instead I saved you, because of what I am. I want you to live, and I know some one of us is going to die. I think it's me. Sometimes I look at myself and I see a horse. There are hounds about me, and I'm following them to death. I'm a dying breed, boy. I can't talk in your riddles. I used to worry even up till today, when you talked to me like that, in case you were setting me up. I don't worry any more. It was yourself you were talking to. But when you talk to me, you see me. Eyes, hands. Not carving. Just seeing. And I didn't save you that day. I saw you. And from what I saw I knew I'm not like you. I am you.

Pyper David.

Craig What?

Pyper Name. Say it. Want to.

Craig More riddles?

Pyper No. Talk straight from now on.

Craig Why?

Pyper Quicker.

Craig Dance.

Pyper The gods are watching.

Craig The gods.

Pyper Protestant gods.

Craig Carson.

Pyper King.

Craig Ulster.

Pyper Ulster.

Craig Stone.

Pyper Flesh.

Craig Carson is asking you to dance in the temple of the Lord.

Pyper Dance.

Lights fade on the island. Lights on the Field. Then Anderson helps McIlwaine out of the drum.

Anderson Content?

McIlwaine Content. Very content. Look (*McIlwaine shows Anderson his hands.*)

Anderson Remarkably fine skin.

McIlwaine Aye, for a man.

They laugh.

Anderson Wash it off.

McIlwaine No way. Never. I can go back now. Georgie?

Anderson Enough's enough.

McIlwaine Did I play well?

Anderson They would have heard you for miles. You've wakened the dead.

McIlwaine I wanted to. I'm a good soldier?

Anderson The best.

McIlwaine A good worker?

Anderson None better.

McIlwaine I want to stay the night here.

Anderson Come on, man, come on.

McIlwaine You didn't do your bit. You didn't speak.

Anderson I listened.

McIlwaine That's not good enough. You're the Grand Master. I have just appointed my friend, Mr George Anderson, to the position of Grand Master of the Orange Lodges of Ireland. I demand silence. He will speak as is his duty.

Anderson Some other day.

McIlwaine No, I want a speech.

Anderson Come on now.

McIlwaine I said I want a good speech. Speak.

Anderson What do you want me to say.

McIlwaine What I want to hear.

Anderson Brethren of the true faith, fellow Orangemen,

comrades-in-arms, the sons of Ulster today give their service and in many cases their lives to the good fight of king and country in many parts of the world. Just as they have often given them before. But we do not lose sight of the battle that rages for our lands, our people, our spirit, our souls in this country where we belong. I do not speak of the Hun, dire enemy though he may be, when I speak of the enemy now. I speak of the Fenian. The Catholic traitor that will corrupt our young, deflower our womenfolk and destroy all that we hold most dear. Our beloved religion.

McIlwaine Where we fought for our glorious religion on the green, grassy slopes of the Boyne.

Anderson The Boyne is not a river of water. It is a river of blood. The blood that flows through our veins, brothers. And this blood will not be drained into the sewers of an Irish republic. We will not recognize this republic. We will fight this republic. We will fight it as we have fought in other centuries to answer our king's call. To answer God's call. We will draw our men from the farms, from the townlands and commerce of our province, our beloved Ulster. And our men will follow that call to freedom. They will fight for it. They will kill for it. They will die for it. They will die for it. Die, die, die.

Anderson starts to fall. McIlwaine holds him up.

McIlwaine Go on.

Anderson No, no more. I've done my bit.

McIlwaine Are you sinking?

Anderson Pyper the bastard was right. It's all lies. We're going to die. It's all lies. We're going to die for nothing. Let me go. It's all lies.

McIlwaine All right, now, all right.

Anderson We'll never be back here.

McIlwaine We'll never leave here.

Anderson We have to go back.

McIlwaine Can you manage walking?

Anderson No. Let me rest. Let me rest.

McIlwaine Right. Right you be.

Lights up on the bridge. Moore and Millen are on opposing sides still.

Moore You'll never lead me again. I'm on my own here, you're on your own there. That's the way it should be.

Millen Who put you there?

Moore You did, I did, they did.

Millen Top brass?

Moore No such thing. Top brass are supposed to give orders. You follow orders. I follow orders. But orders are only orders when you follow them.

Millen If you've stopped following orders, stay where you are.

Moore I haven't stopped following orders. I've started giving them.

Millen You want me to leave?

Moore No. (*pause*) Wait for me.

Millen Why should I? You seem to think I know nothing.

Moore You know enough.

Millen I don't know you.

Moore Who led me? Who saved me?

Millen Who?

Moore Thanks.

Lights up on all areas.

Pyper Well?

Craig Water.

Pyper You're a rare buckcat, Craig. Rare.

Craig I'm a hound, pup. No buckcat.

Pyper Whatever you say, sir.

Anderson We'll never make it home tonight.

McIlwaine Then we'll stay.

Roulston Did I hurt you?

Crawford Yes.

Roulston Good.

Crawford Good.

Pyper Are you ready then?

Craig As I'll ever be.

Anderson This is the place for us.

McIlwaine Just perch ourselves where we are.

Millen Move.

Pyper Coming with me?

Crawford Come on.

McIlwaine Can you not sleep?

Craig To the front.

Anderson I can't sleep, Nat. No sleep.

Roulston Out we go.

Millen Move.

Moore March.

The drum resounds.

Part Four: Bonding

A trench, the Somme. McIlwaine, the Younger Pyper and Millen are awake. The others sleep.

McIlwaine You'd think they were dead, it's that quiet.

Pyper Yes.

Millen When do you think word'll come?

Pyper When we're ready.

Millen What have we to do with it?

Pyper We do the attacking.

Millen We don't do the ordering.

Pyper You above all are not beginning to panic, Millen?

Millen I've been panicking since the last leave, Pyper.

McIlwaine There won't be much of daylight before we're going over.

Millen I think this is it. I think this is going to be the end.

Pyper Millen, for Christ's sake.

Millen I can't help it. I know this time.

McIlwaine Nobody knows nothing here.

Pyper Any officers around?

McIlwaine One passed twenty minutes ago. Told us to get some rest.

Millen I saw him. Useless bugger. Surely to God they're

not going to trust us with that piece of work. Where do they dig them out of anyway? Superior rank, is that it? Superior, my arse.

McIlwaine Keep talking like that and it'll be a court martial you'll be facing, not –

Millen Let me face it and I'll tell them straight.

Pyper Tell them what?

Millen What they're doing to us.

McIlwaine And that will stop them? That'll stop us? Save your breath for running. It's a bit late to start crying now.

Millen I'm not crying.

McIlwaine You're damn near it. Pyper? You come from a swanky family, don't you?

Pyper Why ask that now?

McIlwaine I'm just beginning to wonder what you're doing down with us instead of being with them.

Pyper And who are they?

McIlwaine Top brass.

Pyper I'm not top brass, McIlwaine. Maybe once. Not now. I blotted my copybook.

McIlwaine How?

Millen Should we waken the boys?

McIlwaine Give them time to dream. How, Pyper?

Pyper Just being the black sheep.

McIlwaine Bit of a wild one?

Pyper Bit.

McIlwaine Like myself. I broke my mother's heart.

Pyper I broke my mother's arm. More practical, more painful.

Millen Pyper, how can you laugh at a time like this?

Pyper I'm not laughing, Millen.

Millen Have you contacts up above there? Ones posted to watch over you and make sure you end up in some cushy corner? Is that why you can laugh?

Pyper Get something into that thick Coleraine skull of yours, Millen. Nobody's watching over me except myself. What the hell has got into you?

Millen What got into you the first time we met you. Remember? Knowing we're all going to die. Knowing we're all going –

McIlwaine grabs Millen.

McIlwaine One minute, you. Just one minute. These chaps are having a well-earned kip. Now they're not going to come to their senses listening to a squealing woman keening after death. Do you hear? If you want to make traitors of them, you'll deal with me first. And if you want out, start marching now.

Millen I've never run away from what I had to do. I commanded –

Pyper We all know that. But there's more than sixteen-year-old Fenians you're up against now. Will that hit you once and for all?

McIlwaine I'm warning you.

Pyper Let him go, McIlwaine.

Millen I never thought I was a coward.

McIlwaine You're not a coward. You've done enough to prove that.

Millen But I'm a soldier.

McIlwaine You're a man. The shit's scared out of you. Do you think you're on your own?

Millen No.

McIlwaine Well then.

Roulston wakes up.

Pyper Rise and shine, Christopher.

Roulston Jesus, my mouth feels like a rat's been there.

Pyper It probably has.

Roulston Did you put it there?

Pyper There was a time that I would have.

Roulston Pleasant as ever.

Pyper Full of laughs.

Roulston Any word?

Millen Nothing new.

Roulston I suppose they're saying the same thing over there?

McIlwaine In German?

Pyper No, in Gaelic.

McIlwaine Germans don't speak Gaelic.

Pyper They all learn it for badness, McIlwaine.

McIlwaine Dirty bastards. So that's what they insult you in.

Pyper Couldn't watch them. Fenians, Gaelic speakers.

They get everywhere. Even in the German army.

McIlwaine No way. Not even the Germans would have them. Did you hear about this boy Pearse? The boy who took over a post office because he was short of a few stamps.

Millen He did more than take over a post office, the bastard. Shot down our men until he got what he was looking for.

McIlwaine Let me finish. He was a Fenian, wasn't he? No soldier. He took over this big post office in Dublin, kicks all the wee girls serving behind the big counter out on to the streets. When the place is empty, him and his merry men all carrying wooden rifles land outside on the street. Your man reads the proclamation of an Irish republic. The Irish couldn't spell republic, let alone proclaim it. Then he's caught, him and all hands in gaol. He starts to cry, saying he has a widowed mother and he had led the only other brother astray. Anyway, he didn't plan to take over this post office. He walked in to post a letter and got carried away and thought it was Christmas. Nobody believes him. They're leading him out to be shot. He's supposed to see the widowed ma in the crowd. He looks at her and says, pray for me, mother. The ma looks back at him, looks at the Tommy, he's guarding Pearse, the old one grabs the Tommy's rifle. She shoots Pearse herself. She turns to the Tommy and she says, 'That'll learn him, the cheeky pup. Going about robbing post offices. Honest to God, I'm affronted,' So you see, Fenians can't fight. Not unless they're in a post office or a bakery or a woman's clothes shop. Disgrace to their sex, the whole bastarding lot of them , I say.

Pyper Who gave you this version of events?

McIlwaine Christopher here.

Pyper Roulston?

Roulston He invented quite a few details of his own. The best ones.

McIlwaine I can't help that. I'm very imaginative. I play the drums, you see. An artist like yourself, Pyper. We're a breed apart, us boys. To hell with the truth as long as it rhymes.

Roulston How's Johnny?

Millen All right, Roulston.

Roulston You're keeping up?

Millen Why shouldn't I be?

Roulston That's the spirit.

Millen Spirit?

McIlwaine Thanks, I'll have a double whiskey. Bushmills, if you have it. If not, anything goes. Have one yourself. It'll liven you up.

Millen Doesn't take much to liven you up.

McIlwaine No, not much. Then again, there mightn't be many more chances to be livened up. Don't forget that.

Millen I'm hardly liable –

Pyper All right, enough. Do something with yourself, Millen. Check your stuff, do anything, just keep busy.

Millen Pyper, do you think I have not tried?

McIlwaine I've warned you before –

Millen I've warned myself often enough before and I cannot –

Roulston Johnny, God's good. He's looked after us up to

now. He's with us. He won't desert us.

Millen He deserted us when he led us here.

Pyper We led ourselves here.

Roulston Pyper, leave him. Would it help you if we prayed together, Johnny?

Silence.

Pyper You heard the man, Millen.

Millen It might, I haven't prayed for a long time –

Roulston Neither have I. Together?

Millen What? Pray what? What kind of prayer?

Roulston (*sings*)
From depths of woe I raise to thee
The voice of lamentation.
Lord, turn a gracious ear to me
And hear my supplication.
If thou shouldst be extreme to mark
Each secret sin and misdeed dark
Oh! Who could stand before Thee!

Millen joins in the hymn.

To wash away the crimson stain
Grace, grace alone availeth.
Our works alas are all in vain
In much the best life faileth.
No man can glory in Thy sight,
All must alike confess Thy might,
And live alone by mercy.

McIlwaine begins to sing.

Therefore my trust is in the Lord
And not in my own merit

On Him my soul shall rest, His word
Upholds my fainting spirit.
His promised mercy is my fort,
My comfort and my sweet support.
I wait for it in patience.

Silence.

Pyper Patience. I'm growing tired of waiting. Let it come.

Craig cries out in his sleep.

David?

Silence.

Sleep.

Roulston Maybe you should get a bit of rest, Millen.

Millen No point. Soon have to move.

McIlwaine Nice tune to that one, wasn't there? I could never remember words, but I never forgot a tune in my life.

Roulston You're speaking in the past tense.

McIlwaine What?

Roulston Nothing.

Millen I never recall it as quiet as this.

McIlwaine The smell's different today. Has anybody noticed? Or am I imagining things?

Crawford wakes up.

Pyper No, there's something different in the air.

Roulston Stronger.

McIlwaine What is it?

Millen Fear.

Roulston Are you awake?

Crawford Just about.

Roulston Cold?

Crawford Ice. I'm still tired. Christ, I'm eaten by lice. Give us a scratch.

Roulston puts his hand down Crawford's shirt.

Good man, lovely. Down to the left a bit.

McIlwaine Want some powder?

Crawford Useless bloody stuff. We're still here?

McIlwaine No, we're on our way to Bangor for a bathe.

Crawford Don't tear the face off me. I was only asking.

Roulston You slept all right?

Crawford All right. Up long?

Roulston A while.

Crawford That's enough. Is there time for a quick match?

McIlwaine You have the football with you?

Pyper I have to hand it to your nerve, Crawford.

Crawford Have to practice, man. Any time, anywhere. I want to get into the game seriously when I'm home again. Come on. A quick game.

Millen Not yet.

Crawford Liven you up.

McIlwaine Right. I'm your man.

Crawford starts the game. Anderson wakes up. The game continues through the following dialogue.

Would you like some breakfast, son?

Anderson Fried egg, bit of bacon, sausages?

McIlwaine Soda faral.

Anderson Strong tea?

McIlwaine Name your poison.

Anderson Aye, wouldn't mind.

McIlwaine Sorry, haven't got it.

Anderson What have you got?

McIlwaine Bit of shite.

Anderson Horse's?

McIlwaine Are you mad? Can't get horse's shite for love or money.

Anderson Only human?

McIlwaine Aye.

Anderson No thanks.

McIlwaine Don't turn up your nose at it. It'll soon be scarce enough.

Anderson Not when your mouth's still around.

McIlwaine Compliments flying.

Anderson So's the shite.

Crawford Yous two are pretty sharp.

McIlwaine Lethan, son, lethal.

Anderson We practise in the dark.

Crawford Did yous ever think of taking it up full time?

Anderson Good idea.

McIlwaine What would we do?

Anderson Any suggestions?

Pyper Something sad.

Anderson Damn sadness. Something to make the blood boil.

McIlwaine Battle of the Boyne?

Anderson How the hell can two men do the Battle of the Boyne?

McIlwaine They do it without much more at Scarva.

Anderson Very thing, Battle of Scarva.

McIlwaine They have horses at Scarva.

Anderson We'll get the horses. To your feet, Millen. You're a horse.

Millen Let me be.

Anderson Get him to his feet.

McIlwaine hauls Millen to his feet.

Now, Pyper, you're the blondie boy. King Billy at Scarva always has a white horse. You're his horse, right? Now for King Billy. Who could Pyper carry? Crawford. You, on his shoulders. Right?

Crawford Wait a minute –

Anderson Do as you're told.

Roulston Come on, King Billy.

Crawford gets on Pyper's shoulders. Pyper neighs loudly.

Anderson Raring to go. King Billy and his trusty white steed. Now Millen, you're King James's horse. Who could you carry?

Millen I'm having no part in this.

Anderson Could you carry me?

Millen Go to hell.

McIlwaine Waken Craig.

Millen Craig's like a horse himself.

McIlwaine Moore then.

Anderson Get up, Moore.

Moore What's wrong?

McIlwaine You're King James. Get on –

Moore I'm what?

McIlwaine King James. Get on Millen's shoulders.

Millen I have no part in this.

Moore Part in what?

Anderson Battle of Scarva. Come on, get on.

Anderson and McIlwaine lift Moore on to Millen's shoulders.

Millen Why do we have to be King James? He has to get beaten.

McIlwaine Because somebody has to be King James. And anyway, you're only a horse.

Millen This is not a fair fight.

Anderson What fight is ever fair? Are yous right? Let battle commence. And remember, King James, we know the result, you know the result, keep to the result.

The Mock Battle of Scarva begins.

Music.

182

McIlwaine How can we have music? Sing a hymn?

Anderson Lilt or something. Go on, lilt.

Roulston Lilt?

McIlwaine Lilt.

They lilt.

Anderson King William, Prince of Orange, on his fine white charger eyes the traitor James, James who will destroy our glorious religion should he win the battle. William moves defiantly towards the bitter enemy. His white steed sniffs the dangers but continues to carry his master to glory. James swaggers forward –

Millen On his trusty steed –

Anderson Will his trusty steed shut his mouth when I'm in the middle of the story? Where was I? James swaggers forward, his Papist pride on high. No one shall topple the favoured son of Rome. But look at how King William –

Roulston Come on, King William.

McIlwaine He's going to win anyway. Just lilt.

Anderson Look at how King William, brandishing his golden blade, defies the might of haughty James, minion of Rome. They pass in thick of battle. But the wily James avoids the first attack. Behold, undaunted, our King returns, the loyal steed beneath him devours the ground. This time for the traitor James there is no escape. But luck is on the devil's side. James has swerved in time. Furious and bold, King Billy will not rest. This time James will fall, and with him mighty Rome in this kingdom. They must fight and fight they will until the victor stands poised before the victim –

Pyper trips. Crawford crashes to the ground. Silence.

Millen lets Moore off his shoulders. Roulston and
Moore help Crawford to rise. Pyper lies on the ground.

Moore Can you manage?

Roulston He's just a bit stunned.

Anderson Get up, Pyper.

Pyper I fell.

McIlwaine We saw.

Millen Not the best of signs.

Silence.

Crawford It was as much my fault as Pyper's. I lost
control of his shoulders. That's what happened.

Roulston You're all right?

Crawford I'm grand.

Millen Day's breaking.

Moore Is everybody ready?

Pyper Better waken Craig.

Anderson Better waken yourself, Pyper. Why did you do
that?

Pyper I just fell.

Anderson Did you?

Crawford It's not only his fault.

McIlwaine Let it rest. It was only a game.

Roulston Good sport while it lasted.

Anderson Great. Fair great.

Moore Prepare us for the real thing.

Roulston Yes, it's coming. Better prepare.

Crawford Were yous talking about a smell when I woke up?

McIlwaine Aye, why?

Crawford I find it now. What is it?

Roulston The smell's always there.

Crawford But this is like, this is like –

Millen What?

Crawford I don't know.

Millen I noticed how quiet it was too.

Pyper David, get up.

Millen Did anyone else?

Crawford We were making that much noise, no.

Pyper Come on, man, rise.

Craig What? Are we off?

Pyper Nearly.

Craig Orders come?

Pyper We're waiting for it. It's almost daylight.

Craig Oh God. Right

Moore How did you sleep through all the din, man?

Craig What din?

Moore You must have been dead to the world.

Craig I had this dream. A very clear dream.

Moore A nightmare?

Craig No, no. Good, very good.

McIlwaine What about?

Craig Home.

Roulston Enniskillen?

Craig Yes.

Moore 'Fare thee well, Enniskillen.'

Craig 'Fare thee well for a time.'

Pyper (*sings*)
And all around the borders of Erin's green isle.
And when the war is over we'll return in fine bloom
And we'll all welcome home our Enniskillen dragoons.

Craig 'Fare thee well, Enniskillen.'

Pyper 'Fare thee well for a while.'

Pyper Lough Erne.

Moore Good weather there at the minute.

McIlwaine How would you know?

Moore Letters. Great weather all over. The Bann's fair jumping with salmon at the minute.

Millen Nobody to catch them.

Moore Young lads might.

Millen They ruin a river.

Craig They never know when to stop.

Millen I threw back more fish that I ever ate.

Craig I didn't know you were much of a fisherman.

Moore Oh aye. The two of us. In the summer the banks of the Bann are a second home.

Pyper Beautiful rivers.

Millen The loveliest, and say what you like, Coleraine's at its best point.

Crawford Foyle.

Craig What?

Crawford I'm just remembering the Foyle. I'd forgotten it. Reared by it. Foyle Street.

McIlwaine Well, the Lagan isn't bad either.

Moore Nobody said it was.

McIlwaine It could knock the bloody Erne into the shade any day. And as for the Bann, I wouldn't make my water into it in case it would flood.

Moore Wait one minute. Let me tell you –

Pyper Keep it easy.

Silence.

Jesus, that's it. The source of the strange smell. The river.

Roulston The Somme?

Pyper The Somme.

Crawford How? It's far –

Pyper It carries for miles. It smells like home. A river at home.

Anderson All rivers smell the same.

Pyper Not your own river.

McIlwaine I've never smelt a river.

Pyper You can't stop smelling a river. Anyway, do you not see why it's started to change smell?

Anderson What's that man on about?

Pyper It's bringing us home. We're not in France. We're home. We're on our own territory. We're fighting for home. This river is ours. This land's ours. We've come home. Where's Belfast. Anderson?

Anderson You know as well as I do where –

Pyper It's out there. It's waiting for you. Can you hear the shipyard, McIlwaine?

McIlwaine Your head's cut, man.

Pyper You weren't dreaming about Lough Erne, David. You're on it. It surrounds you. Moore, the Bann is flowing outside. The Somme, it's not what we think it is. It's the Lagan, the Foyle, the Bann –

Craig You're trying too hard, Pyper. It's too late to tell us what we're fighting for. We know where we are. We know what we've to do. And we know what we're doing it for. We knew before we enlisted. We joined up willingly for that reason. Everyone of us, except you. You've learned it at long last. But you can't teach us what we already know. You won't save us, you won't save yourself, imagining things. There's nothing imaginary about this, Kenneth. This is the last battle. We're going out to die.

Pyper No David, you –

Craig Yes, yes. Whoever comes back alive, if any of us do, will have died as well. He'll never be the same. Different men after this, one way or the other. Do you know why we'll risk going through that? Because we want to.

Millen None of us want to die.

Craig I said even to come through this will be the same as dying.

McIlwaine How do you know it's going to be that bad?

Craig The gods told me.

Roulston What did they tell?

Craig The Protestant gods told me. In a dream. On Lough Erne. Get yourselves ready. Make peace with God and man.

The men divide slowly into the pairings of part 3.

Anderson What's got into your man Craig?

McIlwaine Sense.

Anderson He's been hanging around too long near Pyper.

McIlwaine Has he?

Anderson Did you hear that silly chat about rivers?

McIlwaine There's more there than you think.

Anderson I know what I think. That man Pyper's a lunatic.

McIlwaine Remember that night on the Field you thought he was thinking right?

Anderson No.

McIlwaine Good.

Anderson What's got into you?

McIlwaine Maybe I've got sense as well. All right?

Anderson Hi, I'm sorry.

McIlwaine What for?

Anderson I don't know what's going to happen.

McIlwaine You do, Anderson. You do.

Moore Are you feeling any better?

Millen Willy, I lied to you. I lied to you all my life. Was it you or me lost their nerve? Who crossed the bridge?

Moore We did together.

Millen I couldn't have done it.

Moore You have to save yourself today, Johnny, you can't save me. We're on our own today.

Millen You think like Craig we're not coming back?

Moore What do you think?

Millen That it's over.

Moore Go down fighting.

Millen Take me back.

Moore Where?

Millen Home.

Moore This is home.

Millen Death?

Moore You have to look it in the face. Watch yourself.

Millen I need you.

Moore I'm beside you.

Millen Then we'll sink together.

Moore Or swim.

Millen Or swim.

Moore and Millen shake hands.

Crawford It's different to what I thought.

Roulston How?

Crawford Quieter.

Roulston What's done has to be done.

Crawford I thought when this day come you'd have been angrier.

Roulston With you?

Crawford How with me? I meant with God.

Roulston I'm not sure I can tell the difference any more. Anyway, it was always leading to this.

Crawford Don't say that.

Roulston Why not?

Crawford Cowardly.

Roulston Is that not what I am?

Crawford You've proved yourself before. You'll do it today as well.

Roulston Proved what? That I can handle a gun? Stick a bayonet where it's needed? Am as good a man as any soldier? That proves nothing. What you said about me in the church that day was the truth. It was shown to me. You showed me. I accept it. No better and no worse than any of you. None of us are.

Crawford Christopher, do you still believe?

Roulston Yes.

Crawford Would you do something for me?

Roulston What?

Crawford Pray I'll come back.

Roulston No.

Crawford Why not?

Roulston You can do that for yourself. Do it now.

Crawford Do it with me then.

Roulston Wait till the word's given to go.

Craig I'm sorry.

Pyper Why did you do that?

Craig To stop the heroism.

Pyper I wasn't –

Craig You were being stupid. We could do without that, you know.

Pyper Why are you changing?

Craig Because you're going back. You'll go back to your proud family. The brave eldest son. Made a man of himself in Flanders. Damn you, after listening to that bit of rabble-rousing, I saw through you. You're wasted here with us. You're not of us, man. You're a leader. You got what you wanted. You always have, you always will. You'll come through today because you learned to want it.

Pyper I've learned to want you.

Craig No. Tell me this. What kind of life do you see for us when we're out of here? It might be many things, but it won't be together.

Pyper What do you want from me?

Craig What you want.

Pyper I don't understand you.

Craig No. You don't. For the first time, and that's good. I'm your measure. Don't forget that.

Pyper Stop this.

Craig If I'm hurting you, it's about time.

Pyper Don't go out like this.

Craig It's the way I need to go out there. Kenneth, don't die. One of us has to go on.

Pyper David –

Craig Calm.

Pyper Home.

Craig Here.

Anderson Hi, Pyper?

Pyper What do you want?

Anderson We've noticed something missing from your uniform. Something important. We think you should do something about it. It might get you into trouble.

Pyper What's missing?

Anderson Your badge of honour.

Anderson hands out an Orange sash to Pyper.

Well?

Pyper It's not mine.

Anderson It is now. It's a gift. From us. Am I right, McIlwaine?

McIlwaine Right. Very right. Damned right. Anderson gets sensible when he's right, Pyper.

Silence.

Anderson Will you wear it this time, like the rest of us?

Pyper Why?

Anderson So we'll recognize you as one of our own. Your own.

Pyper We're on the same side.

Anderson I'm sure we are. Here, take it.

Silence.

I said take it. Do you want me to put it round you?

Pyper snatches the sash.

That's the man. That's the way.

Crawford Are you ready, Roulston?

Moore What for?

Crawford The last prayer.

Roulston Together.

All (*sing*)
I'm but a stranger here,
Heaven is my home.
Earth is but a desert drear,
Heaven is my home.
Danger and sorrow stand
Round me on every hand.
Heaven is my fatherland,
Heaven is my home.

There at my Saviour's side –
Heaven is my home –
I shall be glorified,
Heaven is my home.
There are the good and blest,
Those I love most and best,
And there I too shall rest.
Heaven is my home.

Therefore I murmur not,
Heaven is my home.
Whate'er my earthly lot,

Heaven is my home.
And I shall surely stand
There at the Lord's right hand.
Heaven is my fatherland,
Heaven is my home.

Moore I can see the others gathering.

Millen It's time then.

McIlwaine All together.

Crawford Better move.

Roulston Every one.

Craig Right.

Anderson Last stage.

With the exception of Pyper, they each begin to put on their Orange sashes. Craig watches Pyper, then takes his sash off, goes to Moore, hands it to him. Moore hesitates, then exchanges his sash for Craig's. At this there is an exchange of sashes, Crawford's for Anderson's, Millen's for McIlwaine's. Roulston goes to Pyper, who takes Roulston's and gives him his own.

Pyper It's come to this, Roulston?

Roulston What's decreed passes, Pyper.

Pyper There's no fight back?

Roulston There's just the fight.

Pyper The good fight?

Roulston The everlasting fight.

Pyper Inside us?

Roulston And outside us.

Pyper Preach.

Roulston No. You preach.

Silence. They wait.

You believe. Believe.

Silence.

Pyper God in heaven, if you hear the words of man, I speak to you this day. I do it now to ask we be spared. I do it to ask for strength. Strength for these men around me, strength for myself. If you are a just and merciful God, show your mercy this day. Save us. Save our country. Destroy our enemies at home and on this field of battle. Let this day at the Somme be as glorious in the memory of Ulster as that day at the Boyne, when you scattered our enemies. Lead us back from this exile. To Derry, to the Foyle. To Belfast and the Lagan. To Armagh. To Tyrone. To the Bann and its banks. To Erne and its islands. Protect them. Protect us. Protect me. Let us fight bravely. Let us win gloriously. Lord, look down on us. Spare us. I love – . Observe the sons of Ulster marching towards the Somme. I love their lives. I love my own life. I love my home. I love my Ulster. Ulster. Ulster. Ulster. Ulster. Ulster. Ulster. Ulster. Ulster.

> *As the chant of 'Ulster' commences rifles and bayonets are raised. The chant turns into a battle cry, reaching frenzy. The Elder Pyper appears. His Younger Self sees him. The chant ceases.*

Younger Pyper Ulster.

Elder Pyper Ulster.

Younger Pyper I have seen horror.

Elder Pyper Ulster.

Younger Pyper They kept their nerve, and they died.

Elder Pyper Ulster.

Younger Pyper There would be, and there will be, no surrender.

Elder Pyper Ulster.

Younger Pyper The house has grown cold, the province has grown lonely.

Elder Pyper Ulster.

Younger Pyper You'll always guard Ulster.

Elder Pyper Ulster.

Younger Pyper Save it.

Elder Pyper Ulster.

Younger Pyper The temple of the Lord is ransacked.

Elder Pyper Ulster.

Pyper reaches towards himself.

Younger Pyper Dance in this deserted temple of the Lord.

Elder Pyper Dance.

Darkness.

INNOCENCE

For Philip Tilling and Patrick Mason

Characters

The life and death of Michelangelo Merisi, Caravaggio

Caravaggio, Michelangelo Merisi, painter
Lena, friend to Caravaggio
Whore, friend to Lena
Antonio, rough trade
Lucio, rough trade
Cardinal, patron to Caravaggio
Servant, to Cardinal
Brother, Giovanni Battisti, to Caravaggio
Sister, Caterina, to Caravaggio

Innocence was first performed at the Gate Theatre, Dublin, on 7 October 1986. The cast was as follows:

Caravaggio Garrett Keogh
Lena Kate Flynn
Whore Pat Levy
Antonio Peter Holmes
Lucio Joe Savino
Cardinal Aiden Grennel
Servant Michael Ford
Brother Jonathan Ryan
Sister Olwyn Fuore

Directed by Patrick Mason
Designed by Joe Vanck
Lighting by Mick Hughes

Life

Music, Vespers, Monteverdi.
   A circle of characters.
   Detached from them, **Caravaggio** *observes, fingering a skull.* **Lena** *caresses a red cloak, like a child.* **Antonio** *and* **Lucio** *caress each other.* **Whore** *rocks herself to and fro, weeping.* **Cardinal** *recites the Offertory from the Tridentine Mass, holding a host.* **Servant** *kneels at Cardinal's feet, with* **Brother.** **Sister** *moves through the circle, repeating her prayer.*

Sister Thine, O Lord, wilt ope my lips and my tongue shall announce thy praise. Incline unto my aid, O Lord. O Lord, make haste to help me.

   Wrapping the red cloak about herself, Lena moves to comfort Whore. Antonio and Lucio kiss. Cardinal raises the host in elevation. Servant and Brother fall prostrate before it. Caravaggio raises the skull. Lena tears the red cloak from herself. Sounds resembling the Latin from the Mass start to pass among the characters. The cloak starts to stretch about them. The noises increase, breaking into animal sounds, eventually becoming a horse going mad, as the cloak now moves wildly through the characters. Caravaggio approaches the cloak-horse, holding the skull before the wild shape. Caravaggio touches the shape with the skull. The shape screams. It wraps itself violently around Caravaggio. Hands start to beat him. Caravaggio falls, roaring. Darkness.
   Light. A hovel. Lena examines a red cloak. Caravaggio sleeps, a bandage around his eyes. A skull lies on the floor beside him. Caravaggio wakes up with a start.

Caravaggio Where am I?

Lena So you're back among the living?

Caravaggio What have you put on my eyes, woman?

Lena What'll cure you. Why?

Caravaggio Nothing.

Lena Had my little goat a bad dream?

Caravaggio spits.

Touchy, touchy.

Caravaggio searches for a goblet on the floor. Lena throws the cloak aside.

That's perfect now. We should invest in a new cloak. I can't keep up repairing this. It's as old as I am. I'm sick seeing the same old ball-covering every time you take a fancy for a fucking John the Baptist. You should learn to sew, you know that?

Caravaggio finds the goblet.

Might keep the cup out of your hand. (*She reaches for a mirror.*)

Caravaggio Fill this, will you?

Silence.

Lena?

Silence.

Lena, where are you?

Silence.

Lena Jesus, I'm getting old.

Caravaggio Old?

Lena Old. Wrinkled. Past it. (*She wails.*)

Caravaggio Yea.

Lena I'm not that past it.

Caravaggio Yea, give us some wine.

Silence.

Look, I pay for my fair whack of the booze in this kip, so where is it?

Lena I hid it.

Caravaggio Did you? Fetch it.

Lena You can wait. You're not getting a drop until you compliment me. Compliment me.

Caravaggio You look grand.

Lena No. I don't. I look old. I am old.

Caravaggio Jesus, preserve me.

Lena It's terrible to grow old.

Caravaggio Jesus, protect me.

Lena You don't notice it happening and it happens.

Caravaggio Right. Two can play at this game, baby.

Lena No, shut it, Lello. Listen to me. (*She sits by Caravaggio.*)

Caravaggio OK, we're off.

Lena I was in Navona today and I saw a midget.

Caravaggio My name is Michelangelo Merisi.

Lena She had a hump, the midget.

Caravaggio Michelangelo Merisi da Caravaggio. (*He strokes Lena's back.*)

Lena I swear to Christ I looked at her and she was happier than me – hump and all.

Caravaggio Michelangelo for the angel and not for that chiselling Florentine cocksucker.

Lena No worries, not a line on her face. Do you know why? What did a man ever matter to a woman like that?

Caravaggio (*stroking Lena's face*) Merisi for my family and Caravaggio for the birthplace of my father.

Lena I don't blame men. I lead the life I want to lead but that midget, she'd have been as content in a convent as me – me content? Where would I be content, Lello?

Caravaggio (*continuing to stroke Lena's face*) I paint with my hands as God intended the eyes to see and to see is to be God, for it is to see God.

Lena I should have entered a convent.

Caravaggio embraces Lena.

Caravaggio In all Rome I stand supremely alone as painter, seer and visionary, great interpreter of man.

Lena I'd have been happier in a convent.

She pushes him away. Caravaggio raises his hands.

Caravaggio I take ordinary flesh and blood and bone and with my two hands transform it into eternal light, eternal dark.

Lena Better than this dump.

Caravaggio For my art balances the beautiful and the ugly, the saved and the sinning.

Lena I wonder do convents take midgets. (*She lays her head on Caravaggio's lap.*)

Caravaggio I am the great Caravaggio and I am keeping up this shit for as long as I need to until I am poured a bloody drink. (*He kisses Lena.*)

Lena I mean I'm no midget but I feel at times as if I've a hump. Maybe it's not too late to become a nun. I was mad about Our Lady when I was a girl. Christ, would you believe that? I used to imagine I was her daughter and Jesus was a right pup who tormented me. The innocence of it.

Caravaggio (*running his hands along Lena's body*) I paint as I see in light and as I imagine in darkness, for in the light I see the flesh and blood and bone but in the dark I imagine the soul of man for the soul and the soul alone is the sighting of God in man and it is I who reveal God and it is God who reveals my painting to the world.

Lena (*sitting up*) What in under Jesus are you rabbiting on about, Lello?

Caravaggio I am Michelangelo Merisi da Caravaggio, called Lello by cretins, who do not know that he with whom they dare to be familiar works with his hands, paints with his hands, and his hands are the hands of God alone.

Lena Lello, should I enter a convent?

Caravaggio You have the hump for it. (*He laughs.*)

Lena walks towards him.

What are you doing?

Lena puts her hand down Caravaggio's trousers.

What are you doing?

Lena starts to masturbate Caravaggio.

I hate women doing that to me.

Lena I am Michelangelo Merisi da Caravaggio.

Caravaggio For Jesus' sake, Lena.

Lena My genius is recognized all over Rome.

Caravaggio I'm a defenceless man.

Lena I am Michelangelo Merisi and I am a wanker.

Caravaggio Lena.

    *Lena pulls Caravaggio's cock roughly. Caravaggio
    yelps.*

Lena That was the hand of God.

Caravaggio You're a rough woman.

Lena I've had to be. Fend for myself. That's what happens
when you've never had a husband.

Caravaggio A beautiful woman like you?

Lena A beautiful woman like me.

Caravaggio No husband?

Lena No.

Caravaggio Not married?

Lena No. Never married.

Caravaggio Do you want to?

Lena Get married?

Caravaggio Why not?

Lena Don't know. (*She pours them some wine.*)

Caravaggio Bit dangerous always, this game.

Lena I love this one. Keep going. Here's wine. Keep going.

Caravaggio You know where it might lead to.

Lena Look, is this or is this not a proposal?

Caravaggio What do you think?

Lena It's a bit sudden. I mean, I hardly know you. You better take me out walking first.

Caravaggio Where?

Lena A girl can't be too safe. Tell me about yourself. Your people, who are they? Who's your father?

Caravaggio Dead. He's dead.

Lena And your mother?

Caravaggio Dead.

Lena Are you from Rome?

Caravaggio No. From Caravaggio. But I had to leave.

Lena And do what?

Caravaggio See the world.

Lena Why?

Caravaggio What?

Lena See.

Caravaggio I like seeing.

Lena I trust you, let's go somewhere.

Caravaggio Where?

Lena Somewhere on our own. Somewhere secret. Somewhere beautiful.

Caravaggio There's a forest.

Lena The forest, yes.

Caravaggio It's very dark. Will you be afraid?

Lena Yes, but I like the dark.

Caravaggio I like the forest, even if it's dark, because you can still see in it always.

Lena The animals.

Caravaggio The birds.

Lena The trees.

Caravaggio The leaves.

Lena Do you see them?

Caravaggio Yes.

Lena Do you know their names?

Caravaggio Sometimes. Do you want children?

Lena How many?

Caravaggio Ten?

Lena Twenty.

Caravaggio A hundred?

Lena Thousand.

Caravaggio Million.

Lena One.

  Silence.

Cut it.

Caravaggio What's his name?

Lena Not tonight. Leave it.

Caravaggio All right.

  Silence.

Lena You on the prowl tonight?

Caravaggio Yea, I better. His eminence has the hot horn again. I've been a bad boy.

Lena How?

Caravaggio Been neglecting him.

Lena What way?

Caravaggio Between one thing and another.

Lena Watch yourself there. A nice line going. We need the financial blessing of father church.

Caravaggio We?

Lena We, sweetheart. Go easy with the Cardinal, boy. Your bread has cheese on it there.

Caravaggio I'll do what I like where I like when I like.

Lena It's like talking to a stone.

Caravaggio That's right.

> *Whore enters, notices the silence. It persists. Caravaggio fingers the skull.*

Whore I love coming into this house. You're so pleasant always.

Caravaggio Remember, woman, thou art dust and unto dust thou shalt return.

Whore That bandage suits you. Why don't you get one for your mouth? Oh, is that wine?

Caravaggio Lady, I wouldn't give you my wine even if there was poison in it.

Whore And I wouldn't piss on you if you were on fire.

Lena I hate to interrupt this sparkling repartee but why are you in here?

Whore Would you ever give us the lend –

Lena No.

Whore You don't know what I was asking –

Lena Money. You're not getting it.

Whore I'm not looking for money. I want a lend of your gold ribbon. The one he got you.

Lena That's the best stitch I possess.

Whore Don't be so selfish. When you went on the streets first, I was like a mother to you.

Lena You robbed me of every penny you could get your hands on.

Whore Exactly. Money ruins young ones. A mother knows that. Lend us the ribbon.

Lena No.

Whore Give us a drink then.

Caravaggio No.

Whore I get the decided feeling I'm not wanted.

Caravaggio Remember, woman, thou art dust and unto dust thou shalt return.

Whore Will you stop saying that to me?

Caravaggio Remember, woman, thou art dust and unto dust thou shalt return.

Whore Fit you better if you said your prayers.

Caravaggio Thou art full of grace and the Lord is with thee. Blessed art thou among women.

Whore Blessed. I know, I know. Blessed.

Silence.

Caravaggio What's the difference between you and a barrel of shite?

Whore What?

Caravaggio The barrel.

Whore Mock on, mock on, God sees you. He hears you. I'm not getting the ribbon?

Lena You're not.

Whore All right. Thank God I didn't ask to borrow a dress. You never know when he might want to wear it. Be good, Lena. You can't be much else with his kind, can you? I'll leave the holy family in peace.

Caravaggio May you die roaring.

Whore Ciao. (*She exits. Silence.*)

Caravaggio When can I take this fucking cloth off my eyes?

Lena When I say so. I had to eat Rome to get the right herbs. The last time you hadn't the patience to lie still in the dark till they were half-way healed. I learned my lesson if you didn't. Coming crying to me. I'm going blind, Lena. I won't see. I won't paint. What's going to become of us?

Caravaggio Well I am a bloody painter and a great one.

Lena You're a dirty shit and a long one.

Caravaggio moves to tear the bandage from his eyes.

Don't dare put your paws near the bandage till I tell you, I'm warning you.

Caravaggio pulls the bandage from his eyes. He roars with pain.

215

Caravaggio It stings.

Lena Pity about you.

Caravaggio My eyes are burning out of me.

Lena God love you.

Caravaggio For Christ's sake, Lena, do something.

Lena Such as?

Caravaggio You're the healer, you know.

Lena Sorry, can't help.

Caravaggio Have I done myself permanent damage?

Lena Who knows? You're the big man. You know it all.

Caravaggio Tell me the truth, cow, the truth.

Lena Moo, Moo.

Caravaggio I'm not laughing, Lena.

Lena Mooo.

Caravaggio Do something.

Lena Mooo.

Caravaggio draws his knife. Lena rises and hits him.

Caravaggio Jesus.

Lena You snivelling pup.

Caravaggio I'm sorry.

Lena Who the hell do you think you are? Who do you think you are dealing with? Some penny piece of pansy rough you scraped off the streets? By Jesus, boy, you should know better than to try that caper.

Caravaggio I'm sorry.

Lena You should know a damn sight better.

Caravaggio I shouldn't have done it. I know. I'm sorry.

Lena Such an action.

Caravaggio It was the first time.

Lena And last time you'll try it with me, whoever else you might terrorize.

Caravaggio I'll make it up to you.

Lena How much?

Caravaggio Not with money. I'll paint you.

Lena You've painted me, goat.

Caravaggio Not for a long time. I haven't painted you as you are.

Lena Yea, the whore.

Caravaggio No. Beautiful and angry. Lena. Look. Watch. Lena.

Lena Yea, Lena the whore.

Caravaggio No, girlfriend.

Lena Girlfriend, yea.

Caravaggio Girlfriend to the goat, to Caravaggio.

Lena My dream goat.

Caravaggio Dream goat.

Lena Unicorn.

Caravaggio Dream.

Lena Unicorn.

Their foreheads touch.

Caravaggio Forest.

Lena Forest.

Caravaggio's fingers start to touch Lena's face.

Caravaggio A bird moves through the forest. A golden bird, and the bird is golden because it carries the sun. The bird sees the tree and it feeds the tree with sun. The tree feeds the leaf, and the leaf loves the tree, and the tree cradles the bird and Lena is the bird who is the sun and the tree and the leaf, for the leaf is the fruit of the beautiful earth. I gather the earth's fruit and the tree's leaf and I plant them in your face for your face is a bowl full of life, full of Lena. Here, Lena, look, your face. (*He holds out his hands to Lena. They caress her face and hair, returning to her face. Then he holds out his hands before his own face, admiring them.*) Your face. Yes, Lena, your beautiful face. (*He blows his nose into his hands.*)

Lena Get out.

Caravaggio You fall for it every time, wagon.

Lena Out.

Caravaggio I suppose a ride's out of the question?

Lena You should be so lucky, queer.

Caravaggio moves to exit, grabbing the cloak as he leaves, while Lena hurls the skull after him. He catches it.

Don't bring that fucking skull into my house, it watches me.

Caravaggio exits, Lena shouting after him.

Jesus, am I glad I put pepper into that eye mixture.

Caravaggio (*off*) Whore.

Lena Goat.

Silence. Lena moves back to the hovel. She lifts up the bandage, scowls, smiles. She throws aside the bandage, picks up the mirror, looks into it, removes it from her sight.

I wonder where's the nearest convent.

Fade.

The street. Antonio and Lucio, rough trade, wait. Antonio bites his nails.

Lucio Stop biting your nails.

Antonio I'm hungry.

Lucio It's a rotten habit and it's bad for you.

Antonio So's whoring.

Lucio So?

Antonio So I'm hungry. I bite my nails. Want a bite?

Lucio Fuck off.

Silence.

I have really long nails. Really nice. Well, so I've been told.

Antonio Mine are disgusting. I think that's why I eat them. Get rid of them.

Lucio This ponce I picked up once, nice bastard, he said to me I had fingers that were carved. He said they had the flow of a musician's hands, they should have an instrument in them. I told him they often had. He didn't think it was funny. Queers have no sense of humour.

Antonio I have.

Lucio You are not a queer. You might be a whore for the

sake of your belly but you're no queer. I wouldn't hang about with you if there was anything wrong with you.

Antonio I like men.

Lucio Don't be disgusting.

Antonio I like their arses. I like biting them. That's what's really wrong with me. My mouth always has to be doing something. Maybe if I'd been born deformed, without a mouth or something, I'd be married. I do know I wouldn't always be hungry.

Silence.

I do think I've a sense of humour though.

Lucio Who said you hadn't?

Antonio You did. You said queers –

Lucio You are not –

Antonio I'm bent as a nail. So are you.

Lucio Well don't go saying it. Bad enough doing it.

Antonio And we're not doing it.

Lucio Funny enough I noticed that.

Silence.

I hate being poor.

Antonio I know. Hunger drives you mad. I saw a ghost last night.

Lucio I think I'll cut out this caper. It's no work for a man.

Antonio It had no head on its shoulders and it knew my name.

Lucio Get a woman or something. This crack can't last for ever. (*He starts to do press-ups.*)

Antonio I wasn't dreaming either. It really had no head, this ghost. I let one roar out of me.

Lucio Women would be less fussy. I suppose there's more of them.

Antonio Do you know what really scared the life out of me? I thought this ghost must be my father or my mother.

Lucio Yea, I'm going off the game. I'm packing this in. I'm packing it in tonight. (*He stops doing press-ups.*)

Antonio So I bent down to pick it up, the head, and see exactly who it was and it bit me.

Lucio What bit you?

Antonio The ghost bit me.

Lucio Ghost? (*He kisses Antonio.*)

Antonio It started to speak. It blamed me. It said I cut off its head.

Lucio Whose head?

Antonio The ghost's, my father or mother.

Lucio How? They're dead. (*He rubs Antonio's hair.*)

Antonio That's why I thought they must be the ghost, stupid. I started to cry. It laughed. No head, and it was laughing. Have you ever heard anything that weird?

Lucio Are you in one of your visions?

Antonio I couldn't believe the sound of it. A ghost laughing.

Lucio Who are you talking to?

Antonio God.

Lucio Why?

Antonio I'm lonely.

Lucio Talk to me then.

Antonio Why should I?

Lucio Why shouldn't you?

Silence.

Antonio Will we try the last resort?

Lucio We tried it last night. Don't want to overdo it.

Antonio It didn't work last night.

Lucio He mustn't have heard us.

Antonio So will we do it?

They kneel.

Lucio You pray.

Antonio Hear us, Father in Heaven.

Lucio We're hungry.

Antonio We could eat each other.

Lucio Not that. Say something religious.

Antonio Such as?

Lucio This is my body.

Antonio This is my blood.

Lucio Turn me into bread, God.

Antonio Me into wine.

Lucio Give us a miracle.

Antonio Give us a man.

Lucio Not even that. Work a reverse job. Flesh and blood into bread and wine

Antonio Give us a feed, Lord, if it's only ourselves.

Lucio Wait a minute, what if he hears us?

Antonio He never hears us.

Lucio But if he does, we're fucked.

Antonio That's the general idea.

Lucio Send us a man, God.

Antonio Send us your son.

Lucio He was a god.

Antonio Send us a god then, we're desperate.

Lucio Don't talk like that. It's a sin. It makes me nervous.

Antonio So?

Lucio He'd strike us down dead if he hears us.

Antonio He never hears us.

Lucio There is a first time for everything

Silence.

Antonio Do you remember the first time?

Lucio No.

Antonio I do. What age was I? Thirteen or fourteen?

Lucio I remember. I called you my little brother. You were beautiful.

Antonio Thank you.

Lucio Keep it down. See your man.

Antonio Where?

Lucio Watching.

Antonio No.

Lucio Standing in the dark. Can't make him out too clearly. Taking in everything though. Wait for the moon to catch him.

Antonio We'll be here all night.

Lucio Think he has a beard. Can't see all his face, but a thick-looking customer. I see him. Give you a hiding as soon as look at you. Face like a horse's arse.

Antonio Fuck it, he'll fancy me. Why me always with the dreamboats?

Lucio Oh Jesus, I think it's the pervert.

Antonio What's wrong with that?

Lucio This boy is something special.

Antonio Know him?

Lucio Had him.

Antonio We're safe?

Lucio Strung to the moon.

Antonio What did he do?

Lucio Never said a word the whole night. Let me rattle on and plied me with drink. Then the props appeared.

Antonio Oh Jesus, for a beating?

Lucio No.

Antonio Then what were the props?

Lucio Grapes.

Antonio Grapes?

Lucio Barrels of them.

Antonio Now that is different. Grapes.

Lucio He squeezed grapes all over me. There was even a bunch hanging from my balls. Then he ate them. I have a good stomach but I swear I nearly took sick. He started to call me Bacchus.

Antonio Who the hell's Bacchus?

Lucio How the Jesus do I know?

Antonio Probably some boyfriend he had one time, foreign with that name. There's ones like foreigners.

Lucio I haven't told you the best bit yet.

Antonio What?

Lucio He had me dress up.

Antonio As a woman?

Lucio As a fucking tree.

Antonio How a tree?

Lucio Leaves all over my head, right? Rotten old fruit dripping all over me. He had fire burning all about me. My big red cheeks burning like two beetroots. Jesus, I felt a right prick.

Antonio Were the grapes still around your balls?

Lucio No, I told you he ate the grapes.

Antonio What was the fire for?

Lucio It was the dead of night and he wanted light to see me. The bastard's a painter. He was painting me.

Antonio As a tree?

Lucio As Bacchus.

Antonio Oh yes, Bacchus. Is he a lunatic?

Lucio He's a painter.

Antonio Does he pay OK?

Lucio I can't remember.

Antonio Oh come on.

Lucio I was pissed out of my head when he had me. My skull was flying.

Antonio And you were that drunk you didn't remember if he paid?

Lucio I was younger then.

Antonio Well, he's still watching.

Lucio He's all yours.

Antonio Are you sure?

Lucio Positive. If he wanted the two of us, he'd have made a move before now. I'll shift. Keep me a bunch of grapes.

Antonio Wait.

Lucio He's for you, Antonio.

Antonio I don't like the cut of him, Lucio.

Lucio He pays well, Toni darling. We need the money.

Antonio But you said you couldn't remember if he –

Lucio I remember he pays.

Antonio Don't leave me yet, Lucio, please.

Lucio Pansy, fucking pansy. Why do I bother?

Antonio Please, big brother.

   Caravaggio enters.

Lucio Fine night.

Silence.

The mate here was just remarking on the moon. A man should enjoy a moon like that. What do you think yourself?

Silence.

Are you taking a stroll like ourselves?

Silence.

I'm heading for my kip. This boy, you couldn't stop him wandering. He's making for a last trip to the river.

Antonio Don't believe him. I'm not. I never hang around the river.

Lucio What are you saying?

Antonio We're not bent. Don't beat us up.

Lucio He won't do that, will you?

Antonio We better get home, Lucio.

Caravaggio You share a home?

Antonio Yes. The wife will be waiting up for us.

Caravaggio You share a wife?

Antonio Yes.

Lucio No. We live by ourselves. Do you feel like joining us?

Caravaggio Join me.

Caravaggio puts a gold coin into his hand, holds it out towards Lucio, who goes to snatch the coin. Caravaggio grabs Lucio by the hair.

Gold.

Caravaggio throws more coins on to the ground and points at Antonio.

You as well. Come on.

He exits. Lucio rapidly collects the coins.

Lucio Come on. Follow him.

Antonio Go home with what we've got. Give him the slip, Lucio.

Lucio For Jesus' sake, there's more where that came from. Come on, Antonio. (*He exits.*)

Antonio Lucio.

Lucio (*off*) Come on.

Silence. Antonio moves to exit, pauses.

Antonio See you, God, you're a right bastard. Good luck. (*He exits.*)

Fade.

The palace of Cardinal Francesco del Monte. Tapestries and paintings. A bench. Cushions on the floor. Meat on a gold platter. A bowl of fruit. Caravaggio carves meat with his knife, the red cloak beside him. Lucio and Antonio watch Caravaggio eat, as they drink wine. Antonio raises the bowl of fruit and approaches Caravaggio, offering him the food. Caravaggio grunts refusal. Antonio turns to go. Caravaggio signals him to stay and watches him holding the bowl, rearranging his hand and pulling Antonio's shirt from his shoulder to expose the flesh. Antonio waits patiently after Caravaggio's attentions. Caravaggio grunts Antonio's dismissal. Antonio shrugs and approaches Lucio with the bowl of fruit, lifting before Lucio's face a bunch of grapes.

Antonio Memories.

Lucio laughs.

Caravaggio What?

Lucio How quickly they forget.

Antonio All the same, men. The whole lot of them. Only after one thing.

Lucio Animals.

Antonio and Lucio Thank Jesus.

They laugh, directing the joke at Caravaggio who does not respond. Silence.

Antonio What's your name anyway?

Silence.

He thinks he knows you.

Silence.

Lucio Can I have some food?

Caravaggio Why didn't you ask before? Are you shy or something?

Lucio Why didn't you offer it?

Caravaggio Not mine to offer.

Lucio Whose is it then?

Caravaggio Your buyer.

Lucio You're not the buyer?

Silence.

You a pimp?

Caravaggio throws wine into Lucio's face.

Caravaggio Sorry. (*He refills his wine cup*.)

Antonio You're a rough man, aren't you?

Caravaggio No. (*He offers Lucio meat*.) You starving as well?

Antonio nods.

Eat. Share it.

They jump on the food.

Eat like Christians. Where's you manners in the priest's house?

Lucio Christ, are you a priest?

Caravaggio No, I'm a saint. I know what Rome's like. Easy to be waylaid by your like. I travel disguised.

Lucio As what?

Caravaggio Guess.

Lucio A woman?

Caravaggio laughs.

A beard works wonders for a woman.

Silence.

Caravaggio What makes you think I'm a priest?

Antonio You have loads of money.

Lucio The way you move your hands. And they're clean.

Antonio Are they? I love clean hands. Give us a look. (*He examines Caravaggio's hands*.) They're really hard.

Caravaggio Soft. Not hard. Soft. (*He looks at Lucio*.) Soft. Like your face used to be.

Antonio No, they're not that clean, not scrubbed like.

Lucio So you remember?

Antonio I mean, I've seen cleaner.

Caravaggio I never forget a face.

Lucio Even when you paint it?

Antonio The hands are a dead giveaway for age.

Caravaggio Clever boy. Strange boy.

Antonio Yea, dead giveaway.

Caravaggio Strange.

Silence.

Antonio Nice place you have here, father.

Caravaggio I'm not you father. Don't call me that.

Antonio You said it was a priest's –

Caravaggio I'm nobody's father.

Silence.

Lucio Who's the buyer?

Caravaggio A rich man.

Antonio Is he nice?

Caravaggio He's rich. All rich men are nice. Right?

Antonio Right. Great. He pays well?

Caravaggio Extremely well.

Antonio Great.

Lucio How do you know him?

Caravaggio He's my buyer too.

Lucio What does he do?

Caravaggio To live?

Lucio Yea.

Caravaggio Prays for your soul before claiming your body.

Lucio Is he a young guy?

Caravaggio You like them young?

Lucio Do you not?

Caravaggio He's young at heart.

Lucio I hate old men. They smell like fish. They should be gutted and fed to each other.

Antonio Pathetic old bastards.

Lucio Slice the wrinkled old shits to ribbons.

Antonio Slowly.

Caravaggio With what? Slice them to ribbons with what?

Lucio My nails.

> *Lucio imitates an animal clawing. Antonio follows suit.*
> *They mock-fight about the room. Caravaggio enters*
> *their game, encouraging them.*

Caravaggio What are you?

> *Lucio roars.*

Lion.

> *Lucio leaps on Caravaggio who avoids him. Lucio*
> *reaches for the tapestries and tears at them with his teeth.*

Hound.

> *Lucio bays like a hound.*

Antonio Can I be something too?

Caravaggio Hare. Gentle hare.

Antonio Just a hare?

Caravaggio pats Antonio. Lucio turns into a wild horse, attacking Antonio, who squeals. Caravaggio throws him off Antonio, and as Lucio kicks out, Caravaggio touches his face.

Caravaggio Steed, trusty steed.

Lucio rises again, breathing fiercely, following Antonio.

Lucio I'm no steed. I'm a dragon, and this is fire.

Caravaggio Fly, boy, fly. Turn into a bird, a fighting bird. An eagle.

Antonio turns into an eagle, landing on Lucio's face. Lucio bellows like a bull.

Bull.

Antonio and Lucio turn into fighting bulls. As they fight, Antonio calls to Caravaggio.

Antonio What are you?

Caravaggio Lizard. Poisonous lizard. Creeping on you. Touching you. Kissing you. Poison. Touching. Kissing. Poison. Kissing. Kissing.

Antonio and Lucio fear the lizard.

Calm, calm, my animals. Come to me. Calm.

Antonio and Lucio come quietly towards him.

Unicorn, unicorns, calm.

Caravaggio captures Lucio and Antonio gently. He holds them both. Antonio breaks away first for more wine. He brings Caravaggio the bowl of fruit.

Antonio That was great.

Caravaggio looks at Lucio's hand. He examines Lucio's fingernails.

Lucio Taste.

Caravaggio puts Lucio's finger into his mouth and chews it gently. Lucio removes the finger and Caravaggio kisses it. Lucio touches Caravaggio's face. He starts to trace the outline of Caravaggio's scar.

What's the mark on your face?

Silence.

Is that why you have the big beard? To cover the mark? Where did you get the mark?

Caravaggio It was worse once than it is now.

Lucio Near your eyes. Were you almost blinded?

Caravaggio I couldn't see much after it, but what I saw, I saw clearly.

Lucio You were kicked in the face.

Caravaggio How do you know?

Lucio It wasn't from a human.

Caravaggio What from then?

Lucio An animal. So was I. Years ago.

Lucio bares his thigh to show a wound. Caravaggio touches it.

Caravaggio Horse.

Lucio Horse. I fell. I scared it. It kicked out. It got me.

Antonio I was bitten by a rat once.

Lucio Were you riding the horse?

Antonio Bit on the ear. I couldn't hear for a month in it.

Caravaggio It was wild.

Antonio Nobody listens to me. (*Antonio lies at Caravaggio's feet, playing with fruit in the bowl.*)

Caravaggio I tried to save it.

Lucio What from?

Caravaggio Itself. I have a way with animals. Innocent at heart. Even the wildest.

Antonio A black rat it was too. It was in my bed. I felt a lump by my leg. I thought I was asleep. But I felt it move. Crawling beside me. Black.

Caravaggio I thought I was blinded.

Antonio I shot roaring out of bed. I hoped it was a lizard. But it was a rat. It ran like mad. (*He curls himself up, closer to Caravaggio.*)

Caravaggio I thought this will be the last thing I see. A horse.

Antonio The rat was probably more scared than I was, but that's no consolation.

Lucio But it wasn't.

Caravaggio strokes Lucio and Antonio.

Antonio My father heard me crying. He lifted me up. Right into his arms. I could never remember him touching me before. I felt all his strength. I loved that. (*He kisses Caravaggio's hand.*)

Caravaggio For the first time I saw.

Antonio Then he dropped me when he found out why I

was crying. He shouted about plague. He threw me into a barrel of rain. It was cold. (*He releases Caravaggio's hand*.)

Caravaggio It touched me, the horse. It saw me. And I could see its touch.

Lucio What about touching people?

Antonio I thought I was going to drown. My father wouldn't save me. He didn't want me. He never had.

Caravaggio Seeing. Touching. (*His eyes closed, Caravaggio tries to touch Antonio*.)

Antonio I couldn't hear myself crying but my face was wet. I thought I was deaf. Maybe he was deaf too, my father. Maybe he couldn't hear me crying either.

Lucio Are you afraid of touching?

Silence. Antonio starts to beat the ground with the gold platter, scattering meat.

Antonio I'm going to get married. Married to a woman, a woman would hear you. Men only hear what they want to hear. Like my father. I hate them. I was bitten by a rat. My father held me. I went nearly deaf. I'm all right now. I can hear. Listen to me.

Lucio You prepare yourself for the buyer.

Antonio He's the buyer, you stupid bastard. He'll do the paying. And he wants you. It's always you. And you said he was mine. But you sit there fucking him with your eyes and hands and ears and every part of you but what counts and you know why you can't do that? Because the horse kicked the life out of them. Your balls are as much good to a man as a cunt.

Lucio What are you calling me?

Antonio I'm sorry, Lucio.

Lucio If you want him, take him.

Antonio Do you want me?

Silence.

Do you not want me?

Silence.

Who are you?

The tapestries open. Cardinal appears, attended by a servant.

Cardinal Caravaggio. His name, my son, is Caravaggio.

Antonio and Lucio kneel in the presence of the Cardinal.

Caravaggio Michelangelo Merisi da Caravaggio, your eminence. And I bring these poor boys to your exalted presence. Feel them. Rough and ready, but to your taste. Bit of sweaty salt to savour the flesh. I know what you want, master. I give your eminence service as painter and pimp and his eminence knows me as a good servant.

Cardinal You are more than usually distressed, Caravaggio. I hope I have not interrupted your little intrigue too early, my friend.

Caravaggio Do not honour me as friend, eminence. I am your humble servant. (*He lifts both boys.*) Receive my gift, cardinal. Caravaggio presents his offerings before his master, most high prince of the church.

Caravaggio throws Antonio and Lucio at Cardinal's feet.

Rough, eh? Like me, no? Take us as you fancy. But I warn you your eyes are bigger than your belly. Your eyes want the lump of tough meat, but your belly needs refinement.

Cardinal I wish you would occasionally defy your reputation.

Caravaggio Eat and be merry, prince, tomorrow we die. Tonight, we die. All life is death, all light is darkness, and from the darkness your boys have crawled to bring you the light of love.

Cardinal You never cease to surprise.

Caravaggio bows.

Caravaggio My only desire is to please his eminence.

Cardinal Poor eminence to have such a disruptive servant. I forgive you. Your behaviour distorts you. I'm afraid you lack – what is it they say? Charmingly vigorous, painfully natural, but lacking perspective? Perhaps not. No, you lack the perfect sense of detail that distinguishes the exceptional from the good. I believe they call what you lack discretion. Your mouth shoots too much poison, Caravaggio. Take care it's not spat back.

Silence.

Sit down.

Caravaggio No peasant would sit in the company –

Cardinal You bore me, Caravaggio. Give me wine.

Caravaggio You heard his eminence. Respect the church. Respect old age. Give the prince his due. Give the old man your wine. (*He grabs Antonio's wine cup.*) Give his dry mouth your cock.

Antonio Father –, eminence –, we –

Caravaggio Don't be ashamed. That's what he'll come round to asking you for. A little more time. A little more

238

discretion. A little more work on it. Then it will be perfectly all right. I know what he wants. How could I not? I serviced him myself when nothing younger was about. I've given him my best. He knows it. He thanks me. He feeds me. He clothes me. And underneath it all I'm a good boy. I know the value of his money. I do as I am told. Painter and pimp. Painter to Cardinal del Monte, pimp to the Papal Curia, whore to the Catholic church. And they need me. For I'm a very special whore. The cardinal is envied for his whore's expertise. Jesus, what I get up to with these hands has to be seen to be believed.

Cardinal If my memory serves me, I asked some time ago for something to drink.

> *On all fours Caravaggio crawls to a wine cup and carries it back in his mouth to Cardinal. Cardinal laughs, takes the cup, gives Caravaggio his ring to kiss. Caravaggio kisses, then pours Cardinal wine. He sits at Cardinal's feet.*

Excuse my fool's manners. He has not welcomed you as friends. Have you visited with him here before?

Caravaggio No.

Cardinal Where did he find you?

Caravaggio In church.

Cardinal At prayer?

Caravaggio Deeply.

Cardinal Good. Your spiritual grace matches your physical beauty. Come here. Sit by me.

> *Silence.*

Come on.

> *Silence.*

239

What are you afraid of? Of Caravaggio? Has he attacked you already?

Antonio Yes, father.

Cardinal Lucky boy, eh, Caravaggio?

Caravaggio bays like a dog.

He's on the leash here. He can only bark. No need to fear him. He has no power in my house. I am a man of God. My house is the house of God. You have no more need to fear me than you should fear God. Would God despise you for your poverty and your profession? No. Do I despise you? No. Come here. Sit. Both of you, sit. You, bring the bowl of fruit.

Antonio goes to Cardinal with fruit bowl. Cardinal selects fruit and eats.

(*softly*) Good boy. Sit down. Are you afraid of me as well?

Antonio No, father.

Cardinal's arm enfolds Antonio. Antonio cuddles towards him.

Cardinal Don't fear my animal either. An interesting animal. He likes to be punished. When he remembers his station, he's the best creature on God's earth. Aren't you, Caravaggio? Stroke him, don't be afraid.

Antonio strokes Caravaggio's hair. Silence.

Give me your knife, Caravaggio.

Caravaggio gives his knife to Cardinal, who holds it before Caravaggio's face.

Look at him. Hear his breathing. Don't be afraid. Look. He carries this weapon but when he makes it my weapon, it could remove his sight for ever. Cut the eye from its socket. Slice the old bastard into ribbons. We know what excites you, Caravaggio? Blood. Can we see blood? If this knife moves into your eyes, what will you be? Where will you be, Caravaggio?

Caravaggio squeals.

If he so afraid? Is it so easy to terrify the wild Caravaggio? Yes, he has his peasant's fear of the dark. It's full of ghosts. Were you boys afraid of the dark when you were children? So was Caravaggio. He's still afraid and not just of the dark and its ghosts. Fear, Caravaggio. Poor Caravaggio. Cry with fear. Cry for me. Cry. (*Cardinal slaps Caravaggio's face.*)

Lucio Leave him.

Cardinal Take back your knife. No fun tonight. These boys, why have you chosen them? Was it for their dirt? Shave him clean. Wash him with your blade.

Cardinal hurls Antonio from him. Caravaggio leaps on Antonio. Antonio screams. To silence the scream Caravaggio grips Antonio's throat. Caravaggio raises the knife. Lucio stays Caravaggio's hand.

Lucio No.

Caravaggio laughs.

Caravaggio Poor lambs. Has the big, bad wolf put the fear of God into your innocent souls?

Lucio Let us go home.

Antonio Please, father. We have the money he gave us. We'll give it to you for masses or something.

Lucio We need that money.

Caravaggio Well said. Oh for Christ's sake, you've been in worse places.

Lucio You've recovered your senses, have you?

Caravaggio A miracle. Thank God for it. Go and offer thanks for saving your lives. This palace is full of chapels. Say your prayers in one before the entertainment starts.

Cardinal Remove them.

The Servant moves towards Antonio and Lucio.

Caravaggio (*sotto*) Don't forget to say your prayers.

Cardinal Bathe them.

Antonio Let us go home, father.

Cardinal Clean them.

Caravaggio God will provide easy pickings.

Antonio Let us go home.

Servant leads Antonio and Lucio out.

Cardinal You'll be the death of me, Caravaggio.

Caravaggio I hope not, Cardinal.

Cardinal Why do you keep coming back here? Have you started to enjoy playing my fool?

Caravaggio I'm not a fool.

Cardinal Then you still must fear me. Why?

Caravaggio Yours is the hand that feeds.

Cardinal You would have bitten it off long ago if that's all it does. Why do you fear my hand? Why, Caravaggio?

Caravaggio Blesses. Yours is the hand that blesses. I fear that blessing and I need it. For I have sinned. And I sin. And I will sin. Forgive me.

Cardinal A dangerous man, aren't you, Caravaggio? You

believe with a depth that is frightening. And with a vision
that is divine. Don't think I am ignorant of your vocation.
You believe, and since you believe you are chosen, not
commissioned. I know you. I know you, Caravaggio.
That's why you fear me. The painter of the poor. Dirty
feet, rags, patches, kneeling in homage to their Virgin
Mary, another pauper, mother of their God. And they
know it and you know it. Who is this God? Why is it
them he has chosen? The beloved poor who will always
be with us, just as their God will be with them, not with
us. You remind us of unpleasant truths, Caravaggio. For
that you may be hated. Your sins may be condemned. But
you will be forgiven, for you are needed. Forgiven
everything eventually. Dangerous words. A dangerous
man. Saving himself by the power of his seeing. And by
his need to tell what he sees. Tell me your sins. Confess,
Caravaggio.

Caravaggio I saw two boys.

Cardinal And you led them astray from God's word.

Caravaggio One looked out at me, listening, and I
watched him looking. Their shirts were white. The body
underneath was brown. I could hear the white of their
shirts touch their flesh. I knew they could see me listening
in the dark.

Cardinal Did they speak?

Caravaggio I heard them whispering and laughing. I
watched them touch each other. Still young, still desired,
and I was angry. I was jealous. They were as near to me as
you are, but in their youth and desire they were as far
away as the stars in the sky. I wanted to raise my fist and
grab them from the sky and throw them into the gutter
where I found them. I wanted to dirty their white shirts
with blood. I wanted to smash their laughing skulls

together for eternity. I wanted the crack of their killing to be music in my ears. I wanted them dead. I wanted red blood from their brown flesh to stain their white shirts and shout out this is painting, this is colour, these are beautiful and they are dead. They are not there. The sin, not there. My sin, not there. Just my painting, not my sin. I didn't touch them. I did not kill them. I desired them. Oh my God, I am sorry for having offended Thee for Thou art the chief good and worthy of all love.

Silence.

Cardinal What am I to do with you, Caravaggio?

Caravaggio Do you not accept my sorrow?

Cardinal I always believed you were alone in this life.

Caravaggio I am.

Cardinal You told me in another confession you were an only child and your parents died many years ago.

Caravaggio Yes, I told you.

Cardinal You had a visitor today.

Caravaggio Who?

Cardinal You've asked for forgiveness. Sometimes to forgive is to punish. I think on this occasion God would declare that your punishment is to meet your visitor.

Caravaggio Who?

Cardinal A fellow priest. I let him wait for you. He claims to be your brother.

Caravaggio I told you I have no living family.

Cardinal Why have you lied?

Caravaggio He's the liar. I have no brother.

Cardinal He claims otherwise. Extraordinary, isn't it? Most interesting. I've given you the courtesy of asking him to wait until you were fully informed of his arrival. I shall be your servant, Caravaggio. I'll bring your brother to you. (*He exits.*)

Caravaggio No. No brother. No father. No mother. Dead. I have no brother. I do not lie. I tell the truth. I paint the truth.

Brother Giovanni Battisti Merisi, enters with Cardinal.

Brother Why have you kept me waiting so long, Michelangelo?

Caravaggio turns his back.

Don't turn your back on me.

Silence.

I've come here to see you.

Caravaggio You've seen. Leave.

Brother Our sister, Caterina –

Caravaggio I have no sister. No brother. No father. No mother. Nobody belonging to me lives. I had a brother. He died and was buried.

Brother Will you leave us together, your eminence?

Caravaggio I won't be left alone with this liar.

Cardinal He says he is your brother. I believe him. He is a priest.

Caravaggio He's a thief. Tell it by looking at him. A man like that is out for what he can get. Believe me, I have no brother. I do not lie.

Brother shows Caravaggio his right hand. Around it are

strung the beads of a black rosary. Brother unwinds the beads and holds them before Caravaggio.

Brother Our sister wanted you to have these.

Silence.

Our sister, Caterina.

Caravaggio No.

Brother You know whose they are.

Silence.

Michelangelo.

Caravaggio No brother. No mother. I have no – I have no – Brother I have none. Leave.

Cardinal reaches to look at the beads. Caravaggio grabs them from Brother's hands. He buries his face in them. Cardinal bows to them both and exits.

What do you want here?

Brother You.

Caravaggio For Jesus' sake.

Brother We didn't know if you were living or dead.

Caravaggio I'm living.

Brother I see.

Caravaggio How did you track me here?

Brother I heard you'd found a good patron.

Caravaggio Oh Christ, so that's it. Well at least you're to the point. My Giovanni, you never stop, do you? Never miss a trick.

Brother That is despicable.

Caravaggio You crawled on your slimy stomach to worm your way into this palace. The brother's a painter, great favourite of his eminence, let me kiss the ring and put a good word in for me where it counts because that's a contact worth developing there, boy, am I right? Fuck off. You're neither needed nor welcome. Find another back to scratch.

Brother Stop denying me like this. Why are you doing it?

Caravaggio Because dear brother, you are a lying, thieving bastard.

Brother Remember my calling. I would remind you the priesthood –

Caravaggio And I would remind you I have been up the arses of more priests –

Brother Shut your filthy mouth.

Caravaggio Don't come crying to me with your holy face, bastard.

Brother Do not call me bastard. Bastard is one word you won't spit at me. You must think little of your own if that's what you have to throw at them.

Silence.

Caravaggio Brother.

Silence.

How is Caterina?

Silence.

I'm asking about our sister.

Brother Caterina prayed long and sore for you.

Caravaggio She might save me yet. She misses me?

Brother She forgave you.

Caravaggio Always. Did she marry?

Brother She married.

Caravaggio Children?

Brother Yes.

Caravaggio Beautiful, like her?

Brother Yes.

Caravaggio Healthy, strong, like the Merisi breed?

Brother Like the Merisi.

Caravaggio Good, good, Caterina. Are they boys, beautiful boys?

Brother Has it sunk to this?

Caravaggio What?

  Silence.

Jesus, do you think that?

  Silence.

Do you really think that?

  Silence.

You must really hate me. All my life I thought it was me who could hate. But it's you. You think that's why I ask after my sister's children?

Brother I'm sorry.

Caravaggio You should be.

  Silence.

No. Spare your sorrow, keep it for our nephews. They'll

need it. I hope their father is a good man. Jesus they have a right pair of uncles, kid. You a eunuch, and me a cocksucker. (*He laughs.*)

Brother Don't call yourself that.

Caravaggio It's true, isn't it?

Silence.

Christ, I believe you're going to start crying for me.

Brother No, I'm not.

Caravaggio You did before.

Brother I was too young when you told me about yourself. I didn't know enough. And you cried as well.

Caravaggio I've stopped.

Brother So have I.

Silence.

Caravaggio Seen any of my work?

Brother The paintings? Yes.

Caravaggio Good?

Silence.

Brother The Cardinal is proud of them.

Caravaggio Why shouldn't he be? Do they not appeal to you?

Brother They would appeal more to the initiated.

Caravaggio The Cardinal is certainly that.

Brother Are you ashamed of them?

Silence.

Are you ashamed of them as well?

Caravaggio As well?

Brother As you are ashamed of yourself. You always have been. I only cried, Lello, because you cried.

Caravaggio Thank you.

Brother And you want me to be ashamed as well. That would give you a perfect reason to live as you live. Hard man. Dirty mouth. Filthy morals. It won't work with me. I won't give you the satisfaction of shocking me. I never will. I know my brother. That's why I've come to see you. I want a straight answer to what I have to ask you.

Caravaggio Risk it.

Brother Come home with me. To our home. To our father's house.

Caravaggio It's yours. Keep it.

Brother Get out of Rome. You'll die here. Look at you. An old man already. Why? No, I don't want to know why, but I do know you must leave this palace behind. Disease and dirt, that is what's here for you. Come home. Live clean. I want you.

Caravaggio Do you ever think beyond the edge of that hole you call home? Do you think it has any hold on me now?

Brother Then why take your name from our village, Caravaggio?

Caravaggio Because I carry too much of it with me. I carry enough of it to know why I hate you.

Brother Lello.

Caravaggio Jesus, man, what did you do to me years ago?

You swindled me out of what little was left to me after Mama died.

Brother No.

Caravaggio Don't deny that. I let you do it. Why the fuck do you think I let you grab what was mine for half-nothing? Do you think I would have given up without a fight if I wanted any place in the pit called home? You got it all, to do as you saw fit. It's all yours, father Giovanni, and you're welcome to it. Come home, me? Tell me where I'll find it first. I don't know. But I do know it's not where I was born.

   Silence.

Brother Come with me.

Caravaggio No.

Brother Caravaggio.

Caravaggio No.

Brother Home, Michelangelo.

Caravaggio No.

Brother Merisi. (*He grabs Caravaggio's hands.*)

Caravaggio I will not live on your land.

Brother Take it. It's yours. Come home.

Caravaggio Go. Go.

Brother Lello.

Caravaggio Go.

Brother Mama.

   Caravaggio weeps.

Caravaggio I'm dirty. Very dirty.

Brother Be clean. Come home.

Caravaggio Mama.

Brother Home.

Caravaggio Mama dead. Clay, her feet in the clay. Dirty, in the grave. Dead. Wanted to die. Lonely. Mama.

Brother embraces Caravaggio.

Brother Lello, don't let us die with you, brother. Merisi, as you love our name, love me, protect me always. Protect our family. I had to take your inheritance for I knew you would sell it to the first bidder for a pittance. You sold it to me, to me, not a stranger. I've kept it for you until you were ready to come home.

Caravaggio Leave the priesthood. Father a child. A son. Healthy sons, plenty of healthy sons. Save our father's name.

Brother There's still the lump of the peasant in you.

Caravaggio We have land. Who will it pass to but another man's sons if you don't breed?

Brother I'm forbidden.

Caravaggio So am I. (*He disengages himself from brother's embrace.*)

Brother Our father's land.

Caravaggio No, priest.

Brother Breed.

Caravaggio I won't.

Brother Can't?

Caravaggio Can't.

Brother So you are what you say you are?

Caravaggio Yes, no, yes, no, yes, yes.

Brother Stay where you belong, stay in the pit of sinners. You paint like a drunkard sees. Badly. It's as if you're asleep. All in the dark. A drunk man imagining in his dreams. Who listens to a drunk roaring? Who looks at him? Noise. You're full of noise. Nothing but noise. You'll leave nothing behind.

Caravaggio My sister has sons. Caterina's sons.

Brother Caterina is dead. The second son killed her at birth.

Caravaggio stuffs his hands into his mouth.

She called for you with her dying breath. To remember her. That's why I searched for you. I hoped God had heard her. I thank God she didn't live to see what she had prayed for. Don't come near her sons.

Caravaggio chokes on his fingers.

Don't come home. Your father died. Caterina died. Your mother is buried. Your brother dies before your eyes. It's as you wished. Your family is dead. You are no one.

Caravaggio I am Michelangelo Merisi da Caravaggio. I am Caravaggio. I am Michelangelo Merisi. I am my brother. I am my sister. My sister –

Silence.

My dead sister.

Silence.

Caterina, I'm afraid of death.

Brother exits.

Giovannni, my brother, don't leave me in the dark. I'm afraid of the night. Mama, don't haunt me. I'll say my prayers. I'll pray for you, sister. Come back to me alive. Come out from the shadows. Take me back. Let me see.

He finds a jug of wine and pours it into himself. He tears tapestries and paintings from the wall, ransacking the room. Lucio and Antonio enter, dragging a bag of booty. Lucio surveys the room.

Lucio Jesus, man, you should not drink on your own. His eminence will have a fucking fit.

Caravaggio Let him have his fit.

Lucio The haul in here is something else, boy. Wait till you see what we landed.

Antonio Come on to hell, get out quick.

Lucio Wait a minute. You know the best place to get rid of good stuff at a fair price?

Caravaggio Yes.

Lucio Would you look after us?

Caravaggio I've the knife.

Lucio And you'd use it?

Caravaggio slashes a cushion, scattering feathers everywhere.

That's what I love about you. You're so demonstrative.

Antonio Lucio, could I have a word with you?

Lucio No.

Antonio Your man's mad.

Caravaggio Trust me.

Lucio We trust you.

Antonio Did you not see?

Lucio I see.

Antonio has noticed the red cloak. He stuffs it into the bag.

Caravaggio So do I. I see clearly. I see this knife. I see the hand that carries it. I curse my hand. I curse my life. I damn my soul. Trust me. (*He exits.*)

Fade.

Death

Lena's hovel.
   The Whore slumps across a table.
   Lena dries her hair. A pitcher of perfume stands on the ground near her. Lena goes and shakes the Whore awake.

Lena Come on, Anna. Rise and shine.

Whore No. Too tired. Sleep.

Lena Sleep if off somewhere else. You've had a fair snooze here. Shift yourself. I'm not your nursemaid.

Whore No, Lena, it's warm here. Let me be.

Lena I'm not running a lodging-house. You staggered in here, now stagger out.

Whore I'm tired, no.

Lena Oh Christ, I give up. I'm too exhausted to argue. Perch there for the night. Don't try to stretch your way into my kip though, do you hear? Sleep where you are.

Whore No, you have me wakened now. I won't sleep.

Lena Then I will, goodnight.

Whore Don't leave me.

Lena Are you afraid of your own company?

   Silence.

Whore Did I tell you who I saw this evening?

Lena You were too drunk to stand, let alone talk.

Whore I was not drunk. I was transfixed. I saw a vision. I saw Our Lord. Our Saviour Jesus Christ. He appeared to me.

Lena That's the second time this month. He's getting to be a regular.

Whore Don't be disrespectful. I met him after hearing mass. Suddenly he was standing before me. Suffused with a golden light. God love him, he showed me the big wounds in his side and his stomach. He let me put my fist into them. They were as big as your boot. I don't know how he survived the beating they gave him.

Lena He didn't.

Whore No, I suppose he didn't. He gave me a message. A secret message.

Lena What?

Whore I can't tell you. It has to be revealed only to the Pope and he has to tell it to the world. So I can't tell you. Only the Heavenly Father can do that. Anyway it doesn't exactly affect you, or me for that matter.

Lena Then why tell you?

Whore He must have taken a liking to me. Nice-looking man. Very tall. Strong fella. Black hair, very thick, but a bit long. Lovely spoken. Do you want to know what the secret message is?

Lena I don't want to spoil things between you and the Pope.

Whore I can tell you, Lena, for you know when to keep your mouth shut. He said to me, and this is strictly between ourselves, that whenever a Pope dies, he goes straight to Heaven. No fear of purgatory nor Hell for them. We always have a living saint on the throne of

Peter. Isn't that great news for them? Jesus is delighted with their great work and he's chosen me to pass on the information.

Lena I'm going to my bed.

Whore Stay up and keep me company.

Lena Get to your own kip.

Whore What house or home have I? Nobody wants me. Not even you.

Lena Not at this hour of the night.

Whore I taught you everything when you first started on the game. I looked after you. Now I'm only a burden.

Lena I know.

Whore I'll die and nobody will miss me. No one will notice me gone. They won't even bury me.

Lena Maybe you'll rise again on the third day.

Whore I'll be fed to the dogs.

Lena They'll die of alcoholic poisoning.

Whore Laugh away. Some day you'll be my age –

Lena And I'll die of alcoholic poisoning.

Whore Have you anything in the house?

Lena Why do I open my big mouth?

Whore Maybe a night-cap would help us sleep.

Lena I don't need help to sleep.

Whore Nonsense, I insist. Where is it?

Lena No, you've had enough.

Whore The day I've had enough, they'll be fishing me out of the river after drinking it dry. Where is it?

Caravaggio (*off*) Lena.

Whore Who the hell is that?

Lena Clear out of here, woman.

Caravaggio Lena.

Whore If it's a client, he might go for the older type.

Lena Just leave.

Whore Fuck off, Lena. I deserve my chance. You have the pick and choice.

Caravaggio Jesus, let me in.

Lena Leave.

Whore No.

Lena Then sit there and say nothing.

Caravaggio Lena.

   Lena exits.

Whore I wonder where she hides the drink?

Lena (*off*) Where are you? I can't see you in the dark. Oh Christ. Lello. Get water. Do you hear me, Anna?

Whore What?

Lena Water. Bring him in. (*She enters.*) Bowl and water. Quick. Cloth as well.

Whore All right. What for?

Lena Bring it.

   Caravaggio enters, supported by Lucio. He is wounded in the back of the head and in the face. His shirt is bloodied. Lena takes him from Lucio. Whore enters with a bowl of water and cloth. Lena soaks the cloth in water and points at the jar of perfume. Whore fetches it. Lena starts to wipe blood from Caravaggio. Whore watches him intently.

Whore Oh, sweet heart of Jesus! Poor Lello. What happened to you, son? An accident?

Lena Keep out of this.

Whore I was only asking.

Lena Mind your own business.

Whore I'll sit here and say nothing, but I warn you, my stomach turns at the sight of blood. Have you anything I could take to settle it?

Silence.

May as well be talking to the wall.

Lena has removed Caravaggio's shirt.

God, you have the stomach of a horse. I couldn't look –

Lena For Christ's sake, Anna.

Whore I know where I'm not wanted.

Lena You're not wanted.

Whore Then just for badness I'll stay.

Lena Can you raise your head?

She examines Caravaggio's head for wounds. She fingers his hair. Touching a wound, she makes him cry out.

OK, it's not deep. You'll live. I'll clean it. (*She washes the blood from Caravaggio's head. She reaches for the perfume.*) You'll smell sweet as a baby. (*She applies the perfume.*) It stings.

Whore He won't care, because he's a brave boy. Aren't you a brave boy? Aren't you?

Caravaggio Fuck up.

Whore Delightful.

Caravaggio Get rid of her.

Whore Do no such thing, Lena. What harm am I doing? You have some cheek barging into a respectable house and giving two decent women such a shock. I have a good mind –

Caravaggio struggles to his feet.

Don't threaten me. I'm warning you. I've met your type. A disgrace to their sex. In my day men were men and respected women. Do you hear me, don't come near me.

Caravaggio grabs her by the neck.

Lena, he's a maniac. He's going to kill me.

Caravaggio drags her to the bowl of bloodied water. He pushes her face into it. Releasing her, he holds her head above the bowl and she spews water back into it. Caravaggio releases her and staggers to a chair.

Fuck you, I've had worse done to me, and I'm still not leaving.

Caravaggio laughs.

You've made a sudden recovery.

Caravaggio Speak when you're spoken to.

Lena What happened?

Silence.

Lucio He –

Caravaggio Shut it.

Lena Is anyone dead?

Caravaggio nods.

Who?

Caravaggio shrugs.

Who is dead?

Caravaggio A man.

Lucio It was a clean fight. Caravaggio was brilliant. Absolute fucking magic, honest to Jesus. And the guy who got it had it coming to him.

Lena What did he do?

Lucio He called us names.

Whore What?

Lucio He called us girls. He picked the wrong man to insult. He insulted you too, miss. That really drove your man there out of his tree.

Lena How did he insult me?

Lucio He called you, well, he said you were . . .

Lena What? A whore? Lena, the whore? The pride of the Piazza Navona? Was that it, the insult? Whore?

Lucio Yea.

Lena He was right. And you killed for that?

Lucio Tempers were high. They were playing –

Lena I don't give a damn what –

Lucio It wasn't just names. He tried to do us out of some money for swag we nicked at the Cardinal's house –

Lena What? What did you take from there?

Lucio Toni's gone off with it. He hates violence, so when the fight got up, he cleared. Better find the bastard or he'll trade the lot for a bowl of spaghetti.

Caravaggio laughs.

Lena You fucking idiot. You fucking idiot.

Caravaggio It was easy.

Lena It was coming.

Lucio He was asking for it.

Lena Who was he?

Caravaggio The less you know the better.

Lena He has connections?

Caravaggio I have better ones.

Lena So, you're safe?

Caravaggio Not that safe. I'd better leave for a while. I need some money.

Lena How much do you want?

Caravaggio Whatever you offer.

Lena You're in no state to run tonight. Lie low here.

Caravaggio They'll soon start looking.

Lena I'll lie.

Caravaggio Her?

Lena She's loyal. Him?

Caravaggio He values his life.

Lena moves to exit.

Where are you going?

Lena To inform. All right?

Caravaggio I need a drink.

Lena That's what you're getting. (*She exits.*)

Whore Lena's a good girl. ·

Silence.

You won't hurt her, will you?

Silence.

I nearly married a man who was killed in a fight. I never recovered. Never.

Silence.

I was beautiful once. It goes, beauty. The wind takes it. I walked through Rome and I watched the world watching me. They still watch, but I never looked back at them. Beauty.

Caravaggio The man was beautiful.

Whore What man?

Caravaggio The dead man.

Whore I never look on the dead.

Caravaggio Are all dead men beautiful?

Whore Stop talking like this.

Caravaggio I didn't notice how beautiful until I saw his blood. It became him. Flesh and blood. Beautiful.

Whore You killed him because he wouldn't have you? You were after him?

Caravaggio I was following him. Waiting to kill him. All my life. Maybe he was following me. Finally, we touched.

Whore What's a queer doing after Lena?

Caravaggio What's a hag doing after love?

Whore I'm not a hag and I'm not after love.

Caravaggio I am a queer and I'm not after Lena, but you're after love.

Whore What makes you believe that?

Caravaggio I can see your face. I can tell what has happened to it. You drowned it in wine and you will drown in water. You were never beautiful. You only imagined it. And what you imagine, you believe. But it wasn't there. Beauty. It never was, woman.

Whore What would any queer know about women? You hate them all because you weren't born one.

Lucio How little you fucking know.

Whore I can smell rot off you already.

Caravaggio The wind didn't take your beauty. It exposed you as ugly. You walked through Rome hoping to be noticed but you were laughed at young and you're laughed at now. You're still looking to be noticed. Well, I have. Do what you have to do with your life. End it. Go to the river. It's where you're wanted, nowhere else.

Whore You are death.

Caravaggio Death, and you are rotten with it.

Lena enters.

Lena Do you want a drink?

Whore moves to exit.

Whore I've had enough.

Lena Where are you going?

Whore To rest.

Lena Say nothing, hear?

Whore Who hears a ghost talking in the river? (*She exits.*)

Lena Anna?

Silence.

Lucio I better move as well. Pour me none.

Lena I wasn't going to.

Lucio Right, I'll try and find your man, Antonio. If I do, can I bring him here for safety?

Silence.

Is that all right?

Caravaggio Get out.

Lucio I'll keep my eyes open, just in case they're already searching for you, and report back. All right?

Silence.

All right. See yous. (*He exits.*)

Caravaggio Drink.

Lena pours wine and hands it to Caravaggio. He kisses her hand and feels her hair.

Lena It's still wet.

Caravaggio kisses Lena's hair. She sits by him, buries her face in his shoulder. Caravaggio raises his hands to her face, pauses, clenches his hands together. Lena rises and walks away.

Where will you go?

Caravaggio Hills, south of Rome. Contacts there from long ago. Likely still there. Then Naples. Fucking Naples. They eat their young in Naples. (*He howls and laughs.*) Come on, Lena. Naples. React. You hate –

Lena Not in the mood.

Silence.

You'll never come back here?

Caravaggio No, will you be glad?

Lena What the fuck does that matter to you, my love?

Silence.

Well?

Silence. Lena hands Caravaggio some coins.

Enough?

Caravaggio counts the money.

Caravaggio No.

Lena All that's going.

Caravaggio No more?

Lena Not for you. I've got myself to look after.

Silence.

Caravaggio I just want –

Lena What you get. What you deserve.

They drink.

Caravaggio My life's gone mad, I've ruined – I've killed –

Silence.

Lena.

267

Silence.

Help me.

Lena Shut it.

Caravaggio You can take my belongings.

Lena Burn them.

Caravaggio Burn.

Silence.

Bury.

Lena The dead.

Caravaggio Our dead.

Silence. Lena starts to cradle an imaginary child.

Lena What will we call it?

Caravaggio Don't call our son it.

Lena All right.

Caravaggio No fights about it being a boy?

Lena If we fight, the noise will waken it.

Caravaggio Him.

Lena Let him sleep.

Caravaggio Who does he look like?

Lena His father.

Caravaggio Come on, he's his mother's son.

Lena No, he's his father's. And he's dead, Lello. The child is dead.

Caravaggio No.

Lena He died. When I wasn't looking he slipped out of me. He fell.

Caravaggio It's not your fault.

Lena I killed him.

Caravaggio He was born dead.

Lena Son. My son.

Caravaggio Lena.

Lena I wanted him. I wanted a child.

Caravaggio It's over now.

Lena Never look at me again. Never touch me.

Silence.

I need to walk through the city.

Caravaggio I'll come with you.

Lena You'll be caught. We'll be watched. Go to bed.

Caravaggio With you.

Lena Fuck off, fuck off, fuck off.

Caravaggio The child.

Lena The child is dead. Do you understand? It is dead.

Caravaggio No. Our son –

Lena Was never born. You couldn't give me a birth. You only bring death. Isn't that why you had to kill? You want to enter darkness. All you really see is the dark. To give life, you must love the light. You love the dark. Leave me. You're a queer. I love you but you're a queer. See the queer. See his darkness. See yourself. Don't see me. Don't see me any more.

Silence.

Caravaggio I'll leave.

Lena Stay.

Caravaggio I'm tired, Lena.

Lena Stay. Sleep. I want to watch you sleep. The last time. See you dream.

Caravaggio Can I stay with you?

Lena opens her lap to Caravaggio. He lays his head there.

Lena Dream. Dream, son. Dream.

The dream commences. Sister, Caterina Merisi, appears as a ghost.

Go to sleep. Dream.

Sister Dream, Lello, take me into your dream.

Lena Sleep, son, your mother is the whore.

Sister Your mother is yourself.

Lena Your father is the goat.

Sister Your father is calling, Lello.

Lena The goat and the whore, the dreamgoat and the girl.

Sister Who is the girl, did you marry her, Lello?

Lena It was our wedding, the virgin caught the unicorn.

Sister Did you have a child?

Lena A child conceived to die, and I want to die.

Sister Sleep, Lena, leave him. Sleep.

Lena sleeps.

Open your eyes. Brother, do you see me. Lello, my brother. look at me.

Caravaggio Caterina. Sister. Caterina. (*He rushes to embrace Sister.*)

Sister Keep your distance, Lello.

Caravaggio Why?

Sister Don't kiss my corpse.

Caravaggio Are we in the grave?

Sister No, in a dream.

Caravaggio Why are you here, sister?

Sister I died. Giving birth to my death. The child broke my body, Lello. I died cursing my son.

Caravaggio Gentle sister –

Sister Gentle? Ever gentle. Too gentle. So gentle they ripped me open to let my husband save his son. Do you remember what I was, Lello?

Caravaggio Silk, you touched like silk, your favourite colour was black. If I were rich, I'd buy my sister silk, black silk and paint her.

Sister I wore black. It was my blood. The child poisoned me. They cut him out and something spilt over me. I couldn't even squeal to stop, but I saw I was covered and it was black. It was my blood. I was dying and had I ever done any wrong?

Caravaggio No.

Sister Why was I punished? Why did I suffer?

Silence.

I did not die cursing my child. I did not curse his father. I cursed all children and all fathers and I cursed God for creating woman.

Caravaggio For creating man.

Sister Show me your hand.

Caravaggio Why?

Sister Show me.

  Caravaggio gives Sister his hand.

Rough hand.

Caravaggio Never stop working. If I stopped, I'd die.

Sister Your hand wants to stop. Your flesh knows what will kill it. Your work will finish you.

Caravaggio It's wrong. My flesh is wrong. My body's all wrong. My mind knows better.

Sister What does it know?

Caravaggio Knows itself. Knows everything. Sees everything. Lets me paint other flesh. Loves it. Hates my own. Hates body. Wants body to die.

Sister Flesh had a dead son.

Caravaggio Mind was glad, mind laughed.

Sister Mind all right alone.

Caravaggio Son had flesh like body and body did not laugh at dead son. Forgive my body.

Sister It does what it must.

Caravaggio Body gets tired.

Sister Poor flesh, wants to stop seeing. Wants to sleep.

Caravaggio And not dream. Not paint. Not all the time.

Sister Stop working.

Caravaggio But mind never stops seeing. I work. I paint. I paint well. I can prove that. I can call on witnesses to prove that.

Sister Call them.

Caravaggio Will they hear?

Sister They already have.

Cardinal appears, in rags, led by his Servant. Cardinal screams.

Servant Keep your voice down.

Cardinal whimpers.

I said enough.

Caravaggio Can he hear us?

Servant He hears nobody but himself.

Caravaggio Cardinal.

Servant Do you hear the man?

Caravaggio Eminence.

Servant Answer him.

Caravaggio goes towards Cardinal. Cardinal screams.

Caravaggio Caravaggio, it's me, Caravaggio. Do you know me?

Cardinal grunts loudly. The grunts develop into a sound resembling 'bread'.

Bread? Do you remember bread? The smell of it? Fresh and brown, like the boys you loved? Do you remember eating? Eating with me? Drinking. Confessing. Do you remember?

Servant Forget it, friend. I've tried often enough to have a sensible conversation with the old bastard. If I have to watch over him much longer, I'll be as cracked as he is. Sometimes he does what you want though. Then he's a good boy, aren't you?

Cardinal Good boy. Good boy.

Servant When you're good, you get food, don't you?

Cardinal Bread.

Servant You kept me hungry in your palace until you would make up your mind to eat. You fed your whores with good meat. I had the leavings from your table. Look what your whores fed you. You laid them in soft beds. I shivered outside your door, waiting to attend you and your bits of dirty cock. Now you ask me for bread. Here's the bread I have for you.

Servant opens his shirt and Cardinal goes to suck his breasts. Servant hurls him away.

Caravaggio Do you know who you are?

Cardinal Good boy, good boy. (*He holds out his hand to Caravaggio.*) Good boy, kiss, good boy.

Caravaggio kisses the hand.

Holy.

Caravaggio Who –

Cardinal Father.

Caravaggio Who is holy?

Cardinal God. God saw. More than you could see, he saw. Good god. Evil god. God saw good and evil. You saw evil. He saw I hid your evil. God saw me in your evil. And father, holy father, hide me from God. The holy father said, save yourself. Sin no more, sin no more. You, pray for me. Paint no more. Paint no more. Pray.

Caravaggio Go from me for ever.

Cardinal Blessed be the hands that anoint me with iron. Blessed be the tongue that spits curses on my head. Blessed be the feet that walk the way to damnation. Blessed be the eyes that see the same damnation, for they have looked on truth and found it lacking. I have looked on God and found him lacking, Caravaggio. There's nothing there. Nobody there. Not even yourself, great painter. It comes to this. Nothing. No one. Beware the sin of pride, my son. Beware the power of God. But do not believe. Do not believe.

Cardinal and Servant fade.

Caravaggio Jesus, preserve me. Jesus, protect me. Jesus, preserve me. Protect me.

Sister From what?

Caravaggio A death like that.

Sister There are other deaths.

Caravaggio Whose?

Sister Those you'll be remembered by.

Caravaggio Who?

Lucio appears, clutching a torn blanket to him. Antonio appears, his face disfigured. Whore appears, drenched.

Whore Caravaggio.

Antonio Caravaggio.

Lucio Caravaggio.

Antonio Hear us.

Lucio See us.

Whore Touch us.

Antonio Paint us, paint us.

Whore Tell him.

Lucio Tell him what he painted, what he touched, he saw, he heard.

Whore Do you see me, Caravaggio? You sent me to the river to drown my sorrows. In the river I found a lover who embraced me coldly. I wept for my life and the tears turned me into salt, for I could not dissolve in that water. I did not fight death, I welcomed it, but death did not welcome me. It fought my sinking and I struggled to die, not live. I did not want the life given to me.

Antonio I tried to win you once when I was beautiful. I was afraid to win, afraid someone one night would kill me. He did. He planted something in me that grew. A terrible flower. Sucking the life out of me. A boy with a bowl of fruit. Do you remember? Beautiful boy, his shirt hanging from him, dying fruit in a golden bowl. A boy with a bowl of beautiful fruit. Dying.

Caravaggio Tell me I did not disease you.

Lucio You saw him. You didn't touch him.

Caravaggio I know your voice.

Lucio You knew my face.

Caravaggio It's different.

Lucio It's starved. It died of hunger. I nursed him through the disease. I was known as his bedmate and when he died so did trade. I could turn my hand to nothing else. I starved to death, Caravaggio. My belly killed me. Hungry. I died wasted. Like an old man. Why didn't you save me?

Caravaggio I couldn't.

Lucio You wouldn't.

Caravaggio Why are you doing this to me? I am innocent of all you throw at me.

Whore Drowned.

Lucio Starved.

Antonio Diseased.

Lucio Your poor, Caravaggio.

Antonio Your models, Caravaggio.

Whore Your bread and cheese, Caravaggio.

Lucio Your genius.

Whore Your reputation.

Antonio Your victims.

Whore Better we had never been born.

Lucio Better we'd never seen the light of day.

Antonio You put our like in the light.

Whore Put us back into darkness.

> *They fade.*
> *Sister takes Caravaggio's hands.*
> *Silence.*

Caravaggio Let me die, Caterina. Let me die. Show me my death. Let me die.

Sister Come home, son. Come home to me.

Caravaggio Who?

Sister I'm here, Lello.

Caravaggio Mama?

Sister Are you hungry, son?

Caravaggio You died, Mama. I buried you. I put you in the clay. Go from me.

Sister My house is empty. Our house. Go and fill it with sons. We need the living in our house.

Silence.

Son.

Caravaggio I filthy your memory with my sin. You know your son. He knows his sin. It is mortal. Go from me.

Sister Do you want your father?

Caravaggio No more.

Sister Talk to your father.

Caravaggio Don't want to see him.

Sister Am I a stranger to you?

Silence. Sister holds out her arms to Caravaggio.

What's wrong, man? Are you too big for petting? I suppose so. I forget easy. I left you early. Why are you crying? Stop. Come to your father.

Caravaggio No.

Sister What brings you home?

Caravaggio Love. Love you, want to see you. I was too young when you died.

Sister But you went on living, and the living mean more than the dead. You belong to them, not to me long buried. Go back. Live.

Silence.

What I'm saying's the truth, hear me.

Caravaggio takes out his knife and points it at Sister.

Too late, son, too late. You may as well put that through your shadow as put it through your father. I'm air now.

Caravaggio Watch me, father. (*He paints the air with his knife.*) This is how I die. How I kill myself. This is how I paint. Living things. In their life I see my death. I can't stop my hand. I can't stop my dying. But I can bring peace to what I'm painting.

Sister Then raise your hand in peace. Paint.

Sister takes the knife from Caravaggio. He raises his hands. Light rises from his raised hands, drawing Whore, Antonio and Lucio from the darkness. Caravaggio speaks to the Whore.

Caravaggio You swallowed a river. They fished you out. You were thrown still drenched into dry clay, wet with sin as we are all wet with sin. Pray for us sinners, now and at the hour of our death. Forgive us sinners, drowned with sorrow for the sins of our flesh, and if I cannot dry your sins, let me dry your flesh.

He dries the Whore's hand in his own.

Dry.

He goes to Antonio.

A boy remembered his father, holding him. Nobody listened. He banged a gold platter to make the world hear. I heard, I saw, a boy with a bowl of fruit. I fashioned you into a golden bowl and whoever eats from you will be clean for you are without blemish.

He wipes the disease away from Antonio's face.

Clean.

He goes to Lucio.

I ate from your body. It was good. We laughed that night. You poured wine on me and lapped it. You were a god, a god of wine, and I wanted to drink your divinity, flesh and blood. Grape. God of the grape, great Bacchus, live for ever.

He kisses Lucio.

Full. Father, as I speak, I see. As I breathe, I fire. As I love, I roar. I open my mouth. I change colour. Come to me, my animals. Open the cage of silence. Come from the forest of your frame.

Light intensifies upon Antonio, Whore and Lucio.

Sister Who is the bird whose song is golden?

Music. Whore, Lucio and Antonio move towards Caravaggio. Whore touches Caravaggio's hands. Antonio touches Caravaggio's eyes. Lucio kisses Caravaggio.

Dragon, breathe your web of fire.
Steed, open your trusty mouth.
Bull, charge with a beating heart.
Lizard, change colour for ever.
Hare, lie with the sleeping hound.
Eagle, see with all-seeing eye.
Hound, play with the wounded lion.
Lion, roar your lament of love.
Who is the bird whose song is golden?
Unicorn, preserve the species.
Unicorn, protect the species.
Unicorn, preserve the species.
Unicorn, protect the species.

Whore Live.

Antonio Live.

Lucio Live.

Caravaggio Light.

Lucio, Antonio and Whore fade.

Da, I'm scared of the dark. I see things in the night-time. I want a story, I'll go to sleep. I met my sister in a dream. She said she was you and Mama. She told me I was going to die like she died and Mama died and you died. I don't want to die. I want to see you. Tell me a story. Father.

Silence.

Father.

Sister What's wrong with you?

Caravaggio He left me. You all left me. It's dark. I want a story.

Sister There was a boy.

Caravaggio What happened to him?

Sister He was born.

Caravaggio Where?

Sister In the pit of his mother's belly.

Caravaggio Then what?

Sister He fell from it and grew into a man alone, the day his father died.

Caravaggio Son of his dead father, he ran away to see the world and see himself and paint the two together.

Sister If he could paint, he could see and speak for ever without dying.

Caravaggio He painted darkness as well as light for he came from his father out of his mother's darkness, and he wished to remember, remember what he was.

Sister He called what his hands spoke and saw, he called it painting.

Caravaggio Only in painting can the light darken and the dark lighten.

Sister His eyes can't stop seeing nor his hands working; they're workers' hands and in working, in painting they find peace.

Caravaggio Calm.

Sister Peace.

Silence.

Caravaggio Shall I die?

Sister Not in this dream.

Caravaggio Then I'll live.

Sister Live.

Caravaggio It goes on. I'll live.

Sister fades.

Caravaggio.

Silence.

Michelangelo Merisi da Caravaggio.

Silence.

Lena.

Caravaggio lays his head on Lena's lap. She wakens. She strokes Caravaggio's back, hair and wakens him.

Lena Come on, animal, the beauty sleep's over. Get up, it's nearly daylight.

Caravaggio What?

Lena It's daylight almost.

Caravaggio Right. (*He rises.*)

Lena I've nothing here to eat.

Caravaggio Want nothing. I'm full.

   Silence.

Lena Where will you go first?

Caravaggio South. The hills.

Lena Then Naples?

Caravaggio Then Naples.

Lena Fuck Naples.

Caravaggio Fuck Naples.

   They laugh lowly.

Lena A kip.

Caravaggio The worst.

Lena Eat their young in Naples.

Caravaggio They say they're delicious.

Lena Better get a move on.

Caravaggio Better.

Lena They know I know you.

Caravaggio Not any more.

Lena Suppose not. Pity.

Caravaggio Pity.

   Silence.

Right. Go.

Silence.

Lena I dreamt I stood in a room, a beautiful room. All bright. Pictures on the walls. All yours. I was in the centre of the room, but I wasn't in the painting. I looked at them and I looked up and I saw you looking down at me. You were happy. It was over. You were at peace. I took my eyes from you and looked around the walls and saw you still in all the pictures. Even if you were gone from me, they were there and you were with them. And I started to laugh because it hit me you were looking at them from above, so you must see them all upside-down, and I knew then somehow we'd won, we turned the world upside-down, the goat and the whore, the queer and his woman.

Caravaggio Lena.

Lena Lello.

Caravaggio Magdalena.

Lena Caravaggio.

Caravaggio Last walk in the forest.

Lena No. Cut down. The forest's gone. No more trees or birds or shapes or colours. The virgin of the forest is a cheap whore and the unicorn's a stupid goat. Jesus Christ, protect the two of them. What are they? Well, this whore's a tired woman and my goat is a broken unicorn.

Caravaggio I see. That's it?

Lena You'll live.

Caravaggio We'll die.

Lena So we will.

Caravaggio It won't be together.

Lena No? Think not?

Silence.

Run. It's nearly morning. And I know nothing. Nothing. Go. Here. (*She gives Caravaggio more money.*)

Caravaggio See you.

Lena See you.

Caravaggio exits. Lena clears up the bloodied cloths. Lucio's voice is heard.

Lucio (*off*) Missus.

Silence.

Caravaggio.

Silence.

Missus.

Lena What?

Lucio Are you there?

Lena Who are you? What do you want?

Lucio It's me, Lucio. I was there earlier. Can I come in?

Lena Who's with you?

Lucio My mate, Antonio. We've got the stuff from the palace. You told me we could bring it here.

Lena Come in.

Lucio Come on.

Lucio and Antonia enter, dragging a bag of booty.

Where is he? Caravaggio.

Lena Caravaggio? Who's he? Oh yes, the painter. Knew

him years ago. Haven't seen him in a long time. No, I can't say I know him now. Wouldn't recognize him even. Do you know him?

Lucio Me? No.

Lena Are you looking for him?

Lucio Why should I be looking for him?

Lena Why should anybody be looking for him?

Lucio Oh I see.

Lena Good. Does he see?

Antonio I don't know what yous two are on about.

Lucio It's OK. He's retarded.

Antonio I'm not retarded.

Lucio That's a sure sign you are retarded when you say you're not.

Antonio What do you want me to say? I am retarded?

Lucio Now you said it. Everybody heard you.

Antonio I'm not fucking retarded.

Lena Will you two bastards keep your voices down at this hour of the night? And what are you carrying?

Antonio I've been carrying this load on my back ever since the killing –

Lucio What killing?

Antonio Your man, the –

Lena What man?

Lucio I know of no man. We haven't seen any killing. Do you remember?

Lena He remembers, don't you?

Antonio Yes, I remember. Sorry. I'm a bit slow. I need things spelt out –

Lucio You see, I told you he was retarded.

Antonio grabs Lucio. They fight. Lena opens the bag of booty. She takes from it a chalice, a gold cross, a silver bowl, and finally a red cloak.

Antonio Do you submit?

Lucio Never.

Antonio Do you submit?

Lucio screeches.

Submit.

Lena You've done well. Good stuff. Worth a bit.

The fight ceases.

Antonio How much?

Lucio Where will we get the best deal?

Lena Navona. Let me introduce myself, gentlemen. Lena, a frequenter of the Piazza Navona. I know who to ask. Safely. Come evening. One thing though. This is mine. (*She holds up the red cloak.*)

Antonio How's it yours?

Lena It belonged to a friend. I'll mind it for him.

Antonio It'll cost you.

Lena clips Antonio's ear.

Lena Will it?

Lucio Is that all you want?

Lena To keep, yes.

Lucio Why?

Lena Memories.

Antonio Who did it belong to?

Lucio Your man?

Antonio Where is he anyway?

Lena Looking down on us, and he sees everything. He sees us now. Yes, he'd like the look of you.

Antonio Would he?

Lena Take your clothes off.

Antonio I beg your pardon.

Lena raises the gold cross.

Lena I command you in the name of the Father and of the Son and of the Holy Ghost to get your clothes off.

Antonio But you're a woman.

Lena I will curse you in the name of Christ if you don't get them off.

Antonio undresses rapidly.

Antonio I've never had it off with a woman.

Lena God moves in mysterious ways.

Antonio Now what?

Lena arranges the red cloak about him, posing his body, placing the cross of John the Baptist by Antonio's side.

Weird.

Lena Weird. (*She admires her composition.*) Yes. Yes. Well, Caravaggio, do you see him? Beautiful, yes? Can you hear me? Can you see us? It goes on and on and thanks be to the sweet crucified Jesus on. See? See. Do you see him, Caravaggio? Do you see? (*She laughs.*)

Music.
Light.
The sound of Caravaggio's laughter. Darkness.

CARTHAGINIANS

For Imelda Foley

Characters

Maela, in her forties
Greta, in her thirties
Sarah, in her thirties
Dido, in his twenties
Hark, in his thirties
Paul, in his thirties
Seph, in his twenties

Setting: A graveyard

Carthaginians was first performed at the Peacock Theatre, Dublin, in October 1988. The cast was as follows:

Maela Roselean Lenihan
Greta Fedelma Cullen
Sarah Maria McDermottroe
Dido David Healihey
Hark Gerald McSorley
Paul Des McAleer
Seph John Olohan

Directed by Sarah Pia Anderson
Designed by Wendy Shea

It was subsequently produced by the Druid Theatre, in a revised version, directed by the author and performed in Galway and Derry in January 1992.

SCENE ONE

Wednesday morning. Music, 'When I am Dead and Laid in Earth' from Purcell's Dido and Aeneas. *Light rises on the burial ground. Three women sit in silence. As if dressing a young girl,* **Maela** *spreads clothes upon a grave.* **Sarah** *is pacing restlessly.* **Greta** *attends to a wounded bird.* **Seph** *sits in silence.*

Greta Poor bird. Bad wing.

Sarah I hope those are the right leaves?

Maela How can you have right or wrong leaves?

Greta You never can tell with birds.

Sarah Tell what?

Greta Their nest, how they build it. You can learn about their flight and how they eat, but where they live, that's a mystery. Anyway, this boy won't live much longer. A goner. Poor old bird. God rest you.

Maela God rest you.

Greta God rest us all.

Maela Don't say that.

Greta What?

Maela You only say that over the dead.

Greta We're all dying.

Maela No, we're not.

Sarah Maybe not.

Maela Sarah, pet, you'll die of sunstroke if you don't take off that big jumper. Are you cold in this heat? Thank Christ for the good weather. How could we stick this place if it was raining? You see, isn't that a sign? Isn't God with us when he gives us this good weather? No matter what they say about what we saw – no, I'm wrong.

Greta What's wrong, Maela?

Maela Talking about it.

Greta About what, Maela?

Maela What I've seen.

Greta What the three of us have seen, Maela.

Maela Aye, the three of us. First I'm living in the graveyard. Then Sarah came to it. Then you, Greta. And all because we believe in the same thing. The dead will rise here. A miracle. But we can't talk about it, for fear if we talk about it, it won't happen.

Greta Charlie, Charlie, chuck-chuck-chuck, went to bed with three wee ducks. Charlie, Charlie, fell asleep, the wee ducks began to weep.

Silence.

Birds have a great way of knowing their own.

Sarah How do they know their own?

Greta They sing.

Sarah We sing as well.

Greta Then sing for me, Sarah.

Sarah (*sings*) In the port of Amsterdam, there's a sailor who sings . . . In the port of Amsterdam . . .

Silence.

Cheer me up.

Greta A joke, Sarah. A dirty joke. The dirtiest joke you know. We'll tell each other dirty jokes.

Sarah A man goes into a doctor's office. He says, 'Doctor doctor, I've got a pain.' 'Where?' says the doctor. 'Where's the pain?' 'Between my legs,' says your man. 'How?' says the doctor. 'It's fallen off,' your man says. 'What's fallen off?' 'It's fallen off.' 'Show me it,' says the doctor. Your man puts his hand into his pocket and hands it over. The doctor looks and says, 'That's a cigar butt.' 'Sorry, doctor, sorry. Here.' 'That's another cigar butt.' 'Here you go, doctor.' 'My good man, that is another cigar butt.' 'Jesus, doctor,' your man says, 'I've smoked it, I've smoked it!'

Greta Not bad, Sarah. You go, Maela.

Maela I know no dirty stories.

Sarah Go on, Maela.

Maela The two of yous can tell the dirty stories. I'll listen.

Sarah Go, Greta.

Greta Three women are sitting in a train. There's an Englishwoman, a Frenchwoman and a Derry woman. Each of them has a banana. The English one takes out her little lunch-box and gets her banana.

> *Greta peels an imaginary banana sideways. She giggles girlishly and then eats it sideways. Delicately, she wipes her mouth.*

The Frenchwoman pulls her banana out from inside her skirt.

> *Flamboyantly Greta products an imaginary banana and devours it in two gulps.*

The Derry woman has a brown paper bag.

> *Greta reluctantly removes a banana from the bag. Raising her eyes to heaven, she sighs. Wearily she peels*

the banana. Seeing it naked she gazes at it with infinite boredom. Suddenly Greta grabs her own hair and repeatedly pulls her head down on the banana.

Sarah That's the worst yet.

Maela I don't understand it but thank God we can laugh.

Silence.

Is he getting better?

Greta No.

Maela Will he die?

Greta Soon.

Silence. Maela has returned to the grave she had been dressing and speaks to it.

Maela You don't know the value of money, you know that? I can't keep up with you. All you think about is style. Isn't that right?

Silence.

Greta What age would she have been?

Maela You mean what age she is?

Silence.

I'm saving for her birthday. (*whispers*) A leather jacket. I'm buying it for her. (*raises her voice*) But we'll see. We'll just have to see. Who knows?

Maela sings.

'Happy birthday to you, happy birthday to you, happy birth . . .'

Silence.

She's not dead, you know. She's not. That's why I saw

what all three of us saw. That's why it's going to happen. It has to, hasn't it?

   Dido *enters wheeling a pram.*

Dido (*sings*)
But if you come and all the flowers are dying,
And I am dead, as dead as I may well be –
Oh seek the spot where I will be lying,
And kneel and say an Ave there pour moi

   Silence. The women look at him.

Yes, heads, still here?

Maela Hello, Dido. How are you, son?

Dido Surviving, Maela. How are yous?

Maela Grand. Surviving.

Greta Where the hell were you?

Dido What do you mean, 'Where the hell was I'?

Greta You were supposed to be here at ten o'clock. It's now half-twelve. I ran out of fags an hour ago and Sarah's tongue is a mile long waiting for her coffee.

Dido Listen, wagon. I'm not running a charity service. Business, baby. I've other commitments. Count yourself lucky I'm here. I had to fight my way to this graveyard through three army checkpoints. There could have been an assault. I could have been detained.

Maela What did they threaten to do to you, Dido?

Dido It was more what I threatened to do to them. No luck though. No score. I think they were on to me as a health hazard. One of them was nice. Blond. From Newcastle. Interested in football. Fancied him.

Greta How can you chat up Brits?

Dido Greta, you know my ambition in life is to corrupt every member of Her Majesty's forces serving in Northern Ireland.

Greta Jesus, that should be difficult.

Dido Mock on. It's my bit for the cause of Ireland's freedom. When the happy day of withdrawal comes, I'll be venerated as a national hero. They'll build a statue to me. I'm going to insist it's in the nude with a blue plaque in front of my balls. (*holds an imaginary plaque before himself*) This has been erected to the war effort of Dido Martin, patriot and poof.

Greta You dirty wee pervert, you –

Dido You're right, Greta. Give us a hug, Sarah. Prove my manhood.

Sarah Give us the grub, Dido, or you're dead.

Dido Leave me in my sin. I ask for woman's love, I'm given –

Greta Give us the grub.

Dido All right, all right. (*He removes three flasks from the pram.*) Sarah, coffee with no milk and loads of sugar. Maela, tea with loads of milk and no sugar. Greta, tea with loads of piss.

Greta Thank you.

Dido Thank you. Maela, ham sandwich with mustard and cheese. Sarah, apples, rolls, tomatoes, fruit juice, book.

Sarah Book?

Dido A gift.

Sarah Thanks, Dido. A hardback. Did it cost a fortune?

Dido Nicked it from the library.

Greta Where's my fags?

Dido *Sporting Life*, packet of chewing-gum, sixty Silk Cut, for Madam.

Maela Are you on a diet? Only a packet of chewing-gum?

Greta I'm giving up fags.

Maela Sixty Silk Cut?

Greta I'm cutting down.

Maela Have you found a place to stay yet, Dido?

Dido Yes. I've found a little place.

Maela Is it dear?

Dido No. It's not dear.

Maela Is it nice?

Dido It will be, Maela. It will be very nice.

Greta (*inhales the cigarette*) That's good.

Maela Nothing like tea.

Greta I meant the cigarette. (*Greta reads from the* Sporting Life) I'm going to do you, young fella. The one o'clock at Edinburgh has a horse in it called Desert Song. I've been following its form all year. I miss it today because you're late. If it wins your throat's cut.

Dido Where's the rare boy? Seph. Your ma sent this.

Dido gives Seph his food.

She says you wanted this as well. (*hands him a guitar*) Guitar. What do you want a guitar for? Are you lonely?

Maela This ham sandwich is lovely, Dido. Where did you get it?

Dido Made it myself. Cuts cost, Maela.

Maela That's very decent of you.

Dido For me, not you. There's no extra dough since you retired to the graveyard and the quiz team disbanded.

Sarah Yous two have a quiz team?

Dido Yup, and a pretty good one.

Maela We were called Sonny and Cher.

Dido She was Sonny, I was Cher.

Sarah How did you meet?

Dido Wandering the graveyard.

Maela We teamed up.

Dido Maela was dressing a grave.

Maela Dido was fasting to death.

Dido In protest. I'd been abandoned by this beautiful stranger. It was a form of suicide.

Maela He was looking for sponsorship.

Dido For the suicide.

Greta Sponsorship?

Dido Aye, every little helps. Anyway, Maela talked me out of it. To pass the time we entered Derry City Super Quiz League and the money we won helped out my dole. But no more. So, what do yous owe me? Sarah, £2.40 plus my commission that's £2.70. Maela, £3.00 plus my commission that's £3.50. Greta, £6.60 plus my commission, you owe me –

Greta £7.70.

Dido No flies on Greta.

Greta No flies on Dido either, but then he doesn't need any.

Dido Watch it.

Sarah (*sings*) In the port –

　Hark *enters*.

– of Amsterdam, there's a sailor who sings. He sings and he sings . . .

Dido Hark. I got you something to eat in case you were hungry. I hope you don't mind.

Hark I have something to eat.

Dido I got you a few beers in case you got dry.

Hark I'm never dry.

Dido You don't have to pay me for them.

Hark I wasn't going to.

Dido Right, right. I see.

Hark I'm glad you see. I'd be very glad if I didn't see you. I am sick of seeing you. Why are you following me? I walk home at night and you are behind me. I walk out the door and you are in front of me. Jesus, when I'm locked in the lavatory I expect to see you dancing under the door. You are known as a queer in this town. I do not like being seen with queers. I do not like queers. I do not like you. Fuck off.

　Hark exits.

Dido I still say there's hope.

Greta Really?

Dido Definitely. He's just playing hard to get.

Greta Pretty successfully.

Dido Who asked your opinion?

Maela Was anybody asking for us in the town?

Dido Nobody. You're kinda stale news now. But the rest of the world's beginning to take an interest.

Greta What do you mean?

Dido flamboyantly produces an Irish Press.

Dido My media bombardment is starting to pay off. Page seven.

Dido gives Greta the paper.

Greta (*reading*) 'Graveyard Girls Greet The Ghosts. Three Derry women have solved those holiday blues by turning into ghostbusters. They are sitting in Creggan graveyard in Derry waiting for the dead to rise. A spokesman for the girls, Mr Dido Martin, said, "They have seen a vision. Forget moving statues and Maggiagore, this is the big one."'

Sarah You should be shot, young fella.

Dido Read on, Greta.

Greta Donations to help the visionaries in their lonely vigil should be sent care of Mr Martin, 7 Ashling Park, Derry.

Maela That's my address. That's my house.

Dido I've moved into it for safety. Don't thank me. You're doing me a favour as well.

Maela Jesus Christ, what will he have done to my house?

Dido It's a surprise. Read on, Greta.

Greta ' "The girls may be suffering from illusions," Mr

Martin added. "They are simple but sincere souls, and each has endured a great personal tragedy," he concluded. We say, good luck, Ghostbusters, and if the dead rise, let us know.' Someone here is about to endure a great personal tragedy, and it's not one of the simple but sincere souls. What the hell are you up to?

Dido Typical, typical. I'm doing my best. I need to rouse national interest. Nobody believes you in Derry, they think you're lunatics. The Catholics think you're mad, and the Prods think you're Martians.

Maela Who cares what anybody thinks as long as we believe it?

Dido Exactly, you said it, Maela. Give it a rest, will you? Sarah, did you find any good flowers for my collection?

Dido produces an album of pressed flowers.

Sarah After what you've done? No.

Dido Jesus, you cannot please some people.

Seph rises and walks over to Dido. He empties on the ground a pile of dead flowers.

Thank you.

Dido starts to sort through the flowers.

Maela You must have a whole collection now.

Dido Yea, it's getting bigger.

Maela It's nice hobby.

Dido Yes. Very butch, very demanding. I haven't time to press them all.

Sarah Stop following Hark and you'll have the time.

Dido Ah, look.

Greta What?

Dido This was a rose, Greta. Isn't it beautiful?

Greta It's dead. I prefer them living. Why do you not?

Dido Flowers are more gentle when they're dead.

Greta Gentle?

Dido Aye. They have more power in them. More magic. You can work spells with dead flowers, did you know that?

Paul enters carrying a refuse sack full of stones.

Paul Pack of whores. Pack of queers. Pack of traitors. Look at the state of this town. Do you know who I blame for the state of this town? Do you know who I blame?

Maela St Malachy.

Paul St Malachy. He saw the end of the world. He prophesied it. He saw the waters rise over Derry. He saw the Foyle and Swilly meet, and that will be Derry gone. He saw it, but will he stop it? No. He sees the state of this town, but so do I see it. And I will search every dump in this town for rubbish. I'm building a pyramid. When the dead rise, I'll walk into the pyramid with them and walk away from this town and the state it's in. And if I find St Malachy hiding in this city, I'll kill him, I'll kill him, I'll knock his teeth down his throat.

Paul exits.

Maela Poor St Malachy.

She continues knitting.

SCENE TWO

Wednesday Night. The women sleep. Seph sleeps. Paul enters.

Greta The bird's dead. The blackbird. I couldn't save it.

Paul Who wrote *Tristram Shandy*?

Greta Black.

Paul An Irishman wrote it. That's your only clue.

Greta It couldn't fly and it wanted the air. It needed wings. The wings weren't there.

Paul Lawrence Stern wrote *Tristram Shandy*. Nobody's read it in this town. Maybe two or three. Why was the bird black?

Greta The bird died. It died from cold. It was black because it was cold.

Paul Go to sleep, Greta.

Greta Charlie, Charlie, chuck-chuck-chuck. Went to bed with three wee ducks. Charlie, Charlie, went to sleep . . . sleep . . . (*She lays the bird in the box.*)

Paul Do you want to talk?

Greta No.

Paul Can you not sleep?

Paul sits beside Greta.

I was at a quiz tonight, but I said nothing. I used to run it. Questions and answers. What's the capital of – ? Who won an Oscar for – ? Who captained Arsenal – ? Fuck sports questions. Selling out. Who wrote the *Aeneid*? Virgil. Who did Virgil guide through the city of hell? That's a tough one, boys. Who will guide me through this city of hell?

Greta Do you not guide yourself?

Paul Through Derry? It's grown foreign to me, Derry.

Greta How's it foreign? Didn't you work in it? Teach in it? We taught together in it. We live in it. Weren't we born in it?

Paul Because I'll die in it. This town.

Greta It's only a town.

Paul A port of sizeable population.

Greta It's only home.

Paul A harbour. An empire. Part of a great empire.

Greta British Empire?

Paul The British Empire is dead.

Greta The Roman Empire?

Paul Roman Catholic Empire. This city is not Roman, but it has been destroyed by Rome. What city did Rome destroy?

Greta Carthage.

Paul Correct. Two points. Carthage.

Greta How are we in Carthage?

Paul Tell them you saw me sitting in the ruins, in the graveyard. I live in Carthage among the Carthaginians, saying Carthage must be destroyed, or else – or else –

Greta What?

Paul I will be destroyed. I would like to go to Carthage.

Greta I would like to go to Rome.

Paul I would like to see the pyramids. I'm building a

pyramid. But I'm no slave. I am Carthaginian. This earth is mine, not Britain's nor Rome's. Mine. Am I right?

Silence. Greta lies down to sleep.

Am I right?

Silence.

Can you not sleep?

Silence.

Good. Who wrote the *Aeneid*? (*Hark enters.*) An Irishman wrote it, that's your only clue. Do you give up?

Hark Virgil. And he wasn't an Irishman, he was a Roman.

Paul Virgil led Dante through the city of hell and Dante said that to remember times of happiness in times of great woe, that's the sorrow beyond enduring.

Hark What times are you remembering?

Paul Sarah's back with us.

Hark I've seen her.

Paul Seph's back too.

Silence.

You haven't spoken to Sarah?

Hark I haven't.

Paul Why not?

Silence.

Hark and Paul and Seph and Sarah.

Hark What about them?

Paul I just want to say their names together. Sarah's back, speak to her. Goodnight.

Hark Where are you going?

Paul I'm staying here.

Hark Where else is for you?

Paul Where else is for you?

Hark That's the same question.

Paul It's still a question. Answer it.

Hark I live on my own in a single room. I keep that clean and I keep myself clean. I want no bother. I'm not involved anymore.

Paul You're still in your cell, John. You should get out and enjoy yourself in the fresh air.

Hark I do get out in the fresh air. Haven't I got myself a grand job in the graveyard? (*sings*) Dig the grave, dig the grave, there were none that was saved.

Paul What happened to us?

  Silence.

You went to jail. I went about mad. Sarah went away and Seph. Oh Christ Seph. Tell me why he did it? Why did he do it? Have you spoken to him?

  Silence.

Is there any hope for us?

Hark Aren't we still alive?

Paul Sometimes. Who wrote *Tristram Shandy*?

Hark Lawrence Stern. He was an Irishman.

Paul That's your only clue. I never read it.

Hark It's shite.

Paul Goodnight.

Paul lies down and sleeps. Hark stands alone. Looks about the women. Silence.

Hark Well, here they all are. The lunatics. They believe in miracles. What are we going to do with them? Mad. Mad as March hares. Lovely way of putting it. Mad. Poor Paul. Poor – poor who? Nobody's poor, son, if you have your health. All the money in the world, but without your health, nothing. (*Dido enters.*) Who am I sounding like? I'm sounding like myself. Myself, myself, myself –

Dido Are you all right, Hark?

Hark How long have you been here?

Dido Not long.

Silence.

Why did you insult me today?

Hark Because you deserved it.

Dido What makes you think that?

Hark Why are you here?

Dido Want to be with you.

Hark You're with me. Why?

Silence.

Dido Do you want a cigarette, Hark?

Hark You don't smoke, Dido. Why offer me a cigarette?

Dido I smoke sometimes.

Hark When other people run out, you smoke. Fags in the pocket to win them over. What do you want, Dido?

Dido To go home with you.

Hark Where's home?

Dido Here in Derry, I suppose.

Hark Derry.

Dido Come home, Hark. I'll walk you there.

Silence.

Are you all right, Hark?

Hark Are you all right, Dido?

Dido No.

Hark Good. You shouldn't be. Have you ever been picked up, Dido? Picked up, by the army or the police? Will I pick you up? Will I show you how to pick someone up? (*Hark touches Dido on the face.*) This is how, Dido. And after that, Dido, do you know what they do? (*Hark kisses Dido.*) Does it not turn you on? Answer to your wildest dreams? Me, Dido. (*Hark caresses Dido's face again.*) Answer me. Tell me the truth. Tell me who you're involved with. Give me names, Harkin. Give me addresses. Just names and addresses. That's all we're looking for. You can walk out of here if you just give me one name and address.

Dido Hark.

Hark Who's Hark? Tell me, who's Hark? Is he your boyfriend? Do you love him? Is he a married man? Would his wife like to hear about it? Would his girlfriend? Who's she? Tell me. Tell me. I'll let you go if you tell me. Tell me what's between your legs. Is there anything between your legs? Is there one between your legs? (*Hark grabs Dido's groin.*) Is the united Ireland between your legs? What happens when cocks unite? Disease, boy, disease. The united Ireland's your disease. Does your cock want a united Ireland? Will it tell me? Would you like it to tell me? Tell me your disease. Tell me. Tell me. Tell me.

Seph Tell him. Tell. I'll tell.

Hark releases Dido and falls to the ground. Dido spits at Seph.

Hark Bad, bad, bad, bad, bad.

Silence.

Now you know. Will you leave me alone now? Do you know my kind now?

Dido I know my kind, Hark. Do you want me to name them? Well, there's me. That's all. That's enough. I know how to use what's between my legs because it's mine. Can you say the same? Some people here fuck with a bullet and the rest fuck with a Bible, but I belong to neither, so I'm off to where I belong. My bed. On my own. My sweet own.

Dido exits.

Hark On your own.

Silence.

Fuck off, Dido.

Silence.

Fuck off, Hark.

Silence.

Sarah Hark?

Hark No.

Sarah What have you done?

Hark What I had to do. It was good for him. Wise him up.

Sarah We need him.

Hark I don't.

Sarah He's a good kid.

Hark There's been better lost.

Sarah Has there, Johnny?

Hark Don't call me that. I used to be called that. But I'm not any more. Johnny is dead now and only Harkin remains. The rest is dead.

Sarah No, he's still inside.

Hark Where he belongs.

Sarah Does he?

Hark Take a pill, Sarah. Take a powder. Forget me. But be careful. You can get hooked on things like that. And you know what hooks do. They tear you. They bleed you. And they can bleed all around you.

Sarah I'm clean, Hark. I've been clean for a while. Believe me.

Hark I believed you before.

Sarah slaps Hark. Silence. Hark sings.

In the port of Amsterdam, there's a sailor who sings, and he sings and he sings to the whores of Amsterdam.

Sarah sits.

Who have promised their love . . . who have promised their love . . .

Silence. Hark sees the dead bird.

Sarah?

Sarah What?

Hark lifts the bird.

Hark Sarah, the poor bird.

Sarah What about it?

Hark It's dead.

Sarah Did you kill it?

Hark No.

Sarah Well, it's not your fault then, is it?

Hark replaces the bird, walks towards Sarah and lies beside her. Seph stands. Maela rises from sleep. She puts a blanket on the grave and speaks to it.

Maela It's cold tonight.

Silence. Maela sees Seph.

Isn't it cold? Don't you find it cold?

Silence.

My daughter's in there. She's waiting for us. Who do you have belonging to you dead?

Silence.

Do you think it will happen? Will the dead rise?

Silence.

Tell me a joke.

Silence.

Will I tell you one?

Seph sits beside her.

A woman walks into a doctor's office and she says, 'Doctor, doctor, I've a pain.' 'Where's the pain?' says the doctor. The woman says, 'In my child, in my child there is a pain. A pain in her heart and in her head and in her hair.' So the doctors shave the child bald and the child dies with no hair. Isn't that a great joke? Isn't it?

SCENE THREE

Paul constructs his pyramid. Maela knits. Hark and Sarah play chess. Seph watches them play. Greta smokes.

Hark (*sings*)
The Flintstones, meet the Flinstones
They're a modern stone-age family.
From the town of Bedrock,
They're a page right out of history.

Paul, do you remember the *Flintstones*? Hit me with a question, maestro, any question regarding the *Flintstones*.

Paul Fred's favourite food?

Hark Brontosaurus steak and cactus juice.

Paul What lodge did they belong to?

Hark Water Buffalo.

Paul Full title, please?

Hark What?

Paul Loyal Order of Water Buffalo.

Hark Jesus, were Fred and Barnie Loyalists? Orange Water Buffalo men?

Paul Yabba-dabba-doo.

Hark Yabba-dabba-doo.

Maela God, aren't men right eejits?

Sarah Your move, Johnny.

Hark ponders on the chess board.

Maela Have you buried the bird yet?

Greta I should have put it out of its misery.

Maela How was it in misery?

Greta It couldn't fly.

Maela It could feel. It could feel you looking after it. I'd say it had a happy death. (*nods significantly at Hark and Sarah*) Poor Dido will be heartbroken.

Greta Where is he today?

Maela Maybe he's sick.

Greta He'll feel my tongue when he strolls in.

Maela You were very good to get us the stuff, Hark.

Hark I'm playing chess, Maela. Shut up.

Paul walks down centre. Measuring distance with his feet. He carries a miniature model of a pyramid.

Paul Am I mad?

Silence.

Sometimes am I mad?

Maela You're definitely not well all the time, son. And you could catch anything handling that rubbish.

Paul It's not rubbish. It's precious. It's stone for the pyramid. Pharaohs constructed pyramids with the hands of slaves. I am not a slave. I construct with my own hands.

Greta Why on under God are you building a pyramid?

Paul I'm building my pyramid, my monument, my hands. My hands, my hands. Am I right, Harkin? Am I right?

Hark You've got a point there, Paul. Point there. (*moves a chess piece*) Get out of that one, girl. (*Sarah moves abruptly.*) Shit.

Paul I won't give up. I'll build on. Everything has to be exact. Every measurement. Through here the dead will find their way back to this world. When I'll finish, they'll rise, the dead. So I'll keep going.

Maela That's the boy, Paul. That's the boy, you keep going.

Greta You're as bad as he is.

Sarah watches Maela knit.

Maela Maybe so.

Sarah That wool looks good and thick.

Maela It'll soon be getting cold at nights.

Sarah It should warm you.

Maela It's not for me. It's for her. She loves pink. It suits her.

Hark She's dead, Maela. She's in the grave.

Maela Maybe to some, not to me.

Hark You buried her, Maela.

Maela She's not dead.

Hark She is. They all are, women. They won't rise.

Maela Stop him talking like that, Sarah.

Hark The dead don't rise. I know. I put them in the earth. Once they go in there, they're swallowed up for ever and ever amen. So be it. Let them rest, girls. Give up your vision. The dead won't rise in Derry graveyard. Go home.

Maela (*shouts*) Sarah, shut up that hateful bugger.

Sarah Move Hark.

Hark moves a chess piece. Sarah immediately counter-attacks.

Checkmate.

Hark The king is dead.

Sarah Long live the king.

Hark God save the king. God save the queen. My favourite song. Morning, noon and night I sing it.

Maela Gaol affected your mind.

Hark My mind. Everybody's mind.

Paul I know what I'm doing this time. I have to follow the shape of the stars. They're telling me something.

Greta They're telling you nothing.

Paul I have to have faith in something.

Greta Have faith in yourself.

Paul Do you?

Greta I'm too tired to have faith.

Hark Do I hear the cry of a lost soul? (*Hark leaps to his feet.*) Why, my daughter, have you abandoned hope? Why do you turn your back on the faith of your childhood?

Greta I blame it on television myself.

Hark Christ, Greta, you're smart.

Greta Think so?

Hark A walking monument to the wit and wisdom of Derry town.

Greta Dear lovely Derry.

Hark Dear drunken Derry, where even the women are too pissed to get it up.

Greta The wit and wisdom of Derry town.

Hark Through wit and wisdom we shall overcome.

Greta 'We shall overcome someday.'

Hark 'Deep in my heart I do believe.'

Greta
'We shall overcome someday.

  Hark and Greta together.

We'll walk hand in hand.
We'll walk hand in hand.'

Maela (*sings*)
'We'll walk hand in hand someday.
For deep in my heart I do believe,
We shall overcome someday.'

Sarah (*sings*)
We are not alone.

  Paul joins.

We are not alone.

  Maela joins again.

We are not alone today
For deep in my heart I do believe.
We shall overcome . . .

Hark Someday. (*affects an American accent*) Brothers and sisters, I have a dream.

Greta What is your dream, brother?

Hark That someday we shall be one.

Greta One people.

Hark One nation.

Greta One country.

Hark Black and white.

Greta White and black.

Hark Brothers and sisters.

Greta Sisters and brothers.

Hark Catholics shall stand with Catholics, Protestants with Protestants –

Maela Should it not be 'Catholics will stand with Protestants.'

Hark I speak of dreams, sister, not of insanity. Let us be like the asshole and let us be apart.

Greta Hallulia.

Hark Let us live apart as we choose to live apart. Let us hate as we wish to hate.

Greta Hallulia, brother.

Hark Let us wander forth into the wilderness of bigotry and let us spread more bigotry. Let us create a nation fit for assholes to live in.

Dido enters, pushing the pram, dressed in football gear.

For as assholes are we known to each other and like the asshole let us forever remain apart.

Hark sees Dido.

Hello, Dido. What kept you? Have they changed the visiting hours? Were you strip-searched? Did you enjoy that? Have you brought me something nice? Books, comics, clothes, change of socks, shirts, underwear? Did you bring me underwear, Dido? Why have you brought me nothing, Dido? Do you not love me? Am I a shite? Am I a fucker? Am I sorry?

During this Dido has stood, silent and unmoved. He then produces from behind his back a handful of sausages.

Dido Pick a sausage, any sausage.

Hark points to a sausage. Dido flamboyantly displays the sausages to the rest of them. Opens Hark's shirt, crams the sausages into the shirt, takes out the resultant mess, points to it.

Is this your sausage? Then have it.

Dido flattens the sausages into Hark's face, rubbing the meat in vigorously. Silence. Sarah laughs.

Maela That wasn't very nice, Dido.

Greta No. Not very nice.

Paul Not very nice at all.

From the pram Dido produces a face-cloth, basin, flask of hot water, stool and shirt.

Dido You're right, Maela. I should make it up to him.

Hark Don't touch me.

Dido Nonsense. I simply insist.

Dido removes Hark's shirt and throws it to Sarah.

You wash, I'll dry. The things I do for you, even if I've lost you.

Sarah So you know?

Dido Everything. I made inquiries ages ago. Don't worry. I've got over worse.

Dido starts to clean Hark's chest.

Alone again. Alone and powerful. Jesus, I wish I could meet somebody. Somebody really rich and wonderful. I need money. Big money. Look at me.

Greta What are you doing in your knickers?

Dido Passing the time. What do you do in yours?

Greta Wait for a miracle.

Dido Seriously, these togs are about the best stitch I possess. How am I ever going to make it dressed like I do? I need clothes. I really need a leather jacket. Leather. I need leather.

Maela Why leather?

Dido Sado-masochism. That's where the future lies, sado-masochism.

Maela What's that?

Dido You fancy somebody, you take them to bed, you beat the shite out of them.

Maela I see. Marriage.

Dido Not exactly. There's pleasure in sado-masochism.

Dido tweaks Hark's nipple. Hark yelps.

Just practising. Shirt.

Dido gives Hark a shirt.

Maela Think of the happiest day of your life and you won't need money.

Greta The happiest day of my life I made money. I backed the Derby winner for the first time. Secreto was the horse's name. It survived an objection. It won. Good old Secreto.

Dido The happiest day of my life is a secret.

Sarah What happened?

Dido All right, I'll tell you. I was that happy I thought I was dreaming. I probably was, for there was a man involved. He was foreign and he was pissed but he was beautiful. I met him when I was wandering the docks.

Maela Was he a sailor?

Dido Likely. I didn't ask. He came up to me carrying red roses and he gave them to me. He said his name was John. He said he was from the Lebanon.

Maela What was he doing in Derry?

Dido Wandering through, like myself. When he gave me the flowers I was sure I'd scored and then he put his hand to my face and I thought, Yippee, but he just knelt down on the ground like this. (*kneels*) He said, 'Listen, listen to the earth. The earth can speak. It says, Cease your violent hand. I who gave birth to you will bring death to you. Cease your violent hand. That is my dream. I pray my dream comes true.' I said, 'I pray your dream comes true as well, but failing that I'll settle for Derry City winning the European Cup.' He smiled and called me Dido. I'd never met him or any like him before. It was like as if he knew me. I turned on my heel and ran like hell. (*He rises.*)

Hark Derry City will never win the European Cup.

Dido Where's your loyalty? We need to build up a good team. Local, loyal.

Hark You need money. Only money talks these days.

Sarah You've changed your tune.

Dido I do need money. How do I make it?

Sarah It used to be a different story.

Hark There's lots of stories.

Dido Everyone has a story, Sarah.

Sarah Tell them.

Dido Could that be the way of making money? An everyday story of ordinary Derry ones. That's it. Tell stories.

Sarah I only know one story. Will I tell it? Once upon a time there were three young fellas, who were pals, best of pals. One of the young fellas, the ringleader it's fair to say, the hard man, he met a girl. Jesus, did they fall for each other. Did they believe in each other. They were the King and Queen of Derry. They were all good mates. They went out walking through the streets of Derry. Hark and Paul and Seph and Sarah. Alone, together, and then in hundreds, and in thousands, and they would overcome someday. They had a dream. Civil rights for all. We would change Derry. And we did. We all changed. There was another dream. A secret one. Go to Europe, see the Alps. One of the gang, the girl, she went away, but not to the Alps. Amsterdam. Now that's another story.

Paul Stop it, Sarah.

Sarah A story of money, of buying and selling. I did the buying and selling. I had a fine old time. A high old time. High as the Alps. I took a pill. I took a powder. And I got hooked. My veins were full of powder. I had my fill and more. I bought it myself and I sold myself to buy it.

Paul Stop!

Sarah (*sings*) In the port of Amsterdam there's a sailor who sings. He sings and he sings to the whores of

Amsterdam who have promised their love to a thousand other men –

She knocks over the queen on the chess board.

The Queen is dead.

Hark Long live the Queen.

Silence. He knocks over the king.

The King is dead.

Sarah Long live the King. I walked by the canals of Amsterdam. I was sinking under the weight of powder. I sank and I sank until I felt hands lift me. I thought they were yours, Hark, but they were my own. I saved myself, Johnny. I saw myself dead in Amsterdam. I've come back from the dead. I'm clean.

She removes the cardigan and shows her bare arms.

Clean. It's true. And if what we saw is true, if the dead are to rise again, then we must tell each other the truth. For us all to rise again.

SCENE FOUR

Friday afternoon. Maela and Seph are alone.

Maela Do you sometimes hear things, Seph? I do, especially when the other two go off for their walk. I hear things and I think it's happening. There's never anything there of course, but it doesn't stop me panicking. I panic very easily. You're like me, aren't you? You're nervous.

Seph shakes his head.

No? I thought you were. Are you afraid even?

Silence.

Of course you are. You should stop this silly nonsense, you know. You should speak. Others did worse than you. Far worse. And if you survived this long, then they'll let you alone now.

Silence.

I wish the two of them were back. Can you imagine if it happened and only you and me were here to see it? Who would believe it? Ah, who cares? As long as it happened. But I wouldn't want the others to miss it. You and Dido and Paul as well. I think yous believe us. As for the other boy, Harkin. What does that woman Sarah see in that brute?

Seph shakes his head.

Oh, he's a brute all right, make no mistake. A bad, bad boy. If my daughter walked into the house with that, he'd be shown the door. Stay away from that kind of fella. Bad news. Do you hear me? I want none of those kinds of boys in my house. You'd think his stint suffering for his sins would have cured him, but he's a bad boy, and he always will be. Did you hear what Mr Harkin said to me yesterday? He as good as called me a liar.

Silence.

I'm sorry, Seph. I can't control my mouth.

Seph laughs.

Oh, laugh away. Go on. Or maybe I should laugh at you. You couldn't control your mouth either. You don't like that, do you? If you're going to laugh at other people, you should learn to laugh at yourself. That's what I've learned. I've also learned that life is very cruel. Isn't it, Seph?

Silence.

I wish them two bastards were back.

Silence.

I suppose you're shocked to hear me saying a word like that, Seph.

Seph shakes his head.

I am. I hate dirty words, though I love dirty stories. But I hate dirty words. Dido has a way with words.

Paul enters.

He's very smart. I wonder what the surprise will be?

Paul Surprise?

Maela You weren't here this morning. Dido said he would have a surprise for us this evening. He's definitely writing something.

Paul Jesus.

Maela He's very smart, you know. The same Dido. Great in the quizzes, do you remember Paul? Paul knew everything.

Sarah enters followed by Greta who pushes on the pram.

Sarah You are not going to believe what is about to descend.

Hark enters.

Hark What is it?

Greta (*to Maela*) Come over here and have a good gawk.

Dido enters in drag. He wears a black miniskirt, black tights, high-heels and beret. He's carrying manuscripts.

Dido Hi.

Maela Sacred heart of the crucified Jesus.

Dido Do you like the new me?

Maela You walked through Derry looking like that?

Dido Aye, I got three wolf-whistles too. All from women. Really, this town has gone to the dogs.

Greta Why are you dressed as a woman?

Dido That's why. (*Shows them the manuscripts.*)

Greta What's this?

Dido Read it.

Greta *The Burning Balaclava* by Fionnuala McGonigle. Who's Fionnuala McGonigle.

Dido You're looking at her, sweetheart. And it's pronounced (*fake French*) Fionn-u-ala Mc Gon-igle. She's French.

Maela With a name like Fionnuala McGonigle?

Dido Oui. I have come to your city and seen your suffering. You city has just changed its name from Londonderry to Derry, and so I changed my name to Fionnuala in sympathy. What I see moves me so much I have written a small piece as part of your resistance.

Maela Can we read it, Dido?

Dido Read it? You're going to do it. Distribute scripts. (*Hands scripts to Paul and Greta. He goes to the pram, humming to himself.*) Hark, you play the heroine. (*He produces a headscarf.*) She is a fifty-year-old Derry mother, tormented by the troubles, worn away by worry to a frizzle.

Hark Why am I playing her?

Dido You have the looks for it. Her name is Mrs Doherty. (*Hands Hark an apron.*)

Hark Surprise, surprise. Everybody in Derry's called Doherty. It's a known fact.

Greta Nobody here's called Doherty.

Hark It's still a well-known fact.

Dido Mrs Doherty has survived the troubles only through her fanatic devotion to the Sacred Heart.

Dido hands Hark a statue of the Sacred Heart.

Sadly, this devotion has led to the neglect of her son Padraig O'Dochartaigh. He is a patriot and idealist. That's you, Maela, here.

Dido hands Maela a tricolour and large flag pin.

Wrap it round you. Padraig is tormented by the troubles of his native land. Should he or should he not take up the gun for Ireland? Should he or should he not speak Gaelic all the time? Should he or should he not screw his girlfriend, a Protestant, Mercy Dogherty. Paul, that's you.

Paul How am I a Protestant with a name like Docherty?

Dido You spell Dogherty with a 'g'. You are a beautiful woman –

Paul I am a beautiful woman.

Dido (*does a twirl*) You move as if on wings.

Paul (*imitating him*) I move as if on wings.

Dido You radiate grace.

Paul I radiate grace.

Dido A Protestant. A social worker. A good Protestant. You are tormented by your desire for a Catholic who might be involved, but you are reassured only by the fact that in bed he is all Protestant.

Paul How do you mean?

Dido Some people are Catholic in bed, some people are Protestant, some people convert, depending.

Paul Which is Catholic and which is Protestant?

Dido What a sheltered life you've led, dear. Mercy is also tomented by guilt, because her father is an RUC man. That's you, Greta. Here.

Dido hands Greta rosary beads and a crucifix.

Greta What would a Prod want with these?

Dido When he interrogates Catholic suspects he beats them over the head with the crucifix and strangles them with the rosary beads. He's a murderous, vicious brute. (*They both giggle.*) Now, Seph, I haven't forgotten you. You play a priest, Father Docherty. You are tormented because your weekly calls from the pulpit for peace and reconciliation have for so long gone unheard you have stopped speaking entirely and now communicate only by means of white flags. Here. (*He hands Seph two large white sheets.*) Wave them.

Seph waves the white sheets together.

Perfect. Sarah, you play Jimmy Doherty, tormented –

Hark There's a lot of torment in this.

Dido It's a tragedy, Hark, shut up. Jimmy Doherty is tormented by the fact that all his life he has been out of work. He's spent his time walking the dog and washing the weans –

Paul And drinking in pubs.

Greta And telling yarns.

Sarah And singing wee songs.

All In the town he loves so well.

Dido Aye. He's a Derry character but don't worry, he's the first to be killed.

Dido gives Sarah a flat cap.

I play two small parts myself. One being Doreen O'Doherty –

Hark Tormented by –

Dido Driven to distraction by the troubles of her native land. But as she is one of life's martyrs who never complains, she is very kind to animals and goes nowhere without her pet dog, Boomer, on a lead. (*produces a stuffed dog on a lead*) I also play a British soldier. (*produces a helmet and toy rifle*) Faceless, nameless, in enemy uniform, in deep torment because he is a working class boy sent here to oppress the working class. Now where are the other guns? The best I could rise to were water pistols, but you'll all need them for there's a big shoot-out at the end. You'll need balaclavas as well. Watch the balaclavas. I had to borrow them from this Provo I know.

Hark Why has he so many?

Dido He has a whole collection. It went to his head a bit when he came third in the terrorist of the year competition.

Paul Terrorist of the year competition?

Dido Aye. You pose once in a bathing costume, and once in a balaclava. It's supposed to be judged on military skills and revolutionary fervour. But the ones that win always tend to be a bunch of poseurs.

Hark Who's won it?

Dido Jesus, Hark, you'll believe anything. I'll give the directions as well as playing the two parts. Now watch the scripts, photocopies cost money. Go. 'The Burning Balaclava' by Fionnuala McGonigle. Our scene begins in a Derry kitchen. A Derry mother, that's you, Hark.

Hark I know.

Dido Put on your apron. Our scene begins in a Derry kitchen. A Derry mother prays to her Sacred Heart.

Hark Yes, Sacred Heart, how's about you? Sacred Heart, I envy you your life. Here's me worn down by the troubles of my native land. What am I going to do with my son? There's you with your fervent heart all burning with love for men, and here's me with my heart scalded, my heart is scalded by that young fella. I may as well talk to the wall as to him. Listen to this, Sacred Heart.

Dido Padraig O'Dochartaigh enters.

Maela Is there any tea in the pot?

Dido He is sullen and rough spoken.

Maela Is there any tea in the pot?

Hark Forget about your belly for once. I'm making you no tea. Say a wee prayer with me to the Sacred Heart.

Maela Stuff your tea then, mother. I don't want your tea. We won't win our freedom drinking tea. I refuse your tea.

Hark I haven't offered you any.

Maela Don't contradict me, mother. Don't contradict a man driven to despair by what he sees. I see dead men and women. I see riots and confusion. I see my city in ruins.

Hark God love you, did you see all that on TV? You never get out of your bed.

Maela I see it with my own eyes, mother, my own eyes.

Hark Turn your eyes to the Sacred Heart, son. He sees all.

Dido They look at the Sacred Heart. Padraig suddenly averts his eyes.

Maela Mother, not yet. I'm not ready to look at him yet.

Hark All right, son. I'll make you a cup of tea.

Dido Our scene shifts to a Derry street. Doreen O'Doherty is walking her pet dog, Boomer. She meets Father O'Doherty.

Hello, Father.

Seph waves a sheet.

Isn't it a lovely day, father?

Seph waves a sheet.

I'll see you at Mass on Sunday, father. You preach a lovely sermon.

Seph waves both sheets.

Bye-bye, father. Say a wee prayer for us all. Doreen sees a British soldier approaching. Oh Jesus, I'm supposed to be playing him as well. What'll I do? There's nothing else for it. I'll just have to play both parts. Right, here comes the Brit.

Dido pulls from his pram the helmet and toy rifle. Playing the Soldier, Dido wears the helmet and brandishes the gun. Playing Doreen, he puts them behind his back.

Soldier Where the fuck do you think you're going?

Doreen I'm going to the fish and chip shop with Boomer here. He's my wee hound of Ulster and he looks after me. I'm buying him a fish supper.

Soldier So you call your hound of Ulster fucking Boomer then?

Doreen Aye, it's short for Boomerang. He might run away from his Mammy, but he always comes back to her. He's a real Irishman.

Soldier Here Boomer, here fucking Boomer.

Doreen Look at the way he runs to you. Isn't it great the way animals know their own? Give a paw, Boomer, give a paw.

Soldier I don't want no fucking paw.

Doreen Wait till you hear him singing. Sing a song, Boomer, sing a wee song.

Soldier I don't want to hear no fucking song. I'm too deep in worry.

Doreen What are you worried about son?

Soldier Oh, the agony of being a working class boy sent here to oppress the working class. Why did I do it? Why did I do it?

Doreen The money?

Soldier It's not worth it. It's not worth the money. I'm going to end it. I'm going to shoot myself.

Doreen Shoot me. Shoot me. Don't commit suicide.

Soldier I can't shoot you, madam. I'm a British soldier. We never shoot on sight.

The others groan.

(*Dido interjects*) It's only a play. (*He resumes as the Soldier.*) Tell you what. Is Boomer working class?

Doreen No, he's a cocker spaniel.

Soldier shoots Boomer.

Jesus Christ, you've shot Boomer. You've shot poor Boomer.

Soldier Maybe I can bring him back to life. (*Starts kicking Boomer.*)

Doreen What are you doing? What are you doing? You've killed him, now you're kicking the lining out of him.

Soldier Typical. Fucking typical of you Irish. We Brits never get any thanks.

Doreen I'm joining the IRA. I'm joining the IRA for Boomer.

Hark Doreen O'Doherty, did I hear you say you were joining the IRA? Don't do it. I saw what they did to Boomer. But offer it up, Doreen. Offer it up to the Holy Souls in Purgatory. I know how it must break your heart. You've had Boomer since he was a young pup.

Dido I brought him home in a wee box, tied with string. I had to open it with a razor blade and I cut my finger. Little did I think that the pain I had bringing him into the house would be anything like the pain I have taking him out of it.

Hark Come on back and I'll make you a cup of tea.

Dido Thanks. I'll just have a cup in my hand.

Hark A nice cup of tea.

Dido Our scene shifts to a Derry bar. Padraig and Mercy are drinking.

Paul Padraig?

Maela What, Mercy?

Paul Padraig, I am a beautiful woman.

Maela Mercy, you are some woman.

Paul I move as if on wings. I radiate grace.

Maela You radiate, Mercy. You radiate.

Paul But I am a demanding woman as well.

Maela You know your own mind, Mercy. You are a feminist.

Paul Do you know my mind, Padraig? For me, Padraig, would you burn your balaclava?

Maela What makes you think I wear a balaclava?

Paul I know, Padraig. I watch the news on TV. Oh, Padraig, what's going to happen to us? Where is there for people like us. A Protestant and a Catholic in love?

Maela There's a place for people like us.

Paul Somewhere.

Maela Sometime.

Paul Some place.

Maela A different place.

Paul A new place.

Maela A new province.

Paul A new province?

Maela A province where Catholics and Protestants can go to bed together and talk dirty.

Paul I think I'm going to cry.

Maela Mercy, remember, feminists don't cry.

Dido Mercy and Padraig look at each other. It is love.

Paul It's your round, Padraig.

Maela I got the last one.

Paul No, you didn't.

Maela I did. We've had three. I got the first.

Paul Padraig, why do we always end up fighting? Do you hate me because I'm Protestant?

Maela Of course not. I'm a Catholic, how could I be a bigot? But your father is an RUC man. You know what you must do.

Paul What?

Maela Kill him.

Paul Ahh.

Dido Our scene shifts to an RUC interrogation centre.

Greta Who exactly are you, mister?

Sarah Sure everybody knows me, wee Jimmy Doherty.

Greta What's your religion, wee Jimmy?

Sarah Religion, religion, isn't it a great wee thing, religion? Where would we be buried if it weren't for the wee religion?

Greta Together.

Sarah Aye, in death, as in life, apart. Why have you hauled me in here?

Greta To beat you up.

Sarah Sure I never refuse a body. Away you go.

Greta beats Sarah's head with a crucifix.

Greta What's your politics?

Sarah The man in the street.

Greta I want this man's name and address. What do you do? Who do you work for?

Sarah I sing wee songs and tell wee jokes. Have you never heard me? (*sings*) 'In my memory I will always be – '

  Greta strangles Sarah with the rosary beads.

Greta One more note and you're dead.

Sarah (*defiant*) 'In the town that I love so well.'

  They all shoot Sarah.

You'll never get away with this.

Greta I was putting you out of your misery. No jury of sane men or women would convict me.

  Sarah dies dramatically.

Dido Just die, Sarah.

Greta Do I kill anybody else?

Dido Loads.

Greta Great.

Maela Dido, isn't there enough killing on the streets of Derry without bringing it into the graveyard?

Dido On with the play. Our scene shifts to the Waterside. A Catholic priest walks through Protestant areas on his mission of peace.

  Seph walks across, waving white sheets.

In their Protestant home Mercy has told Daddy she is to marry a Catholic. She is weeping.

Paul So you see, Daddy. I have a terrible choice.

Greta About your future family's religion?

Paul Yes, Daddy. The Catholic Church will never agree to me bringing them up as children.

Greta Don't you mean Protestant?

Paul No, Daddy. Catholics are conceived at the age of forty. That way there's no sex. What am I going to do, Daddy? I love him.

Greta Kill him.

Paul Ahh.

Dido Our scene shifts to a Derry street. Quick, everybody, pistols and balaclavas. Not you, Hark. You're in the middle of an ambush. Run through it with the Sacred Heart. Don't worry, he'll protect you. Right, everybody. Ready. Run, Hark, run. Squirt, everybody, squirt. Get that Sacred Heart. Get that Sacred Heart. Stop the fight. Our scene changes to a Derry kitchen. A Derry mother nurses her broken Sacred Heart.

Maela Ma, ma, has there been an ambush?

Hark There's been an ambush, son. Look, look.

Maela Ma, your Sacred Heart.

Hark My Sacred Heart, son. My Sacred Heart. Son, son, where were you when my Sacred Heart was riddled with bullets? Where were you?

Maela I was having a quick pint with the girlfriend, ma.

Hark Take away these quick pints, take away the girl . . . girlfriend? Who?

Maela I meant to tell you about Mercy –

Hark Mercy? She's a Protestant with a name like that.

Maela I want to marry her, ma. I love her. What will I do?

Hark Kill her.

Maela That's dirty, ma.

Hark It's your duty as a Catholic.

Maela Ah ma, no.

Hark Then do it for me, son. Do it for your mother.

Maela All right, Mammy.

Dido Our scene changes. A Derry street. On one side Mrs Doherty and Padraig, on the other Mercy and her Protestant daddy.

> *Dido switches on a cassette recorder and plays 'Do not Forsake Me Oh My Darling' from* High Noon. *They pace back and forth.*

A priest appears.

> *Seph wanders between both parties, waving white sheets.*

Dido They fire. They get the priest.

> *Seph dies.*

Maela We've shot a priest, we've shot a priest.

Paul He's not a priest, he's not a priest.

Maela How is he not a priest?

Paul He's wearing a balaclava.

> *Maela shoots Paul.*

Maela Blasphemer, you've shot a priest.

> *Greta shoots Maela.*

Greta Catholic bastard, you've shot my daughter.

Hark shoots Greta.

Hark You murdering RUC madman. Look at this, all dead. Dead. What could I do? I had to kill. I depend on the dying. Nobody knew it, not even my son, but I knit all the balaclavas. The more that dies, the more I'm given. Violence is terrible, but it pays well.

Dido shoots Hark.

Dido What could I do? I'm only a soldier. A working class boy, just a boy. What does Ireland mean to me? What does it all mean?

They all rise and shoot Dido.

They've got me. I join the dying. What's a Brit under the clay? What's a Protestant in the ground? What's a Catholic in the grave? All the same. Dead. All dead. We're all dead. I'm dying. They've got me. It's over. It's over. It's over. (*dies*) That's it. What do you think?

Silence.

Tell me the truth. Isn't it just like real life?

Silence.

Did yous like it?

Hark I'm searching for words to describe it.

Dido Did you think it was too short?

Hark It's not short. It's shite.

Hark hurls the script and props on the floor.

Shite.

Sarah Dido, you know Hark. He can be a bit rough at times. He just says things straight out. I think this time he's right. It's shite.

Sarah throws her script and props at Dido.

Paul Shite incredible.

Greta Shite incarnate.

They throw their scripts and props at Dido.

Maela Dido, there's some people who take great delight in running other people down. You have great courage, I think. (*Maela hurls her script and props on the floor.*) If I'd written that shite, I wouldn't show my face for a month.

Hark Your skirt's lovely though. It suits you.

Dido Borrow it, shitehawk, borrow it.

Dido tears off the skirt and throws it at Hark.

Fuck yous. Fuck yous. Fuck yous.

Paul Ah, Dido. It was shite but it was a good shite.

Dido Fuck yous.

Hark It was a bit of crack. Livened us up. We all enjoyed ourselves.

Maela Ah Dido, calm down. It wasn't that bad.

Hark Even old Seph enjoyed himself. Good old Seph. A good laugh. I could break my heart laughing at old Seph.

Seph Can I have a cigarette?

Silence.

Can I have a cigarette?

Greta gives Seph a cigarette. Hark grabs and breaks it in two.

Hark Long, short. Long, short. Pick a straw, Seph. Long or short. Live or die. Do you remember the hunger strike, Seph? Has your tongue been on strike? Not speaking? Not smoking? You'll kill yourself, Seph. Smoking.

Seph Can I have a cigarette?

Sarah Why have you come back home, Seph?

Paul She asked you a question. Answer her.

Seph I talked. I ran away. And I came back. I went to those I informed on. I said, kill me. Let me die. They said, live. That's your punishment. Life, not death. Live with what you've done.

Paul Why did you talk?

Sarah What did you know?

Seph Live with what you've done. But you see, I talked because I lived with what was done here one Sunday. I was here that Sunday. I saw it. I was in Derry on Bloody Sunday.

Greta Bloody Sunday. Where were you on Bloody Sunday?

Paul I was here on Bloody Sunday. We were all here on Bloody Sunday.

Hark On the march.

Sarah Through Derry.

Seph Bloody Sunday. Everything changed after Bloody Sunday.

Maela Nothing changed. Nothing happened that day. Nobody died. I should know, I was at the hospital. If there had been anyone dead I would have seen them, and I saw no one dead. (*jumps to her feet*) I saw no one dead. I saw no one dead. You're telling lies. You've driven away the dead. I hope you're satisfied. I hope you're satisfied with your lies. (*She exits.*)

Dido Leave her alone.

Sarah Maela.

Dido Leave her.

Greta Maela.

Dido Leave her!

SCENE FIVE

Greta and Sarah alone. Greta fingers Maela's knitting. Sarah is fixing her hair.

Sarah Do you like Hark, Greta?

Greta I don't know him.

Sarah Who does?

Greta Paul.

Sarah Old mates.

Greta Old pals.

Sarah Yea. Friends. Them and Seph, they knocked about together. Reunited. Funny life, eh?

Greta Hysterical.

Silence.

Have you come back for him?

Sarah Yes.

Greta Do you think he'll save you?

Sarah What from?

Greta Yourself.

Sarah He has to save himself first.

Greta Does he?

Sarah We all have.

Greta Are we worth saving?

Silence.

Do we ever get what we want?

Sarah What makes you ask that?

Greta When I was a girl, the one thing I wanted most was a brother.

Sarah Were you lonely as a kid?

Greta I was, I suppose. I didn't like many people. And they weren't falling over themselves about me. My parents were well on when they married. I was the only one. They kept themselves to themselves. I did imagine once I had a brother. (*She laughs.*)

Sarah What are you laughing for?

Greta Do you remember the first time you became a woman? Did you know what was happening?

Sarah Just about. I had sisters.

Greta Well, I didn't. I didn't know what was happening. And do you know what I did, Sarah? I asked my father.

Sarah Your father?

Greta Yes. The poor man nearly died. He murmured something about asking my mother. My mother was cracked, Sarah. Cracked. She never stopped cleaning. They called our house the doll's house on High Street. People used to stop and look into it through the window. The woman polished the footpath. She wallpapered the dustbin. Cracked. When Mammy wanted to tell you anything secret, she would whisper it to you very lowly. Up to her dying day she did that and she spent more and more time whispering because she began to find this life more and more secret. But I digress. I asked my mother what was happening to me. My mother said, you have been paid a visit by the tooth fairy.

Sarah The tooth fairy?

Greta You heard me, girl. The same ones that came to take away your teeth came at a certain age to wee girls and gave them what was known as a woman's complaint. She had a bandage and I would be right as rain in no time. I was fourteen, I knew nothing, but I knew the tooth fairy was pushing it. So what was happening? Are you ready for this? I thought I was turning into a man.

Sarah You're the weirdest kid I've come across, Greta.

Greta Don't knock it if you haven't tried it. Whenever I was feeling lonely, it was some consolation to think I'd grow into my own brother. And I grew out of it.

Sarah Are they dead, your parents?

Greta Yup, within six months of each other. Rough time. But it was quick. I nursed them, or I tried to. My sad father, my mad mother. All for the best. Quick. Mammy, daddy, gone. I still kept on the family home. It's not like a doll's house anymore. Anybody who looks in my window wishes they hadn't. Sorry, mother. I'm not the most pleasant of women.

Sarah Good.

Greta Good.

Sarah kisses Greta's hand.

What's that for?

Sarah A gift from the tooth fairy.

Greta Fuck the tooth fairy.

Sarah She's better than nothing.

Greta I suppose she is.

Sarah Why did you come to the graveyard, Greta?

Greta Do you really want to know?

Silence.

I'm waiting for a miracle.

Sarah What kind?

Silence.

I want Hark back, that in its own way is a miracle. Maela wants her daughter back, that would definitely be a miracle. What do you want?

Greta I want myself back.

Sarah How do you mean?

Greta I would like to be what I used to be.

Sarah Which was?

Greta I've told you. Myself. Jesus, I hope they find Maela.

Sarah Dido will find her.

Greta Paul's more reliable, when he's in his right mind. He might handle her better.

Sarah Do you think she's stopped believing?

Silence.

Have you stopped believing?

Greta No, Sarah, no.

Maela enters followed by Paul, Dido, Seph and Hark.

Maela, thank Christ.

Silence.

Maela She's dead, isn't she?

Silence.

My wee girl's dead. They're running mad through the streets of Derry and my daughter's dead. Do you not understand that?

Dido Understand what, Maela?

Silence.

Where were you, Maela?

Maela Nowhere. Nowhere. I went for a walk. Through Derry. Everybody was crying. What was wrong with them? All shouting. I couldn't hear what. Was it at me? I wasn't listening to them.

Dido What were you listening to?

Maela They said, 'She's dead. I'm afraid she's dead. We can get you home safely in an ambulance. There's a lot of bother stirring in the town.' I said, 'What do you mean she's dead? There is a dead thing in there and that thing is cancer, that thing is not my daughter. My daughter's at home. I better get back to her. I don't know what I'm doing out.' The town's gone mad today, hasn't it?

Dido She's dead, Maela. Your daughter's dead.

Maela No, doctor, you're wrong. My daughter is alive. My daughter is not that thing. I'm going home.

Dido I'll go with you.

Maela Nonsense. I'm perfectly capable of walking home.

At my age I should know my way around Derry. I've walked through it often enough. William Street and Shipquay Street and Ferryquay Street and the Strand and Rosville Street and Great James Street. I'm walking home through my own city. Everybody's running and everybody's crying. What's wrong? Why cry? Two dead, I hear that in William Street. I'm walking through Derry and they're saying in Shipquay Street there's five dead. I am walking to my home in my house in the street I was born in and I've forgotten where I live. I am in Ferryquay Street and I hear there's nine dead outside the Rosville flats. They opened fire and shot them dead. I'm not dead. Where are there dead in Derry? Let me look on the dead. Jesus, the dead. The innocent dead. There's thirteen dead in Derry. Where am I? What day is it? Sunday. Why is the sun bleeding? It's pouring blood. I want a priest. Give me a priest. Where am I? In Great James Street. It's full of chemists. I need a tonic for my nerves. For my head. For my heart. Pain in my heart. Breaking heart. I've lost one. I've lost them all. They had no hair. She had fire. She opened fire on herself. When I wasn't looking she caught cancer. It burned her. She was thirteen. It was Sunday. I have to go to Mass. I have to go to Mass. I have to go to Mass. Dido, take me to Mass, Dido.

Dido Who wrote *The Firebird*, Maela?

Silence.

Who, Maela?

Maela No.

Paul *The Firebird*, who wrote it, Maela?

Maela Stravinsky.

Paul What nationality?

Maela Russian.

Sarah Where is the *Venus de Milo?*

Maela Paris. She has no arms.

Dido Someday we'll head for Paris, Maela. We'll learn French. Where do we live, Maela?

Maela That's a hard one.

Dido Do you want a clue? Derry is –

Maela Doire. Doire Colmcille.

Dido What does that mean?

Maela The dove. The bird of peace.

Greta Where do we live in Derry?

Maela The graveyard.

Greta Why?

Maela It seems to be where we belong.

Hark Every question correct.

Paul You're some woman.

Dido No stopping her.

Maela Is it over?

Dido Not to the final.

Maela Will we make it?

Dido What do you say, Paul?

Paul Sonny and Cher are back in action.

Dido Get the questions ready, Paul.

Hark I'm game.

Dido Thanks, Hark. Maela, you're not to get drunk before it starts. Bottle of sherry, dry?

Maela nods.

The rest of yous?

Hark Couple of six-packs?

Seph Aye.

Greta Vodka.

Sarah Tonic.

Paul Nothing for me.

Dido Couple of Britvic 55s?

Paul OK.

Dido Throw in what's going. Remember the small commission.

Maela Young fella, you have a heart . . .

Dido Like a cash register. Ring-a-ding, dear, ring-a-ding. Show us the colour of your money.

SCENE SIX

Saturday evening. Light rises to find them in party mood.

Hark Give me a D.

Chorus D.

Hark Give me an E.

Chorus E.

Hark Give me an R.

Chorus R.

Hark Give me another one.

Chorus R.

Hark Give me a Y.

Chorus Y. D.E.R.R.Y. D.E.R.R.Y. D.E.R.R.Y. D.E.R.R.Y. D.E.R.R.Y.

Hark What have you got?

Chorus DERRY.

Paul Order, order, order.

Hark (*sings*) The referee's a bastard, a bastard, a bastard. The referee's a bastard, e-i-o.

Paul shows Hark the yellow card.

What did I do? What did I do? (*He appeals innocently to the others.*)

Chorus The referee's a bastard, a bastard, a bastard. The referee's a bastard, e.i-o.

Paul OK, I give up, I give up.

Chorus Booooo.

Paul Roar among yourselves for a while. I'm sorting out questions.

They organise their drinks.

Hark Paul, where was the last time we were in a crowd like this?

Paul The one and only pub.

Hark Not the Derry Renaissance?

Paul Where else, big fella?

Dido What Derry Renaissance?

Hark The Derry Renaissance was strictly confined to

pubs. Correction, one pub.

Dido Which pub?

Hark You wouldn't remember it. It was closed down.

Dido Was it raided?

Paul Yea.

Dido By the army?

Hark No.

Dido Police?

Paul No.

Dido Who raided it then?

Seph Cruelty-to-animals people.

Dido What?

Seph It was closed over a cat.

Paul Mustard Arse.

Hark Poor Mustard Arse.

Dido Who the hell was Mustard Arse?

Seph The cat that closed the pub.

Dido How could a cat close a pub?

Paul That's a story in itself.

Dido Tell us.

Paul It was a rough place.

Seph Rough owner.

Hark Not that rough, he loved the cat.

Seph Siamese, beautiful.

Hark Grey, great colour, moved like a dancer, in and out of the glasses on the counter, graceful. That was its downfall.

Dido Its grace?

Hark Not exactly. Some rough customers drunk there. How did we survive holding arts evenings?

Seph We were together.

Paul They served brilliant sandwiches.

Hark Great chunks of ham, thick as your fist.

Paul One day this big guy eating a sandwich asked for the mustard.

Hark Cat came waltzing along the counter.

Seph mimes the cat.

Seph Miaow.

Hark Your man sticks the knife into the mustard.

Seph Miaow.

Hark Cat walks past tail in the air.

Paul Your man spreads a streak of mustard on the cat's arse.

Hark Cat went bananas.

Seph Miaow. Miaow. Miaow.

Paul Leaps from the counter into an alcove.

Hark A stag's head's hanging in the alcove.

Paul Cat starts rubbing its arse on the head.

Hark The head falls on these three old fellas.

Paul Kills one outright.

Hark Knocks the other two senseless. That cat's still going bananas.

Paul Send an ambulance.

Hark Send a priest.

Seph Send a fucking vet.

Paul All arrived at the one time.

Seph The vet got the place closed down.

Hark We did our bit as well.

Paul I was the compère.

Hark I was the poet.

Paul And Seph played the guitar, and sang.

Hark And he sang, and he sang, and he sang.

Dido has a bowl of lemon slices and salt before him. He pours salt on his hand. Licks it, and sucks the lemon followed by the tequila.

Greta What the hell are you drinking?

Dido Tequila.

Greta What's it like?

Dido It's rotten, but it's great for the image.

Greta Are you going to drink that the whole evening?

Dido No way, I've got bottles of Guinness for when I want a drink.

Greta Are you OK for vodka over there, Sarah?

Sarah Grand, thanks, Greta.

Greta Just come over here and help yourself –

Dido She will not come over here.

Maela She will not come over here.

Dido There's no conferring between teams.

Maela There's no conferring between teams.

Greta Are you two parrots?

Maela Come over here, have you ever heard the like?

Dido Amateurs. Why have we got her on the team?

Maela Think of her as a kind of mascot.

Dido Yea, a big cat. We'll call her Fluffy.

Maela and Dido roar laughing.

Maela God forgive us, Greta, we're just taking a hand at you.

Greta Are yous?

Dido Listen, Greta, you better know how we work. Maela answers on geography, mythology, art and music –

Maela I do classical, Dido does pop.

Dido I also do sport, current affairs, film, literature and history, Roman and Renaissance being my two strongest areas.

Greta What am I supposed to do?

Dido You just sit there and look fluffy, pussycat.

Maela and Dido go hysterical.

Greta I'm warning you two bastards.

Dido No, seriously, we're weak in cookery.

Maela And cricket.

Sarah We haven't a hope in hell.

Hark We are going to pulverize those two bigheads.

Paul Are we ready to kick off?

Hark Fire away, Paul.

Paul Gather round. Gather round.

Dido Hark, if your team needs a few points start –

Hark How's your balls, queer boy?

Dido Swinging. How's yours?

Hark Stiff.

Dido Jesus, listen to once in a lifetime.

Paul Alright, alright. First question. Dido's team, who wrote the *Canterbury Tales*?

Dido Geoffrey Chaucer, 1340–1400.

Paul Correct.

Maela Well done, Dido. Beautifully answered.

Paul Hark and Sarah's team, in what century did Chaucer live?

Hark Geoffrey Chaucer, let me think, if we only knew his dates –

Sarah 1340–1400.

Hark Would it be the fourteenth century?

Paul Correct.

Maela Just answer the question, Dido, and stop showing off.

Paul Which famous family ruled Renaissance Florence?

Dido The De Medici family.

Paul Correct.

Dido Easay-peasy Japanesy, yawn yawn.

Paul Other team, spell Medici.

Hark M-e-d-i-c-i

Dido I hope you're not wearing out your brains.

Paul Identify the source of these lines:
The moon shines bright in such a night as this,
When the sweet wind did gently kiss the trees
And they did make no noise, in such a night –

Greta It's *The Merchant of Venice*.

Paul Correct.

Greta
In such a night
Stood Dido with a willow in her hand
Upon the wild sea banks and waft her love
To come again to Carthage.

Dido How flattering. Thank you, Greta. Piss off.

Greta I remember it from A-level.

Paul Sarah, who wrote these lines?
Lay your sleeping head, my love,
Human on my faithless arm –

Sarah
But in my arms till break of day
Let the living creature lie –

Paul
Mortal, guilty, but to me
The entirely beautiful.

Dido I have a funny feeling she knows this one.

Sarah Auden.

Paul Correct.

Sarah W. H. Auden. Wystan Hugh Auden.

Dido Excuse me.

Paul What is the capital of Bolivia?

Maela La Paz is the capital of Bolivia.

Dido Other team, spell La Paz, and there's a 'z' at the end of La Paz. Am I right?

Paul What is the capital of – sorry, the Judicial capital of the Netherlands?

Sarah The Hague.

Paul The European Court of Justice is in the Hague. There will be justice, and there will be peace, but there will be no peace without justice.

Dido Paul, get on with the quiz, please.

Paul Where is the English FA Cup Final played?

Dido Wembley Stadium.

Paul Correct.

Dido What's this, high infants?

Paul Hark's team, what was the size of the crowd at last year's FA Cup Final?

Hark A hundred thousand?

Paul Near enough. Dido's team, a hundred thousand attended the final. Name them.

Dido What?

Paul You have ten seconds; ten, nine, eight, seven, six, five –

Hark – four, three, two, one, zero.

Paul I won't pass it over. In the 1963 film *Cleopatra*, a well-known couple –

Dido I know this. Elizabeth –

Paul – Taylor and Richard Burton were the leads. Cleopatra died by means of an asp bite. What was the name of the asp?

Dido What was the name of the asp?

Greta Would it be Doris?

Dido How the hell would it be Doris?

Greta Maybe it was Sammy?

Paul Sammy, the asp, is correct. All equal. Einstein's Theory of Relativity has never been set to music. Four points for the first version.

Hark (*sings*)
I woke up this morning, there was something in my head.
I looked out of the window. I see e equals mc squared.
I got the blues, baby. I got the blues, baby.
I got the Theory of Relativity blues.

Paul Not bad, Hark. Not bad. Two points for that. Dido's team, who captained the 1971 Arsenal League and FA Cup Double champions?

Maela Frank McClintock.

Dido Hold it, Maela, that's enough.

Maela It was Frank McClintock.

Dido That's enough, Maela. Paul, I demand to answer that question. It's not fair to expect poor Maela to answer a football question.

Paul How do the opposition feel about that?

Hark Let him answer.

Dido Thank you, Hark. A nice touch from the opposition. Seventy-one. Arsenal Double team, let me think, captain? Charlie George?

Paul Wrong. Other team?

Hark Frank McClintock.

Paul Correct.

Dido You dirty bollocks.

Hark Thank you, Dido. Nice touch from the opposition.

Dido Shut up, Hark.

Maela I knew that, Dido.

Dido Shut up, Maela.

Paul Easy one. Which queen of Carthage ruled there until deserted by Aeneas?

Dido Dido, Queen of Carthage.

Paul Correct.

Hark Dido, Queen of Derry.

Dido At least I admit it, sunshine.

Hark Bitch, bitch.

Paul Hark's team, what does Carthage mean?

   They confer.

Hark We don't know.

Dido It means new city.

Paul Correct.

Maela You know a lot about Carthage, Dido.

Dido (*whispers*) I know a lot about the question master, Maela.

Paul I declare the quiz a draw. Congratulations.

Dido Tie-breaker, tie-breaker, we demand a tie-breaker.

Paul All right, all right. Hark's team, which admiral died at the Battle of Trafalgar?

Hark Nelson.

Sarah Nelson.

Paul Correct. Dido's team, who else died at the same battle?

Silence.

Dido Was there a Sammy?

Paul Wrong.

Cheers from Hark's team.

Paul I declare Hark's team the clear winners after the tie-break.

Dido Fix, fix, fix. That quiz was a complete fix, a fix.

Paul You had your chance to win and you blew it.

Dido Fix, fix, fix.

Hark He's just a sore loser.

Dido I am not a sore loser.

Maela We'd have won if you'd let me answer the Frank McClintock question.

Dido I am well aware of that, Maela. How did you know about him anyway?

Maela You showed me him in your scrapbook. He had lovely legs.

Dido So he did. God, how could I have forgotten. Frank McClintock's legs. Where are they now?

Hark Where are they now, those we have loved? Joni Mitchell?

Paul Joni, still going strong.

Sarah Bob Dylan?

Paul Bobby? Still going strong.

Hark Don McLean.

Chorus A long, long time ago, I can still remember.

Hark He had another one.

> *Seph starts to sing 'Babylon'. Sarah, Hark and Paul join, followed by Greta and finally Maela and Dido. They repeat the lyrics. Sarah is left humming alone. The others clear away the bottles etc. Silence.*

Sarah I'd like a kid.

Greta Charlie, charlie, chuck-chuck-chuck, went to bed with three wee ducks.

Sarah I want a kid, Hark.

Hark Put it out of your head.

Greta Charlie, charlie, went to sleep, the three wee ducks began to weep.

Sarah I'd like a child.

Hark It's not going to happen.

Greta When the sun did greet the morn, the three wee ducks, they were all gone.

Sarah I want a child.

Greta Are you telling the truth, Sarah? About the child? Is it the truth? Wasn't it your big idea to tell the truth?

Paul Leave her alone, Greta.

Greta Why do you go mad, Paul?

Hark Leave him alone, Greta.

Greta Leave him alone, leave her alone. Leave me to tell the truth. What about telling the truth? Why do you go mad, Paul?

Paul I go mad when I have to.

Greta When you have to?

Paul Leave me alone.

Greta You're never going to build that stupid pyramid. It's only in your own head it even looks like a pyramid. And if you do build it what are you going to do with it?

Paul Be buried in it. With the dead. When they rise.

Greta Wash your brain of that shit.

Maela Long ago they talked of washing the dead.

Paul It's not shit.

Maela It was for the Last Judgement. For them rising.

Paul The dead can rise.

Greta How can the dead rise?

Paul You saw them, not me.

Greta Was I mad when I saw it?

Paul Stop talking about madness.

Greta grabs the plastic bag.

367

Leave that.

Greta Why? What is it?

Paul A coffin.

Greta starts to rip the black plastic bag apart.

Stop it. Stop. Stop it. (*grabs the plastic bag off Greta*) The plastic bags. They threw them over the dead. Bury them decently. Put them in the ground. Carrying the dead like a pile of rubbish through Derry on Bloody Sunday. Don't tear the plastic bags. Don't defile their coffin. Don't, please, don't. Don't let them die. Don't let me go mad. If they die, I'll go mad. I have to keep carrying them. That's where I keep them. Give them back to me.

Greta Why are they in there?

Paul Hiding.

Greta From what?

Paul The war.

Greta What war?

Paul In my head. The war in my head. It's driven me mad.

Hark There's another war outside your head.

Paul It's driving me mad. I'm losing a grip on myself.

Hark The war I fought.

Paul I was a good teacher. I was popular with people.

Hark And I fought it for good reason.

Paul I run two quizzes in different pubs to save a bit of money. I want to see Egypt. I want to go to Carthage. But I'm losing a grip on myself. I don't want to go mad.

Seph Why are you mad, Paul?

Paul Derry destroyed.

Hark For good reason.

Paul Every bullet, every boot put through it –

Hark For good reason.

Paul I've felt them all.

Seph Can you feel any more?

Paul The pain comes and goes and I go mad with pain. The living can't heal it, but the dead might. I believe they'll rise because I am mad, for if the dead don't rise to meet me –

Hark Enough.

Paul I will meet them for I cannot last much longer in this town.

Silence.

Greta Why the hell do you put yourself through this? (*She takes the plastic bag.*) I don't believe you're mad. I don't believe you. I think you're full of lies. Full of shit.

Hark And you're not?

Greta If I am, I don't go around squealing for pity.

Hark But you go around squealing for truth?

Greta Why shouldn't I?

Seph Be full of pity?

Hark Why would you want pity, Greta?

Seph For being herself. She hates herself.

Greta Do I, traitor?

Seph Being a traitor –

Greta And you are.

Seph I know. I know what I am. I hauled this from the mast and I danced on it. (*grabs the discarded tricolour*) That's the way I made sense of it all. Would it have been better to have been shot on Bloody Sunday? Did I want that to happen? Why did I want that? Why did we all want it? Did we want Bloody Sunday to happen?

Hark How the hell could we want Bloody Sunday to happen?

Seph So we could make sense of it all, make sense of our suffering. (*starts to wrap the tricolour around the guitar*) Thirteen dead on Bloody Sunday. It could have been thirteen hundred. Thirteen thousand. Thirteen million. One. One left alive, that one is me and I'm going to tell.

Hark You've told enough.

Seph Have I told you this? (*puts his fist through the guitar*) That's the war in my head. They said after Bloody Sunday they wanted to avenge the dead but they wanted to join them. And I would tell on the living who wanted to join the dead. I'd save them from themselves. I'd save them from the dead. I'd save you, Hark.

Hark You're a traitor, Seph. Nothing more. Who gives a damn if you live or die.

Paul Do you give a damn who lives or dies now?

Hark No.

Sarah You did one time.

Hark Long ago.

Dido What changed you?

Hark I changed myself. That's life, eh, Sarah?

Paul No, that's luck.

Hark Pick a straw, the luck of the straw. The loser goes hungry, the loser goes on strike.

Paul You never went hungry.

Hark Pick the long straw, pick the short straw.

Paul You were never on the hunger strike. You were never on it, Johnny.

Hark I got the long straw.

Paul You never volunteered.

Hark I didn't go hungry.

Paul You didn't want to.

Hark I didn't die.

Paul Lucky boy, eh? You lived, Harkin. Others died. You never volunteered. What were you, Harkin? What are you? A glorified look-out man who got himself caught. What have you done we haven't all done?

Hark Coward, you're a coward, Paul.

Paul Big hero, Harkin. Hard man.

Hark Coward.

Paul Keep saying that word, Harkin, and then start asking who's the coward, boy?

Hark No.

Paul Who went on missions and couldn't kill? Coward who couldn't kill? Coward.

Hark No.

Paul A glorified lookout man, a coward who ran away. Coward.

Hark Not true.

Paul Then what is true, Johnny? Tell me.

Hark (*takes a water pistol from his pocket*) I couldn't use the gun. I wasn't man enough.

Paul You're in the middle of an ambush. Run, Hark, run.

Hark Somebody's coming. Hide, hide.

Paul You never used the gun, Hark. Give it to me. It's only a toy.

Hark I want to use it, Paul.

Paul hauls the gun to Hark's mouth.

Paul Eat it then. Eat it. Eat it. Eat it before I shove it down your throat.

Hark throws Paul's hand away.

Hark I can't. Can't fire, can't kill, can't eat. Coward. I'm a coward. Want to eat. Want to live, I want to live. And I can't face the dead. Will the dead go away and stop haunting me? I cannot kill to avenge you. All I could have killed was myself. And I couldn't. I can't. Come back to me, Sarah. I'm dead. Come back and raise the dead.

Sarah I'm back, Johnny.

Hark I've told the truth, Sarah.

Paul Johnny?

Hark Paul.

Seph Johnny?

Hark Seph.

Silence.

Greta Tell a joke.

Hark Tell the truth.

Greta A dirty joke.

Hark Tell the truth, Greta. You said so.

Greta A doctor joke. A woman walks into a doctor's office. She says, doctor, doctor, I've a pain. I've a pain. The doctor says, where? She tells him. She needs an operation. She has a pain. A pain.

Maela She is very young to have this operation.

Greta So she thinks, but they say in the hospital it could happen at any age. And they were very good to her all the time she was in hospital. They tell her it is not the end of the world. She left the hospital.

Sarah Where did she go then, this woman?

Greta She was an only child, this woman. She kept herself to herself. And her parents, they were both dead. So she went to her parents' grave. She said, Mammy, Daddy, I'm afraid. And she saw the dead. She saw herself. She saw nothing, for she is nothing. She is not a woman anymore. She's a joke. A dirty joke. Charlie, Charlie, chuck-chuck-chuck, went to bed with three wee ducks. Charlie, Charlie, went to sleep, the three wee ducks began to weep. When the sun did greet the morn, the three wee ducks, they were all gone. No wee ducks. There will be no wee ducks. Laugh. It's a joke. This woman has no pity anymore. She had an operation. A woman's problem. I blame the tooth fairy myself. Right, Mother? Gone. All gone. All gone. Mammy, Daddy, I'm afraid. Mammy, Daddy, I'm afraid.

Sarah Greta.

Greta Mammy, Daddy, I'm afraid.

Sarah Greta.

Sarah goes and puts her hands gently on Greta's breasts.
Greta screams. Sarah comforts her. Greta calms.

Greta It's tonight, Sarah.

Sarah I know.

Maela So do I.

Greta They will rise tonight, the dead will rise tonight.

SCENE SEVEN

Saturday night. They sit in a circle.

Dido Do you ever get afraid in this place?

Greta What of?

Dido Ghosts.

Greta Do you believe in ghosts?

Dido Yes. Do you?

Greta Why do you think we're here?

Silence.

Dido I'm scared shitless.

Silence.

I hope there are not going to be any poltergeists. I saw a film once about a poltergeist. It bit people's heads off and disembowelled them. I had to be nearly carried out of the cinema every time I saw it.

Sarah How often did you see it?

Dido Five times. It was brilliant.

Hark You have great taste in films.

Dido Yea, I know. I see everything.

Hark Nothing like a good western.

Dido When you were a kid, Hark, playing Cowboys and Indians, which were you?

Hark The Indian.

Dido You get weirder by the minute.

Hark What's wrong with Indians?

Dido They always got beaten.

Hark Not always.

Seph I liked the Indians as well. Their head-dresses were great.

Hark They had the best words.

Paul Firewater.

Hark Medicine man.

Seph Peace pipe.

Paul Great words. Like poetry.

Maela When I was young, at school like, I quite liked poetry. I don't remember any poems. I tell a lie. I do remember one. How did it go?
Is there anyone there, said the Traveller –

Paul
Knocking on the moonlit door

Greta
And his horse in the silence champed the grasses
Of the forest's ferny floor
And a bird – and a bird –

Sarah
– a bird flew up out of the turret,
Above the Traveller's head:
And he smote on the door a second time;
'Is there anybody there?' he said

Hark
But no one descended to the Traveller;
No head from the leaf-fringed sill
Leaned over and looked into his grey eyes –

Seph
Where he stood –

Dido
– perplexed –

Paul
– and still.

Greta
But only a host of phantom listeners
That dwelt in the lone house then
Stood listening in the quiet of moonlight
To that voice from the world of men . . .

Seph
And he felt in his heart their strangeness –

Paul
Their stillness answering his cry . . .
For he suddenly smote on the door, even
louder, and lifted his head.

Sarah
'Tell them I came, and no one answered,
That I kept my word,' he said.

Maela
Never the least stir made the listeners,

Though every word he spake –

Greta
Fell echoing through the shadowiness of the still house
From the one man left awake.
Aye, they heard his foot on the stirrup,

Maela
And the sound of iron on stone,

Sarah
And how the silence surged softly backward,

Women
When the plunging hoofs were gone.

Silence.

Seph Do you ever write poetry now, Hark?

Hark I wrote doggerel.

Paul Some good stuff. Heady days back then.

Hark You would have been only a kid, Dido.

Dido There were no kids after Bloody Sunday.

Paul Do you remember their names? The dead of Bloody Sunday?

Silence.

Paul Bernard McGuigan, forty-one years, Inishcairn Gardens, Derry. Patrick Doherty, thirty-two years, Hamilton Street, Derry. Michael Kelly, seventeen, from Dunmore Gardens, Derry. William McKinney, twenty-seven, from Westway, Derry. James Wray, twenty-three, Drumcliffe Avenue, Derry. Hugh Gilmore, seventeen years old, Garvan Place, Derry. Jack Duddy, who was seventeen, Central Drive, Derry. William Nash, nineteen, Dunree Gardens, Derry. Michael McDaid, twenty-one, Tyrconnell

Street, Derry. Gerald Donaghy, seventeen, Meenan Square, Derry. John Young, seventeen, Westway, Derry. Kevin McElinney, seventeen, Philip Street, Derry. Gerald McKinney, Knockdara House, Waterside, Derry.

Hark Perpetual light shine upon you. Rest in peace.

Seph Bloody Sunday.

Sarah Sunday.

Greta Sunday.

Sarah Sunday.

Greta Wash the dead.

Paul Sunday.

Maela Bury the dead.

Seph Sunday.

Sarah Raise the dead.

Hark Sunday.

Dido Do you see the dead?

Greta The dead beside you.

Maela The dead behind you.

Sarah The dead before you.

Greta Forgive the dead.

Maela Forgive the dying.

Sarah Forgive the living.

Paul Forgive yourself.

Hark Forgive yourself.

Seph Forgive yourself.

Maela Bury the dead.

Greta Raise the dying.

Sarah Wash the living.

Light breaks through the graveyard.
Birdsong begins.
Light illuminates them all.
They listen, looking at each other, in the light.
They lie down and sleep.
It is now morning.
Dido alone is awake in the graveyard.

Dido What happened? Everything happened, nothing happened, whatever you want to believe, I suppose. What do I believe? I believe it is time to leave Derry. Love it and leave it. Now or never. Why am I talking to myself in a graveyard? Because everybody in Derry talks to themselves. Everybody in the world talks to themselves. What's the world? Shipquay Street and Ferryquay Street and Rosville Street and William Street and the Strand and Great James Street. While I walk the earth, I walk through you, the streets of Derry. If I meet one who knows you and they ask, how's Dido? Surviving. How's Derry? Surviving. Carthage has not been destroyed. Watch yourself.

Dido drops flowers on the sleepers.

Watch yourself, Hark and Sarah. Watch yourself, Seph. Watch yourself, Paul. Watch yourself, Greta. Watch yourself, Maela. Remember me. Watch yourself, Dido. Watch yourself, Derry. Watch yourself. Watch yourself. Watch yourself.

Dido caresses Seph's guitar, half-covered with the tricolour.

Play.

Dido exits as the music plays.

BAGLADY

For Eoin and Maurean

Baglady was first performed at the Peacock Theatre, Dublin, in March 1985.

Baglady Maurean Toal

Directed by Patrick Mason
Designed by Frank Hallinan Flood
Lighting by Tony Wakefield

The **Baglady** *wears the heavy clothes of a farmer, rough trousers, dark overcoat, boots. She is feminized only by a grey scarf protecting her head, hiding her hair completely. On her back she carries a grey, woollen sack. The Baglady walks along the edge of her space.*

Baglady I saw someone drown once. I was carrying them in my arms. When I looked behind me, there was nobody there. I'm walking to the water. This place is full of it. The river's everywhere you look about you. Here's the very edge. I want to put something into it. If you take one step too close you fall in. I saw someone drown. I saw. But I didn't tell. Tell me now. Tell me to the water that took you. Throw it in for what it's worth.

The Baglady sings as she continues walking.

Who's at the window, who?
Who's at the window, who?
A bad, bad man with a bag on his back
Coming to take you away.
Who's at the window, who?
Who's at the window, who?
Go away, bad man, with the bag on your back,
You won't take me with you today.

The Baglady stops.

Go away from me. Don't look at me. Don't come near. I'm not dirty. Do you hear? Go away. I'll tell my father what you call me. He's a respected man in these parts. A decent man. He'll nail you for the stories you tell about me. He hears you. He hears everything. Go away.

The Baglady walks.

I had a dream. I went to sleep. Nice and warm. I was all
blood. My mother cleaned me up. The white interlock
went red. When you're clean, that way they can't smell
you. They won't follow you. Nobody finds you. Just
yourself alone.

The Baglady stands.

When you're on your own, you know everything. You can
go anywhere. Look at me. I know this place like the back
of my hand. (*holds out her palms*) See these? I walk on
them. I call one home and the other here. That way you
can't get lost. Watch when your two hands meet. Like this.
That's a bridge where I stand watching the river beneath
me and the people about me crossing the bridge on their
business. Now I separate my hands. The bridge goes away,
but the place goes on. It doesn't have a name for it's
written on my hand, and your fingers can't talk. (*holds up
her ten fingers*) I carry places with me. These are all streets.
I walk through them every day on the way to the river.
They're full of people too, but I wouldn't look at them. I
just carry them with me. They're my mark. They'll be
buried with me. My father is buried. Dead and buried. I
carry him as well, here on my back. Every stitch behind
and before me, it belonged to him. Whatever I didn't need,
I buried with him. A good-living man, he worked hard for
what he got in this life. He never touched me, never raised
his hand, never. I haven't a bad word to say against him.
He played cards but he deserved respect. Respect his
grave. This is it. Don't touch my father, don't walk on his
grave. Walk on a grave, you desecrate it. You turn into a
thief. Thief! I saw you. I saw.

The Baglady walks.

Be careful where you walk these days. Everywhere's
dangerous. Full of corners you wouldn't know what's
hiding behind. Lock your doors. Lock your windows at
night always. Lock yourself up. If you keep walking,
nobody follows you here or home. They might watch you
but they won't follow you. I need none of them. I walk on
regardless. Let them look. I want nobody. I live on the
bridge. I look down into the river. I saw somebody drown.
I was carrying him in my arms, he started to cry because I
was leaving our house with him. When was that? I don't
remember. I remember before leaving I was bleeding, but
where was it coming from? I can't remember. I remember
our house full of people. They were talking with their
mouths and teeth, and I saw my father's tongue. He was
laughing one evening. He won the cards. My father was a
good man. Not one of you are fit to tie his shoes. Not one
of you. Don't dare tell me otherwise. My father was a
gentleman. I give him my blessing. Our house was white, it
had black windows at night-time and the door was red. It
was never closed. We were an open house. Tramps of the
day stood in a line outside our house, looking in at me and
my father and my mother. One man had a fit. He was like
a dog, a big, black dog. He had water coming from his
mouth. Burntoes or Crumlish, that was his name. They
were tinkers. They begged money. I remember big slices of
toasted bread in their hands, butter running from it like
blood from a cut. Burntoes, he was lame. He walked on a
crutch. It had the shape of a man with a big head. My
mother said to me that Burntoes was lame because one
night he got drunk and because he had no house to live in
he walked the streets. One night he met the devil. It was so
cold that Burntoes let the devil lay hands on him. Burntoes
felt the devil's touch haul him down to hell. When he put
one foot into the devil's fire, Burntoes jumped that hard to
get out of hell, he left part of his foot behind to burn.
That's why he limped. That's why when he saw you at

night he cut the sign of the cross on himself, in case you were the devil. In the name of the father. And of the son. My father was not the devil. (*Beat.*) They slept in our byre. They had the smell of the cattle. Straw all over their clothes. When they got drunk, Crumlish beat the life out of poor Burntoes. Crumlish was a bad brute, but Burntoes never left him. Nobody could separate them. When Burntoes died, Crumlish squealed like a pig. He sounded like a woman. They were like a married couple my mother said.

The Baglady stops walking.

My mother was married. She was a married woman. My father and my mother lived in our house. It was white with a red door, and there were black windows everywhere. Even the door had a window. The windows were cut from glass. Sometimes you could look into the window and see your face. It moved, not like your face in the river swallowing you for ever. You could take your face out of the window. I looked through my face one day in the window and I saw my father and my mother. My mother wasn't there, and my father was moving. He called me by my name. It was my mother's. My mother. My mother told fortunes. She could read people's cards. Their faces told her stories.

The Baglady walks.

I can walk for miles without limping. I never stop. See my hands, they make a bridge when I link them. Beneath the link there's water running. I stand on the bridge and look over. I see. I saw the river. It flowed beside our house. When I stood beside the river, our house looked a long way away. That's where I lived then, in our house, and my son lived in the river. Sit down, I'll tell you about the house.

*From her coat pocket the Baglady takes a slice of bread
and a bottle of red lemonade. She sits, eating and
drinking.*

We had electric in the house. Different colour in every
room. I liked red the best. The same colour as this
lemonade. No, red's never the same, no matter what way
you look at it or see where you see it. When you look into
the sun, the red blinds you. Blood can do that too, if you
cut your head badly. The electric light's a different red
again. It was never black when you put the red light on .
You could see out through the windows even in the night-
time. And you could see in. I used to breathe on the glass
and write my mother's name and my father's name on it.
In the morning it was never there, the names. The sun
wiped them out. It was red too. But you can't drink the
sun nor blood nor the electric. This is all I touch, red
lemonade. All I eat, white bread. I like the colours of them.
You need money to buy the colours. My father had money.
Wads of it lying on the table or smelling in his hands.
Sometimes there was a picture of a woman in his smell.
She looked like a mad woman, dressed all strangely, all in
green. A green lady. I held her once in my hands the only
time I was trusted with money, because money's a man's
responsibility. When you get married, make sure it's to a
man who knows the value of money. If you don't, and you
have money, give it away. Give it away because money is a
man's thing. Watch the way money moves to a man's
hand. Pound notes, fivers, tenners, down on the table. I
don't want it. It smells. Take it away from me. Keep away
from me. I'll tell on you, I'll tell. We had electric in our
house. It lit the whole room. I could see everything. I could
see the money. I don't want it. Don't put out the light.
Don't leave me in the black room. If I can't see, I can't
talk, and if I can't talk, I can't tell. And I'm going to tell.
I'm going to tell.

The Baglady buries her face in her hands, then speaks to her hands.

My father gave me money. Where is it? What did I do with it? Have I lost it? Where would I have spent it? Should I throw it into the river? How was it got rid of? Answer me. You know. You were there. Have you got a tongue between you? Have you lost that as well? I'll tear you apart. I'll cut your tongue out, if you don't tell me what happened to me. Tell me everything. Tell. Clap if you're going to tell me. Clap. Clap.

The Baglady claps her hands.

You were walking towards the water. You were carrying something in these hands. We tried to tell you not to. You couldn't hear what you were carrying. Your Father was with you. He thought you were carrying him. So he took himself from your arms and he walked into the river, turning into a black dog, shaking the water from his hair. You held us out to him, but he wouldn't stop. Do you remember? Can we stop telling you now?

The handclapping stops. The Baglady rises suddenly.

Get away from me. Get away. Take that dog away. I hate dogs. It's a killer. It jumps on you and eats you up. Take it away. Red. Red. Out of my sight. Foot. Hand. Moving in the river. Don't bring it any nearer to me. Chase it far away. Stomach. Blood. Neck. It doesn't move any more. It's gone away. Say the dog's gone away. Stop him following me. I'll shoot it dead. I'll drown the bastard. Give me peace. I deserve peace. I don't care what happened, just give me peace. Get this out of my sight.

The Baglady tears the bread into bits and throws it about her.

Melt.

The Baglady sits.

When things are torn, you can't put them back again. When something's taken from you, you can't get it back. You can try, but what use? Look, do you see that dog who keeps following me, what do you think he's after? Wanting to be fed? I've nothing for him. He knows, but will he go away? No. What then does he want? Does he want me to tell him something? Or is he telling me? Are you asking or telling? Are you looking for this?

The Baglady takes from her pocket a deck of playing cards. She kneels. The Baglady holds up the king of diamonds.

Here is your beginning. It is always a sign of water. No matter what card is drawn, it says the same always. Why do you back away from it? Do you fear water? Do you fear birth? Do you fear it more than death? Or did someone die in troubled water? Your hand's shaking. Are you trying to catch them?

The card drops from the Baglady's hand.

Did you hear that falling? Was it a crack? It could have been your heart, it could have been your mind. Still, the sound was breaking, like a glass on the ground. Can you see into it? Tell me who's there, watching out? Do you see yourself? I see a man's reflection. He looks like yourself. It could be your father. Wait. There's another with him, standing by him. It's another man. A man younger than yourself. Could it be father and son? I might be wrong but they share a resemblance. They share a name. A family name. You have no name. You are not married. You have no family. Could these men be brothers? If so, are they friends now? Why is one of them drenched? Is he crying? Is the other dead? But which is doing the crying? Watch yourself beside water.

The Baglady holds up another card.

The five of clubs. A bad card. Don't worry, it's over. It's youth. But is stands for suffering, because it means sorrow. Five black wounds of sorrow. They're healing since they're black, but you have something to confess. It happened long ago. Somebody did something, and you did. Did whoever it was tell you to say nothing? When you tried to tell did nobody believe you, so you stopped believing although you saw it all?

She places the card down.

Maybe your cards will tell you it wasn't your fault. You'll forgive. You'll forget. We all do. Forget, that is. That's what living's about. Forgetting. I believe you. I forgive you.

The Baglady raises the queen of hearts.

This is the queen of hearts. She comes without king or jack. Alone, this is a lucky card, for it shows you have a heart, good heart. She asks questions you'd never expect. She knows there is something hidden in your heart, a secret she could guess at, but she won't. All she'll say is that she too had a son. He was taken. The queen left her country in disguise as a beggarman, searching for her son. Every time she came to the place where she might find him all she found instead was the same answer. Your son is dead, his father killed him. She couldn't say my son is my father and my father is my son. She could not say it, but that was all she possessed, the truth. She wants you to receive. She knows you. Look. See who comes after.

The Baglady raises the queen of spades.

A black lady. Bitter. The quiet card. This one keeps her counsel because she's angry, and no one knows that anger's source. She has the face of a corpse. Is she woman at all? There's some doubt about it. Does she remind you of anybody? Do you remember the queen of hearts? She had a son. Did he look like this? Is that why his father killed him? Do you see this one's cheek? There's a track across it. It could be the track of a fist. This woman's received a blow that will shut her up for ever, but she's with you through all your life.

The Baglady shows the seven of diamonds.

A seven for good luck, and here it's diamonds. That's for marriage. I know who's next to arrive. A man in black.

The Baglady holds up the knave of clubs.

You see, I thought there'd be a priest involved. When he asks you to do something, you can't say no. It might be at a funeral you met him, or else a wedding; there's very little difference between them, weddings and funerals, because they're all tied in some way to money. Let me see which is which here.

The Baglady looks at the ace of spades.

Oh Christ, I see death. You'll be attending a funeral. A young woman or a child's funeral. It's definitely somebody young. Don't panic. Taking all the cards together, I'd say there's good news in them. I shouldn't have mentioned death. But I saw it. What I see I have to tell. I have to say it.

The Baglady starts to spread the cards in patterns on the ground.

I knew a man once, God rest him. (*lifts one of the seven cards*) This is him here.

As the Baglady tells his story, she manipulates the cards as characters.

You'd think he had everything. He ruled the roost in his

house. His wife and child walked in fear of his body and its strength. He had that much strength he wanted more. He wanted his wife's, he wanted his child's. Some nights he turned into a black dog and took himself out walking. Walked for miles, walked the feet off himself, walked himself into his grave. When this man died, the dog lived on. It went mad with grief. It knew who was master and one day this dog grabbed the man's daughter by the throat. She went hysterical but the dog wouldn't let go. It chained her up. Then one night the dog changed back to the man. When he spoke to his daughter she thought he was the devil. He said she was his wife. He'd come back for her. She got such a shock she jumped that hard from her chain that she tore her head away from the rest of her and all that was left behind was her skin and bones. The man whistled for his dog and it came running. He set the dog on his daughter's body and it ate all that was left of her. (*Beat.*) The first man I saw standing in the cards, the man beside water, the man at your beginning, the man with a family, I know now for sure that's my father.

The Baglady rapidly gathers the cards together, returning them to the deck, shuffling it rapidly.

I see the five of clubs. I see the queen of hearts, she knows the queen of spades. I see a man in black. That man is not your father, but you must call him father. The queen of spades starts smiling. She thinks she is your father. The five of clubs is love, but it will bring you sorrow. You will love your son but you must love your father. In the name of. In the name of. Jesus, he's dead. My father is dead.

The Baglady howls. From her sack she hauls an iron chain. She beats it violently on the ground around her.

Get out of my way. Do you not hear me? I'll knock you out of my road with this boy if you don't move. This is what I'm cut from. This is my fist. It will teach you respect for what I say to you. Watch where I'm going. I'm on my way to a wedding. This is my dress. It cost a fortune. Do you hear that? This is all I own, so I value it. It was left to me in a will. It was left by respectable people. A good man. A good woman. I gave the world a good child.

The Baglady sings:

Who's at the window, who?
Who's at the window, who?

The Baglady gathers the chain into her arms.

It's yours. Take a good look at him. That's him in front of you. Yours as much as mine. He's come to see you. Hold him. He's yours. (*drops the chain*) That's my body. That's your mother's body. Your mother's dead as well. (*fingers the ring of the chain*) In our house there's a room made from windows. I'm not allowed in, even to see out of it. But I can see it clearly. That's where they sleep, my mother and father. The room only appears when they're lying in it. They can change the shape of our whole house. They have magic. Sometimes my mother is my father and my father is my father too. Sometimes they turn me into each other when they think I don't know what they're doing but I do. I always do. I watch them. I see them through the window. I stand in the yard with the cattle and the dog on the chain. I know what they've done. I saw through the window. But I won't tell what I see, because it's a secret. I promised myself.

The Baglady tries to snap the chain in two.

Tell me my name. Do I have a name? Is it a girl's name? Is it a good name, a clean one? I wash my name like myself every morning. I wash my face and my neck. I wash my breast and my woman. I wash my legs. My feet. When I touch myself, I'm clean. I'm not afraid of drowning in a basin of water. If you don't go near water, you get dirty.

Black as your boot. Black as your baby. In the water. My name is my father's. I lost it after him. He washed it away. I saw it all. I jumped through the window. It cut me in two. My father pulled me. I was all dirty. I roared out. I knew what happened to dirty girls. He knew. Dirty, dirty. Get away from the water. Don't leave me under it. I can't breathe. Let me go. My neck, it's sore. Your fist's like a knife. It's cutting me. I can't breathe. The water will rise and take me. I can't run away. I'm sore. I won't tell. I won't open my mouth. Let me go. I'll stay quiet. I'll be good. Let me out. I'm soaking. I'll turn into water. Let me go.

The Baglady howls. She grows silent. She starts to rock her whole body gently.

Ssssh, ssssh. Stop that crying. Hear me? Stop it. Be a good girl. Your daddy does it for your own good. You can be a bad girl. You have to do as your daddy tells you. Don't you? Stop that crying. Stop. Look at this. Look. (*takes a ring from her pocket*) Isn't this lovely? See the way it shines, even at night? You've never seen this before, have you? It's a ring, a ring for a wedding. That's for you. I gave it to your mother. It's gold, like your hair. When you grow up and get married, I'll buy you a wedding ring too. And a long white dress. And a big white cake. And lemonade to drink, red lemonade. You'll be crying when your daddy gives you away at the altar. Take the ring. See if it fits you. Does it fit? Good. You can keep it. Put it around your finger. They say if a girl sleeps with a wedding ring in her bed she will have lovely dreams about the man she'll marry, the house they'll have and all their children, boys and girls. Boys and girls together. Do you ever dream, Daddy? Do I ever dream? Will I tell you about my dream? It's about a good girl. She did as she was told. And she could keep a secret. A big secret. And because she could keep secrets, her father gave her a golden necklace. He trusted her with his life. When she kept her mouth closed, the necklace shone like the sun and she was beautiful, very beautiful. But if she breathed a word of their secrets, the necklace grew black, blacker and blacker, and it tightened about her throat, tighter and tighter, twisting her face up, so she hardly had a face and she couldn't breathe again until she said she was sorry. Are you sorry? Are you a good girl? Are you? Are you?

The Baglady holds out her arms. She embraces the air. Her embrace turns into a grasp. Her hands start to beat against her body. She fights her hands away. They reach for the chain. She curbs it with her foot. Her hands free the chain and raise it to her neck. It starts to coil itself tightly about her. She bites her hand as it coils the chain. It starts to uncoil. She holds the chain in her lap.

Was it dead or was it alive? Was it a boy or was it a girl? How can you tell if it were alive or dead? Did you hear it breathing? Did it cry out? Did it have a name? Can I give it a name? Can I give it a kiss? A big kiss? A big kiss for Ma? A kiss for Daddy too?

Lifting the chain from her lap, the Baglady winds it into a heap before her. She gathers up the scattered cards as she sings.

Who's at the window, who?
Who's at the window, who?
A bad, bad man with a bag on his back
Coming to take you away.
Who's at the window, who?
Who's at the window, who?
Go away, bad man, with the bag on your back,
You won't take me with you today.

The Baglady raises the queen of hearts, questioning it.

Mother?

The Baglady drops this card on to the heap of chain.
She raises the king of diamonds.

Father?

The card drops on to the chain. The Baglady raises the
queen of spades.

Daughter?

The card drops on to the chain. The Baglady raises the
ace of spades.

Son?

The Baglady tears the card in pieces. She drops the
pieces into the red lemonade bottle. She shakes the
mixture. She pours the contents on to the chain.

Son.

The Baglady places the bottle on top of the chain. She
shuffles the remainder of the cards.
The Baglady leaves the cards on the heap of objects.

They're dead now, dead and buried. I buried them. I
married them.

The Baglady removes her scarf, showing her hair. She
places the scarf on the pile of objects. The Baglady takes
a white dress from her sack and holds it against her.

A man visited her once. He said I am your father. He held
her, his daughter, in his arms, his two arms. She couldn't
move away or near to him. He gave her a kiss. His mouth
cut her tongue like glass. She was all torn. She cried for a
drink of water. She wanted to wash herself, to wash the
dirty girl she was. But she stayed a dirty girl for ever. Face.
Neck. All red for ever. Breast and woman. Pouring. Legs.
Wet. Feet. She called on God to take her out of her father's
house. A man in black came to the house and said she was

a liar. But he forgave her because he took her with him to
the house of God. Women in black washed her. In fire, not
water. They nailed her son to a river. When the water
graved him, she heard her father crying. To please her
father the woman died as well. They wouldn't bury her,
she had to bury herself. She got up and walked into her
coffin. But she saw. I saw. God forgive me. I saw.

*The Baglady takes the dress from her, dropping it into
the heap. The Baglady takes the ring from her finger.
She raises it to look at in the light.*

With this ring, I thee wed. This gold and silver, I thee give.
With my body, I thee worship. And with all my worldly
goods, I thee endow. In the name of the Father and of the
Son and of the Holy Ghost.

The Baglady drops the ring.

Drown.

FABER CONTEMPORARY CLASSICS

The Faber Contemporary Classics series
aims to provide a body of work, in collected form,
for all the Faber playwrights.

Alan Ayckbourn
Alan Bennett
Brian Friel
Trevor Griffiths
David Hare
Ronald Harwood
Sharman Macdonald
Frank McGuinness
John Osborne
Harold Pinter
Tom Stoppard
Nick Ward
Timberlake Wertenbaker